The Toxic Meritocracy of Video Games

The Toxic Meritocracy of Video Games

Why Gaming Culture Is the Worst

Christopher A. Paul

University of Minnesota Press
Minneapolis
London

Published by the University of Minnesota Press
111 Third Avenue South, Suite 290
Minneapolis, MN 55401-2520
http://www.upress.umn.edu

Printed in the United States of America on acid-free paper

The University of Minnesota is an equal-opportunity educator and employer.

23 22 21 20 19 18   10 9 8 7 6 5 4 3 2 1

Library of Congress Cataloging-in-Publication Data
Names: Paul, Christopher A., author.
Title: The toxic meritocracy of video games : why gaming culture is the worst / Christopher A. Paul.
Description: Minneapolis : University of Minnesota Press, 2018. | Includes bibliographical references and index.
Identifiers: LCCN 2017018695 (print) | ISBN 978-1-5179-0040-3 (hc) | ISBN 978-1-5179-0041-0 (pb)
Subjects: LCSH: Video games—Social aspects. | Merit (Ethics)—Social aspects. | Video gamers—Psychology.
Classification: LCC GV1469.34.S52 P38 2018 (print) | DDC 794.8—dc23
LC record available at https://lccn.loc.gov/2017018695

For Erin, Piper, and Ingrid

Contents

Introduction
Growing Up Gamer

Games, video games in particular, are special to me. I am the grown-up version of one of those kids who went to the arcade on a regular basis, who graduated from Atari to Nintendo to PCs, PlayStation, and Xbox. I have spent my life bouncing back and forth among computers, consoles, and mobile devices. There were points where I didn't have time to play much, like college, prompting an evolution in what I could play and fit into my daily life. I have transitioned from the massive time investment of *World of Warcraft* to choppier, more flexible games that can be better compartmentalized, like *FIFA* and *Clash of Clans*. However, through almost all of my life, video games have been primary elements of my recreational experience and a base for my social interactions, both offline and on.

I have often had to defend video games from concerns about what they would do to me or worries about how I could be better spending my time. When I was young, teachers told me that video games were a waste of time; when I was older, other scholars told me that video games were trivial and need not be studied. Fortunately, I had parents who enabled, or at least allowed, a fair chunk of my play, and supportive colleagues who helped me advance my work. I understand that there was a time when video games were marginalized, relegated to arcades you weren't supposed to go to, and subject to scorn and concerns about your brain rotting, how much time you were wasting, or the violence they might inspire in the susceptible. However, while

1

those complaints can still be seen on occasion, we are no longer in the same kind of cultural moment.[1] Video games are now a part of everyday life, serving as both touchstones for how we construct who we are as a people and as an economic engine that generates billions of dollars (more than the music or movie industries) and attracts the investment of millions of hours of time by people around the world.[2]

Despite this move from marginalized activity to accepted part of mainstream culture, my shame about what video games are and what game culture has become is far deeper than ever before. Maybe it is a part of getting older, but there are parts of the culture around video games I simply cannot defend.[3] My interest in and commitment to video games is far more conflicted because I see what has happened in and around the games I have enjoyed so much. From the limited depictions of women and people of color in games to ongoing campaigns of harassment, like GamerGate, the current state of culture around video games is dark, and I think those of us who recognize problems have an obligation to address them.

A huge part of the problem with video games exists in the interactions between how they are designed and how we think about what they are. Video games, like all technologies and media forms, express ideologies. The games that are made and played are important artifacts that shape the culture around games, yet many of their ideological implications are not openly discussed. Both the narratives within video games and the way most AAA games are designed celebrate merit, which leads to significant problems. Videogame design is predicated on an extreme focus on rewarding skill and effort. Merit is a key part of the code within games, effectively becoming a central ideology that shapes what games get made and how they are played. Leveling systems within games sort characters into clear hierarchies of power while providing a set of objectives for players to follow in cases ranging from *World of Warcraft* to *NBA 2K* to *Kim Kardashian: Hollywood*. Game design is praised when it achieves proper balance, which leads to a fetish for situations where players are free to choose multiple paths through a game, secure in the knowledge that games from *Street Fighter* to *BioShock* to *FIFA* are structured so that different choices still lead to equitable experiences for players. Those of us playing video games all too frequently believe that one of the good things about games is that, as one journalist celebrates, "online games remove our physical identity, and all the traumas and inhibitions that come with it; everybody starts equal, everyone is judged on their contribution."[4] However, believing that kind of positive spin on games requires ignoring all the structural inequalities that ensure players never start from the same place.

The clearest ancestor for contemporary online games is *MUD1*, Richard Bartle and Roy Trubshaw's 1978 game that is described as being created by "two angry young men, feeling oppressed," who designed "an escape with their own two hands; a place where the laws were fairer, where the experience was not so unkind."[5] Elements of *MUD1*'s lineage can be seen in almost every online game, particularly in fantasy role-playing games like *EverQuest*, *Ultima Online*, and *World of Warcraft*. *MUD1* was explicitly designed as "a place in which players were able to succeed according to their actions and intelligence rather than an accident of birth into a certain social class or fortune."[6] Bartle contends that he and Trubshaw "were creating a true meritocracy. Not because I thought a meritocracy was the one true way, but that if we were going to have a system in which people ranked themselves, then a meritocracy was the least-worst approach."[7] *MUD1* gives contemporary games a complex inheritance, one where video games have long been designed around principles of ranking players based on skill and effort, seemingly replacing the importance of birthright, but ignoring the structures around this approach that advantage some and disadvantage others.

Pursuing merit as the paramount system of ranking players has spread beyond online games. Most competitive multiplayer games are designed to enable the best players to win, on the assumption that a video game should be an assessment and adjudication of a player's skill, which is a core tenet of eSports and tournament play. Skill is a vital part of discussions about video games, which can be seen as integrated into discussions surrounding them. In one small example in July 2016, about six months after the public launch of Supercell's *Clash Royale*, players sought to assess the state of the game. The central thesis of Chief Pat, a prominent YouTuber with over two million subscribers, was that *Clash Royale* would be different from other mobile games, that it would be the place where true skill had a chance to shine through play. *Clash Royale* features elements of deck building, battle arenas, and competitive play, but for the purposes of this argument the game is far less important than the kinds of appeals that are made about it. Contextualizing his story to his first experience with the game, Chief Pat notes that within five minutes of playing he saw a game that would be 100 percent fair because the play would be all about skill.[8] Similar arguments are easy to find throughout the community of *Clash Royale* players, as they lament the evolution of the game, design decisions, and what they see as a general devolution of play toward a preference for luck or legacy, rather than a promotion of player ability.[9] The dominant presumption of notable and outspoken players is that competition in video games is supposed to be an evenly matched battle, with the most talented player winning. This kind of argument dominated that particular discussion about *Clash Royale*, but the general appeal is common in many different kinds of videogame genres. This is a particularly notable instance as players are making clear appeals justifying, rationalizing, and advancing a meritocratic approach to videogame play and design.

Issues with game design also reach into the industry itself, which tends to be far whiter and male dominated than society at large. In 2005 the International Game Developers Association (IGDA) released a thorough report on the demographics of those who make games, finding that over 83 percent of developers identify as white and 88.5 percent identify as male.[10] The IGDA now collects demographic data as part of its annual "Developer Satisfaction Survey"; in 2015 it found that 75 percent of developers identify as male and 76 percent identify as white, and described the "prototypical game industry worker/developer as being a 32 year old white male with a university degree who lives in North America and has no children."[11] Age is more accurately reported in more recent data, where 67 percent of the respondents in 2015 fell between the ages of twenty-five and thirty-nine. The developer and academic Robin Potanin puts the lack of diversity in stark terms based on her experience, recounting that "at one stage in my game production career I was the only female on the production floor in a development team of 60."[12] A lack of diversity in people and background portends to a lack of diversity in new ideas, as those who grew up with games make the games they would most enjoy playing. The journalist Matthew Handrahan sums up this position from an industry point of view in reporting an interview with the creative director of Ubisoft: "Be it *League of Legends*, *Destiny*, *The Division* or *Overwatch*, the majority of gamers are actively seeking out experiences that will be consistent and—to varying degrees—predictable over long stretches of time."[13] Even as the industry has diversified somewhat over time, large game developers and publishers are structured to encourage a conservative approach to game development, one that replicates the meritocratic dependency and audiences of past successes rather than striking out on new paths. The growth in development costs creates a situation where companies betting $100 million or more on a game focus more on what has worked than on what could be.

Focus on meritocracy reaches beyond the design of games and into the narrative stories they typically tell. Most major game storylines, from *Grand Theft Auto III* to *Uncharted* to *Restaurant Story*, enable players to grow from a relative weakling into a strong, powerful demigod. In *Grand Theft Auto* games players start out at the bottom of a criminal organization or ostracized from the people they used to work with; *Uncharted* features Nathan Drake, an orphan seeking to prove his familial connection to famed explorer Sir Francis Drake; and *Restaurant Story* is predicated on an avatar who sets out to build a restaurant and starts without an oven to call her own. In all these games, if the player keeps playing (with at least a modest amount of skill) he or she will become a criminal mastermind, a famed treasure hunter, or the operator of an exceptionally successful restaurant.

Grand Theft Auto III epitomizes this kind of development, as the story begins with the protagonist, later discovered to be named Claude, left shot and betrayed by his girlfriend while robbing a bank together. Claude manages to survive but is captured, placing players in a position where they are alone and on their way to a ten-year prison sentence for bank robbery. The game's narrative unfolds from rock bottom for Claude, who transforms into a leader of the underworld who successfully outfoxes the mafia, a Columbian drug cartel, and the Yakuza in the space of a few hours of player-led intervention and exploration. By the end of the game, Claude has eviscerated the cartel and exacted his revenge on both the mafia don who sought to kill him and the girlfriend who initially betrayed him. Claude lets players experience being a strong, silent killer, and the narrative of the game lets them take credit for Claude's ascension from the bottom of the underworld to kingpin. It is notable that this version of *Grand Theft Auto*, the one with the clearest development of a meritocratic narrative arc, changed the face of video games and, in the words of one game journalist, makes Claude and his leather jacket "as important to a generation of gaming as 8-bit Mario and his blue overalls."[14]

Frequently complemented by the designed progress of leveling, games tell tales where the character starts at the bottom, often worse off than the player, until the player propels the character's rise to the top. The narrative growth of the character may be interrupted and stalled in a dramatic second act, but the thrust of the story told in most large-scale games omits problems with structural imbalance or differential access to resources, and focuses instead on how the person behind the controller facilitates the character's success. In *Grand Theft Auto III* Claude is a one-man wrecking crew, routinely besting everyone around him and thriving against all odds. However, all of Claude's success is due to the intervention of the player, as someone must successfully complete missions and move the narrative along. The story many games tell players is that if you work hard enough, if you are good enough, you can follow a straightforward path to power, wealth, and resources. As Arthur Chu writes, video games have often been seen as a refuge, "a magical world where, despite the violence and horror, *winning was always possible.* Where enemies could always be slain. Where gaming experience always led to leveling up, as opposed to a real world where trying seemed to get you nowhere. Where the capricious unfairness of real human beings was erased and your princess was always waiting at the end of World 8-4."[15] Video games depend on these meritocratic tales, like Mario's obsessive quest to clear levels and save the princess, and although other media may appeal to similar tropes, the reliance on player valor and individual talent in video games is striking and clearly linked to the role of the player. Video games are a place where a particular ideology—meritocracy—runs rampant and largely unchecked.

Video games are a key point of insight into what is happening in the world and a potential site to realize substantial change. Video games are a harbinger of things to come, a model of the world we inhabit, and an extreme where certain behaviors and practices were honed before being integrated into contemporary political movements in the United States and the United Kingdom.[16] Video games offer a unique space of insight into the interests and practices of white men of means. They are a place where meritocracy is made real through consistent interaction and reinforcement. However, they are also an excellent place to explore low-risk, high-impact experiences where players can see, explore, and feel a different subject position. Video games are a platform for experimentation and a place for intervention. Video games give space for new perspectives and a chance for reflection while offering a way to intervene in modern life. They are a location where what they have made can also be unmade—but to do that it is necessary to understand what exactly is going on with, in, and around them.

This project contends that the dependence on meritocracy within videogame narrative and design is a substantial problem. Meritocratic norms limit the potential audience for video games and structure how players and designers interact. The meritocratic focus of games is self-insulating and self-replicating. Those who are successful believe they have attained their status through the quality of their effort, a compelling ground on which to build the impression that they are simply better than others are. The prevalence of meritocratic myths in games also encourages players to want more meritocratic games and deride video games that do not fit that template as lesser, bad games, and sometimes even to contest whether non-meritocratic efforts are even proper games at all.

In her study of online trolls, Whitney Phillips makes a clear case for how systems and structures matter in any attempt to address online culture. She argues that the reason we can't have nice things is because "trolls are born of and embedded within dominant institutions and tropes, which are every bit as damaging as the troll's most disruptive behaviors."[17] In detailing the reason for problematic behavior, a huge part of Phillips's argument is that it is not just the people that are a problem, but also the systems, structures, and norms that support and enable their behavior.

Any step to address larger issues in video games and game culture requires subverting meritocratic norms and expectations; falling back on meritocratic practices ensures a limit on how much videogame culture can change. Fixing game culture would also help develop the norms, systems, and structures to create a more positive environment that can spread beyond the limited space of games. Addressing the issues in video games would provide a road map for how to deal with similar behaviors in other realms and perhaps get us on a path building our own new, nice things. Reconstructing videogame culture requires recontextualizing how we think about games in the first place. However, a first step in this process is accounting for the obligations of those who are privileged enough to play, write and think about, and make video games by pointing to some of the structural inequalities that ensure we are not all starting from the same place.

I am an incredibly lucky person. I was born straight, white, and male into a two-parent household in a rich country, which is pretty much winning the genetic lottery. I had the opportunity to go to college and graduate school and now get to teach, think, and write for a job. I quite literally play video games for research purposes. That doesn't suck, but it also offers me a platform to create change. More pointedly, all those benefits leave me with an obligation to leverage my advantages to help make the world a better place.

Although my position and obligations are specific to me, if you are reading this book I expect there is also a context for the obligations you carry as well. One of the ways of framing where we fit and how fortunate we are is to think about the world as a village of one hundred people, with the same distributive ratios that we have for the seven billion people who inhabit the world at large.[18] Over the past decade the number of people with a college degree in that hypothetical village has grown from one to seven (at the time of this writing), but if you are one of those people with such a degree you still have ninety-three fellow villagers who have not had the same opportunities. If you have access to a computer, you would be one of twenty-two that do, numbers that are largely matched by the seventeen who are unable to read and write, the twenty-three with no shelter from wind and rain, and the thirteen who do not have safe water to drink. At the point that you are fortunate enough to be in a position where you can have the ability, the time, and the resources to read a book about video games, you are one of a very small group of people in the world with that opportunity. To me, this is one way of thinking about how we all carry an obligation to make the world a better place and of reflecting on how imbalanced access to resources subverts any attempt to measure merit. Video games are not everything, but they are important; therefore, committing to improving the culture around video games is one place to start fulfilling some of our obligations.

One of the key problems with meritocratic ideology is that it self-replicates in a way that discourages critical reflection about the privilege a person possesses. A key piece of the meritocratic myth is that it seduces the successful to believe they earned their position in society. It is far more comfortable to think that your skills and effort account for your accomplishments than to think it was gifted to you through a cornucopia of accidents or elements of good fortune. Success in a meritocratic system creates a cocoon that encourages a lack of critical reflection about the breaks and luck that lead to a variety of advantages enabling a person to ascend to the heights he or she reaches. From gender, race, and class to national origin and ability, all the intersections of our identities circumscribe where we start in meritocratic systems. Those who succeed under meritocracy are often talented, smart, and thoughtful—I would surely like to think that I am—but the successful typically benefit from a series of structural head starts that help them climb the social hierarchy. Thinking you are talented, gifted, or better than others is certainly more comfortable than realizing you are simply luckier. Self-insulating meritocratic norms are a key part of what has made the culture around video games so negative, so isolated, and so problematic, because many of the games we have teach players that they are special and have earned their success.

Perhaps the biggest takeaway of my career is that those of us who have benefited from the current system have an obligation to do more than simply sit back and observe. Those fortunate enough to be in a position to speak out have a job to do just that. There are not always good platforms on which to critique contemporary society; therefore, when a person stands on one, he or she should use it to make the world a better place. As a person who benefits from a system that largely gives me a job for as long as I would like one, as a previous author who has contacts with publishers, as a player who has spent a lifetime playing video games, and as a person who has benefited from structural privilege throughout my life, this project comes directly out of my obligation to try to make a difference. Although your story may not line up perfectly with mine, I encourage you to do your own accounting of how you ended up where you are and how accidents of birth and inherited advantages may have moved you forward on your path. I believe the culture surrounding video games has gotten too bad to simply sit back and watch any longer; the status quo must change, and the concept of meritocracy is a formative part of the toxicity found in the culture around video games. We need to spend more time thinking about the ideological implications of video games, enough to match the effort put into our obsessions over frame rates, hours played, and drama about downloadable content. The beginning of this change requires briefly explaining the concept of meritocracy, going on a shallow dive into the current state of the culture around video games, and then providing an overview of the book as a whole.

Meritocracy, in Brief

Perhaps the most prominent meritocratic narrative is the American Dream, according to which people, especially those new to the United States, can pull themselves up by their bootstraps and succeed based on hard work and perseverance.[19] By convincing immigrants to come to the United States and persuading those who struggle that if they work hard enough their fate will improve, bootstrapping narratives individualize responsibility, erase structural barriers, and advance a meritocratic story that is typical in contemporary Western society and actualized in video games. Meritocratic game narratives partner perfectly with elements of meritocratic game design to make video games one of the purest spaces of meritocratic rhetoric. Video games are a place where the abstract ideology of meritocracy is actualized and solidified. In a broader context, meritocratic narratives cover up structural inequality and personalize responsibility to make each individual appear to be responsible for his or her own success or failure, resulting in recognition by critics that meritocracy functions more like a myth than as a coherent ideology.[20] However, as meritocracy has become more widely accepted it is increasingly difficult to recognize where it came from and how inherited position is often more meaningful than any individual talent.

Meritocracy makes it seem like people are responsible for their own success or failure, even when the wealth of someone like U.S. president Donald Trump is far more likely to be the result of inheritance than individual investment savvy.[21] Trump is a case study in how we do not actually live in a meritocracy. Substantial parts of his success were based on being a connected white man. He is able to say things that a woman or person of color simply would not be allowed to, while showing little awareness that the body he inhabits gives him a much wider latitude than that given to others.[22] He appeals to his talent and attempts to promulgate it through his books and his brief attempt at a "university." He minimizes the resources gifted to him by birth as a "small loan" to help bolster an argument that he achieved his status based on his own merit, when the reality is that he grew up in one of the richest families in the United States.[23] Instead of developing real estate and creating some of the most amazing buildings in the world, the Trump Organization is mostly a rent-seeking endeavor, making its money based on leasing out the name "Trump."[24] Donald Trump certainly has talents and puts in work, but his merit is magnified and facilitated by being born into a rich family that was already prominent in New York real estate. His advantages are magnified by his status as a straight, white man who uses his performance of masculinity as a way to appeal to voters. He has since passed many of those advantages to his children, who continue to perpetuate a system where their jobs are part of a familial inheritance, rather than an achievement based on their talent and hard work. The Trump family success demonstrates how meritocracies break down as parents pass privilege to their children, lessening the amount of skill or effort they need to have in order to be successful.

Systems, ideologies, and cultures that seem natural are produced through regular social interactions, and neither meritocracy nor video games are exceptions to those dynamics. We are in a moment when we have to look critically at meritocracy and take it apart. The increasing inequality in which we are living undercuts, subverts, and prevents meritocracy from working, while appeals to meritocratic ideology give moral justification to the winners.[25] Meritocracy eliminates any focus on structural problems and systems, focusing us on individuals instead. The hallmarks of meritocracy and its effects can be seen in areas ranging from the Brexit vote, to criticism of the Black Lives Matter movement, to the 2016 Trump presidential campaign. Meritocracy depends on an equal starting position for all, and the world around us features constant reminders that equal opportunity is not available for everyone. In this light, it is relevant to briefly examine where the idea came from and how it came to be so widely accepted in many parts of the world.

Popularized by its use in a satirical novel by Michael Young in 1958, "meritocracy" refers to a society where people rise and fall based on their personal skills and effort. Prominent supporters of meritocracy, like Daniel Bell, see it "as an emphasis on individual achievement and earned status as confirmed by one's peers."[26] In the 1990s, as the term was becoming more widely used, Peter Saunders expounded that a meritocracy is a system "based upon a competition in which the achieved rather than ascribed characteristics of individuals determine the outcome. It is a system which depends upon genuine equality of opportunity but which generates unequal outcomes."[27] In specific application to his native Great Britain, Saunders writes that "the principle of meritocracy is widely understood as a 'fair' and 'just' principle, and for most people (even if not most sociologists), evidence that ability and effort are increasingly being recognised and rewarded in this country would be positively welcomed."[28] In the most basic sense, "a meritocracy is a social system where individual talent and effort, rather than ascriptive traits, determine individuals' placements in a social hierarchy."[29] Jo Littler, a prominent critic of the ideology, states that "a meritocracy is nowadays understood as 'a social system which allows people to achieve success proportionate to their talents and abilities, as opposed to one in which social class or wealth is the controlling factor.'"[30] The idea of a meritocracy generally concerns social order and how to allocate resources. Backers of meritocratic norms typically believe that skill should be measured, that effort should be tracked, and that those who demonstrate the best combinations of talent and hard work should rise to the top of the social ladder. By assessing these individual traits, meritocracies aspire to cut out considerations of social class, race, family background, or other characteristics in order to dole out rewards to those judged to be the most deserving, allowing them to ascend the social hierarchy.[31]

Saunders is correct is his belief that meritocratic norms have become widely accepted in many contemporary societies, but there are fundamental structural problems inherent to a meritocratic system of organization. The most basic implication of sorting people based on a combination of talent and drive is that meritocracies are predicated on "unspecified levels of inequality, but with equal opportunities to compete for advantageous positions within it"; yet, as Ruth Levitas notes, "you cannot, in fact, have equality of opportunity when there are large substantive inequalities."[32] Jo Littler lists three key problems of a meritocratic order: one must consider "'talent' or 'intelligence'" to be something that "is inborn from birth"; "that it endorses a competitive, linear, hierarchical system in which by definition people must be left behind"; and that it requires a "hierarchical ranking of professions and status."[33] Meritocracies require sorting people into categories where some are adjudged more worthy than others based on effects of their life circumstances, not their skill and effort. It is a system predicated on inequality, where those who are less successful are supposedly struggling because they either are not talented enough or are too lazy to improve their lot in life. Meritocracy isolates, individualizes, and strips out context. In the contemporary world there has also been a lack of attention paid to equality of opportunity, as those at the top pass their inheritance to those like them, while yanking the ladder away that helped them up in the first place.

As an ideology, meritocracy affects people in many different ways. Embracing meritocracy makes allocating resources seem straightforward: as soon as a system for judging merit is established, it becomes easy to assess who finished at the top and is most deserving of the greatest rewards. In addition to its utility in economics, supporters of meritocracy argue that it "is considered by many to be an ideal justice principle, because only relevant inputs (e.g., abilities) should be considered and irrelevant factors (e.g., ethnicity, gender) should be ignored when distributing outcomes. Thus, meritocracy is bias free and can be seen as creating social mobility; this is the American dream."[34] Meritocracy is about making clear, self-rationalizing decisions. For those who buy into the principle that merit can be properly assessed, meritocracy functions brilliantly. Meritocracy makes decisions clear, as it offers up a straightforward rationale while ensuring decisions appear fair and proper. These twin dynamics make a meritocratic ideology self-reinforcing for those who believe in it.

As an "ideally" just way to make decisions, meritocracy folds nicely into decisions about how to best design reward systems in games, as systems relying on evaluations of merit are generally interpreted by players as fair. This can translate as the simple lesson that video games teach: that killing the boss proves a player's skill, which means the princess is a proper reward for demonstrating merit in play and evidence of a player's superiority over others. However, in practice meritocracies are plagued with problems, as any structural biases that create inequality of opportunities short-circuits the ability to properly judge merit. Meritocracy is a kind of social organization that seems sound in a design document; however, as soon as it moves into practice it becomes impossible to isolate merit from other factors in the process of evaluating people. Meritocracy works as a magnifier for any sort of structural inequality stemming from differences in things like sex, gender, race, class, sexual orientation, age, or many other factors. A common critique of standardized exams, like IQ tests, the SAT, and the ACT, is that they carry cultural biases. I contend that much of the same baggage applies to the skill- and effort-based challenges found throughout video games, as both kinds of exams set the terms for engagement, whether the interaction is about getting into college or devoting hours to successfully completing a newly released video game. Properly judging merit requires starting at the same place, so any existing barriers hinder certain people, and those shortcomings are then blamed on the individual affected, rather than on the society around them. By individualizing people, meritocracy has the impact of making people judgmental and rude, while making individuals more likely to attribute their status in life to their own efforts or lack thereof, which makes us less sensitive to others. These cultural dynamics are both a natural outgrowth of meritocratic systems and are regularly displayed in the culture around video games.

The State of Game Culture

There are problematic parts of any culture, and there are ways in which technology enables troublesome behavior.[35] Anonymity and norms of online communication have led to a situation where being outspoken and a woman, or sometimes just being a woman, on the internet will lead to death threats and persistent harassment.[36] Other media, like television, use rape and harassment of nameless women as a way to show that characters are complicated or that the show is edgy.[37] The connections between meritocracy and problematic culture aren't just present in the realm of games either: they can be found throughout tech culture, where a meritocratic ideology often limits diversity in hiring and retention throughout the careers of those who are not white and male.[38] Sexism is prevalent in college computer science programs, online harassment has led to women retiring from writing careers because public attention sets the stage for harassment, women are fleeing jobs in technology because of a generally "hostile and unwelcoming environment for women," and research on GitHub has found that code written by women is considered lesser as soon as a woman's name is attached to it.[39] The dynamics lead to a clear argument that women are not welcome on the internet, but harassers are. It is impossible to extricate the problems in video games from broader cultural issues with sexism and racism, but these are precisely the kinds of obstacles that undercut a meritocratic order. Instead of starting from the same place with a relative equality of opportunity, those from marginalized groups typically face substantial obstacles simply to catch up to the starting line of those born with advantages tied to their sex, gender, race, and/or economic and social status. All of these elements and so many more set the stage for a culture where what matters is not just merit, but also all the structural advantages or disadvantages one faces. Despite this, there are some promising, positive steps within sectors of game culture to take on problematic norms, from industry-led conferences on diversity to academics seeking to change conversations and cultural norms around games to major gaming news outlets that recognize how important it is to cover the dark side of the game industry, even though any progressive move faces criticism from some readers.[40] However, looking more closely at the state of the culture around video games shows just how bleak the situation is and why more must be done to address existing problems.

Ranking hate speech or trying to assess which oppression is worse is a regressive activity that does not fix problems, but analysis of virulent sexism is perhaps the easiest starting point for a discussion of toxicity in games. The use of the term "rape" is omnipresent throughout the discussion around games, popping up almost any time certain players either win or lose in spectacular, or sometimes even ordinary, fashion. Those who lose to computer-controlled opponents may talk about how the game raped them, while victors in battle might mention how they raped their opponent. The prevalence of the term, especially in conjunction with racist and homophobic speech, can counter efforts to make games more inclusive and welcoming to a broad population of potential players. Specific examples of misogynistic language that has become a hallmark of online games are documented on websites like *Fat, Ugly, or Slutty* and *Not in the Kitchen Anymore*, with the former starting in response to the widespread belief among a certain type of player that all women who play games online must fall into one of those three categories and the latter documenting audio clips from online games to "raise awareness and educate others about the issue of harassment in online gaming, as well as provide a safe place through various social media outlets for people to vent about their own experiences."[41]

Game culture's issues with women can be clearly seen in the case of Anita Sarkeesian and her efforts to develop a Kickstarter-funded video series called *Tropes vs. Women in Video Games*. The positive lesson to take from the campaign was that it raised almost $160,000, well more than its $6,000 goal. However, part of the reason for the massive amount of fund-raising was a widespread campaign of misogynist abuse where, according to one journalist, "every access point they [online critics] could exploit was used to get at her."[42] A game was created where the objective was to punch Sarkeesian in the face and, when attempts were made to shut down hate speech by locking down comments on particular messages or videos, the speech simply moved to other articles and venues.[43] The example of Anita Sarkeesian is sometimes chalked up to issues with online misogyny as a whole, but it is more specific than that. As Leigh Alexander astutely notes, the discourse around games is different from other media and, when it comes to sexism, "games have it bad. Anita Sarkeesian has done a number of video series about gender stereotypes. Only when she tried her hand at games did the monsters come."[44] Games are similar to, but different from, other media and technology in general. Arthur Chu writes, "I've spent time in a lot of places that draw the opinionated and the zealous. I hang out with artsy theater people, with angry political activists, and with nerds of all stripes. And never have I met a group of people as doggedly convinced that their opinion is 'objectively' correct as gamers."[45] A similar sentiment is shared by the media critic who writes under the pen name "Film Crit Hulk," who observes, "hulk can tell you with confidence that the culture of video games has a much, much, much, much higher rate of all the 'bad stuff' than everything else (save politics)."[46] GamerGate has become the epitome of this culture, the dynamic that prohibits critical analysis and assessment of the structural issues surrounding access to video games. Research into online harassment by the Pew Research Center has found that "while most online environments were viewed as equally welcoming to both genders, the starkest results were for online gaming. Some 44% of respondents felt the platform was more welcoming toward men."[47] Although 44 percent is a minority of respondents, only 51 percent of respondents felt online gaming is equally welcoming to both men and women. Other online activities had a minimum of 66 percent of those polled who viewed the activity as balanced. Although hate speech and exclusion are suffused throughout society, some places are worse than others, and if you have ever played an online game or spent time reading news about games you likely experienced enough of the "bad stuff" to know it.

Beyond actions and discussion in the culture surrounding games, the representation of women within games is frequently disappointing, from the visual representation of individual characters to the way avatars of women are used as props within games. One commentary contends that "gaming's obsession with breasts is part of a juvenile medium's awkward process of floundering towards mature themes," but concluded with an analysis of how "public calls for realistic proportions are sometimes at odds with consumer demands."[48] Effectively, public lobbying or designer desire to check unrealistic portrayals in games are rapidly shut down because of ambiguous appeals to players' interests in ridiculous representations of bodies. When questions are asked, notable designers often attribute the issue to "cultural differences" in an attempt to find a get-out-of-jail-free card to evade criticism.[49] Beyond how women are bodily represented, women face grave limitations in the roles they are given in games, frequently receding into the background. A widespread belief throughout the game industry is that games with female protagonists don't sell as well as those with men on the cover, despite a lack of data to back up the presumption.[50] Developers play an interesting role in this process, both advocating for putting female characters in prominent positions on game box art and contending that it would be too much work to add women as playable characters or arguing that masculinity is so crucial to the story being told that women need to fade into roles as background, non-playable characters.[51] The eventual inclusion of women characters into the popular soccer title *FIFA 16* is a particularly instructive example of the role of women in games. Noting that adding women to *FIFA* took years and demonstrates how a system explicitly designed to house men "struggles to accommodate women even when it makes efforts to," the game journalist Nathan Ditum concludes that "our industry is one in which it's possible to conceive of women being something that might appear on a checklist of stuff we'd ideally like to include. Women, an optional extra dropped from this particular reality due to a lack of resources."[52] Women are frequently left out of games or included as an afterthought, which substantially limits the amount of diversity in video games and creates a baseline condition that ensures inequality of opportunity for many, instead of a perfectly balanced platform from which to judge merit.

Troubles with racial depictions of characters in video games also run throughout the medium. As Evan Narcisse puts it in the introduction to an e-mail conversation with a number of black critics and game developers, "Video games have a blackness problem. . . . When they appear at all, black characters are often reduced to outdated, embarrassing stereotypes."[53] Narcisse and those with whom he e-mailed go on to discuss that there is no single answer to solve these problems; instead, it will take a number of conversations and smaller steps to move the industry and the audience for games forward. As evidence of Narcisse's premise, one 2015 release encapsulates many of the issues around racial depictions in games. *The Witcher 3: Wild Hunt* was highly praised in reviews, with the critic Tauriq Moosa contending that "it's one of the greatest games I've ever played," yet also noting that "not a single human in the game is a person of color."[54] Moosa argues that the dominance of white men in positions as both game developers and game critics leads to a situation where "we got a hundred articles confronting the *Witcher 3* devs about less pretty grass physics, but not a single article asking them about no people of color."[55] The crucial point of Moosa's essay focuses on responding to the defense made by backers of the game that a narrative based on Slavic mythology requires using white characters. First, Moosa argues that with so many stories about white men in games, it is crucial to note these moments when women and people of color are written out of the stories told within them. Second, for games set in a fantasy world, players are often asked to believe in dragons, wraiths, and magic. Why are racial depictions the mythical step that goes too far? In the aftermath of Moosa's essay many in the game community quickly spoke out in criticism, to the point where a piece in defense of his article began by positing, "Are non-white characters in fantasy games less 'realistic' than dragons? Plenty of video game fans seem to think so."[56] Eventually, sustained harassment led Moosa to delete his Twitter account, although several prominent game developers and critics voiced support for his position under the hashtag #IStandWithTauriq.[57] Moosa did an excellent job of pointing out the blind spot video games have with regard to race, and the reaction to his essay emphasizes just how limited consideration of race in games is.

Game culture and game design often work in a circular, self-reinforcing loop on issues of inclusion. Games that do not attract a diverse audience lead to the creation of more games that will not attract a diverse audience. Robin Potanin argues that "publishers are predominantly concerned about what will sell best in large family retail chains" and that the economics of the industry "does not encourage diversity" because publishers are largely interested in games "that promise to be strong sellers."[58] In addition to the economic structures of the industry, Potanin argues that there is a correlation between the "predominance of young white males represented in games and young white males making games," creating an environment where "videogames are unique in their extreme gender disparity. No other media under-represents the female population to such a degree as games."[59] Construction of video games as a space for white males of means has a long history, as Carly Kocurek writes; nostalgia about videogame arcades is "populated almost exclusively by young white men with both the time and the money to play video games as much as they wanted."[60] And though issues about representation of women are beginning to be discussed within the industry, there is far less focus on race, class, and other intersectional issues that similarly ensure unequal starting points.

Looking at representation in games, Kishonna Gray argues that many games "illustrate race and gender in stereotypical terms," which has the impact of devaluing those who are not white and male, confirming their marginalized status when it comes to video games.[61] Detailing the role of voice in online gaming, Gray argues that the need to talk and the speed at which nonwhite players are identified and called out for not conforming to dominant expectations places them in a position to be harassed and marginalized throughout their play.[62] This bias reaches beyond casual play and into highly visible contexts like eSports tournaments, where prominent black players are subject to racist harassment at least in part because their presence is judged by a vocal segment of the community as abnormal and unwelcomed.[63] Building games around repetitive tropes and narratives limits the community of people likely to play games, both online and off, putting players in a position where troublesome speech is more readily normalized. Normalizing hate speech limits the audience for video games and repels people who would diversify the audience for games and change community norms. Changing the culture of games requires taking a step back and asking a critical set of questions about what video games are and how they could look, work, and tell stories differently.

Working from the premise that video games are a significant cultural object, it is important to ask two key categories of questions about them. The first type of question is about what counts as a video game: Are video games limited to the realm of consoles and PCs? What about mobile devices, web browsers, or Facebook? Perhaps more important, are these games placed in a hierarchy where some kinds are deemed more valuable or worthy than others? Pressed hard enough, many players will express a preference for one type of platform over another, and many reading this can think of examples of what they don't consider a proper video game but that could fit as a "real" game for others.[64] Genre also intersects with this question in interesting ways as different regions of the world have different values, but *World of Warcraft*, *League of Legends*, and *Destiny* often count differently than *Madden NFL*, *Candy Crush Saga*, and *FarmVille*. Further, how do we consider board games, role-playing games, computerized versions of games like solitaire, and interactive experiences like *Gone Home*?

The second group of questions is about who counts as a gamer or player. The term "gamer" itself is contested, as many people who play video games do not identify with the term, but this is a crucial question when it comes to thinking about game culture, meritocracy, and changing the existing order of games.[65] In the course of this project, the word player is used when talking about the broad, heterogeneous group of people who play games. Gamer is used to convey a subset of that group, a person whose core identity is often defined around video games and who tends to be deeply invested in contemporary videogame culture. Who gets privileged and is given a voice shapes what gets counted as a game, as some votes are rendered valid and others are not considered at all. In a world where large publishers and marketing teams play an outsized role in how games are presented, the question of who counts as a target audience is tremendously important. When considering these issues, it is crucial to think about how they intersect with one another: How frequently are the kinds of games least likely to be considered proper video games played by the kinds of people least likely to identify as gamers? How likely are the borderline games to resist meritocratic norms in game design and narrative? Do they show us a different path? What kinds of spaces can be explored if meritocratic game design is resisted in favor of something else?

Games in general and video games in particular offer the opportunity to explore new and different possibility spaces. They give players the chance to enact roles that they are not likely to experience in ordinary life, from ruler of a great empire (*Civilization*; *Populous*) to streetwise criminal or outlaw (*Grand Theft Auto*; *Red Dead Redemption*) to professional athlete (*FIFA*; *Madden NFL*; *NBA 2K*). They also open space to explore experiences typically rendered outside of core games, like fashion model or boutique owner (*Kim Kardashian: Hollywood*; *Fashion Story*), service-industry employee (*Sally's Spa*; *Cook, Serve, Delicious*), or student (*Persona 4 Golden*; *Bully*). Video games give players a chance to actualize subject positions, to become a new kind of person, which could make games a perfect place for experimentation. Video games could give us a chance to explore almost anything, yet cultural constraints limit what ends up actually being made and marketed. What counts as a game and who counts as a potential player set the bounds for what kinds of experiences are likely to be available. Meritocratic norms limit what kinds of stories are told and, by extension, who will become part of videogame culture. Video games offer the promise of resisting dominant social narratives, but they can also easily fall into the trap of reinforcing a narrow set of perspectives. Rethinking what counts in videogame culture offers a platform on which to challenge troublesome elements of video games and key issues in society at large, particularly when one considers the surging, rapidly diversifying audience of people who play video games and the widening number of platforms on which games are played.[66]

The fragmentation of media in contemporary society has created a situation where mass culture experiences are relatively rare. Audiences can seek out individually matched content that suits their interests, at the cost of dividing groups of people into smaller and smaller pools. Audiences for hit television shows have shrunk considerably, and movies, when adjusted for inflation, tend to gross less money today than they did historically. Video games offer an opportunity to contact an influential audience, often one that can be better reached in games than in other media. The limited number of experiences in mainstream games also offers a perfect opportunity to challenge what has existed thus far. Video games are a relatively new medium and, while other media have had a chance to tell a range of stories, video games tend to repeat the same tropes over and over. The dependence on meritocratic expectations likely stems from a range of causes, but other media, like books, music, and board games, have had the time and the back catalog to depict a variety of tales. This existing limitation in the kinds of experiences within games, combined with the simultaneous rise of video games and meritocratic norms in society more broadly, makes those who play games a key audience for destabilizing meritocratic norms. A key, requisite element of detoxifying game culture is encouraging reflection about the structural inequities that exist within videogame culture and society at large.

Dear Game Designers

Escaping a meritocratic thought process is terribly difficult. It is quite likely that everyone reading this book has benefited from a number of structural advantages and also faced notable challenges in their life. It is also more comfortable to think about how our successes are tied to our merit than to advantages we were gifted. However, the challenge I am seeking to lay out in this book is to encourage critical thought about the assumptions we regularly make and the implications of those assumptions in practice.

Think for a moment about the beginning of Bethesda's *The Elder Scrolls V: Skyrim*. Often cited as one of the best games ever made, *Skyrim* can readily consume over a hundred hours of game play. The opening minutes of the game are largely cinematic, as the player regains consciousness and begins to learn of his or her situation.[67] Engaging from a first-person perspective, players slowly learn clues of where they are and who they are perceived to be. The player is a convict being led to the headsman to be executed along with the leader of the rebellion, a rebel, and a horse thief. Players can look around to the other four white men in the horse-drawn cart with them, one of whom is driving the prisoners somewhere. Upon arrival, names are read off of those who are to be executed. The horse thief seeks to run and is shot down by archers. The player is then mysteriously missing from the list of prisoners to be executed and is thrown into a character-selection process with a dizzying array of options. It is notable that the first choice for race in the game is for "Nord," which features an in-game description reading, "Citizens of Skyrim, they are a tall and fair-haired people. Strong and hardy, Nords are famous for their resistance to cold and their talent as warriors. They can use a battle cry to make opponents flee." After personalizing their character, players are led by the Captain, the first woman depicted in the game, into a lineup to be executed. One non-player character is led to the headsman and executed. Then the player is called out, but shortly after his or her head is placed on the block a dragon shows up and wreaks havoc. Players are able to escape with the help of the rebel on their original prison cart and make their way through the early section of the game, learning the basics of play, picking up equipment, and battling the Imperials, largely in hand-to-hand combat. As players seek to escape from the Imperial soldiers, they learn through background discussion that the dragon is a harbinger of the end times. As players progress throughout the game they become more powerful, discovering they have special abilities and a key role in the future of the world.

The assumptions and game-design choices made in the early part of the game are notable and important. Players start out as disempowered, about to be executed, but over the course of the game the avatar grows increasingly powerful and, with the help of the player, becomes crucial to saving the world and averting disaster. As the game unfolds, the player's effort means that his or her avatar moves forward, almost on rails, in an effort to defeat the dragons and reach his or her potential. This straightforward progress in character development stands in stark contrast to the narrative design of the game, which is hailed for the number of options and possibilities present. It is notable that all the early characters are light skinned, coded as Nordic, and that they are overwhelmingly male. This likely speaks to the established audience for the game, but it also limits the potential audience for what the game could be. Granted, with three and a half years of development time and $85 million in development costs, *Skyrim* needed to reach an established audience, but the game takes few risks in how it chooses to represent those early non-player characters.[68]

The point of considering *Skyrim* critically is to think more deeply about the assumptions the game makes about its audience. The game effectively assumes a white, male player. The game assumes a person who can relate to a modified Nordic mythology. The game assumes the player is someone who wants a story that mixes violence, rebellion, dragons, magic, and the ability to save the world. All these things can be compelling, but they are telling a particular story for a particular audience. Additionally, the game is designed in a manner to celebrate the player's intervention in the world. Without the player the world would be destroyed, but based on the player's skills and effort he or she is able to avert catastrophe. It is vital to work through the implications of the assumptions games make.

The game normalizes whiteness and maleness through the choice of early non-player characters and the centrality of the Nord. The number of races and key women characters can disrupt this over the run of the game, but the introductory moments are meaningful. One of the most substantial lessons of the game, however, is that hard work and skill pay off in substantial rewards. As long as the player plays hard enough and well enough, they will save the world because of their merit. The game need not address structural barriers or inequity, as the player has ascended from a convict about to be executed into the only person who can avert apocalypse.

A single game designed in this manner would be one thing, but *Skyrim* is both an exceptional game based on its critical reviews and a typical one based on its focus on merit, men, and whiteness. Repetition of a single approach makes it real and concrete, which also offers promise and potential for games that seek to structure things differently. The point of this book is to help you think through the implications of the choices made in game design. Video games matter, and the decisions made about what to represent and how to do it are impactful. It is possible to disrupt and change what has been, and hopefully this book will demonstrate why things need to be different and how that can happen. *Skyrim* is a great game, but it is a symptom of the meritocratic traps that are found all too commonly in video games.

What's to Come

Beyond accounting for the background information for what inspired this project, it is important to work through the foundational steps in my argument. The first key piece to this work is a deeper analysis of where the term "meritocracy" came from and how, in contemporary society, it has been stripped of its context and twisted to seem normal and natural. Understanding the context for meritocracy is vital because it sets up space for reflection about how games both are and are not special. Games are different from other media in some important ways, but the dominance of meritocracy as an ideology was something they inherited. Backstory and context for that complicated relationship helps illustrate how video games actualize meritocracy and why that matters, and suggests ways to find an alternative path forward. Critically examining meritocracy requires detailing how Western society has gotten to a place where merit is something to be celebrated and also finding the spaces in which meritocratic expectations clearly do not work. Recent cultural analysis provides excellent examples of where basing a culture on merit simply breaks down, cases in which skill and talent serve as a pleasant-looking veil to obscure what lies underneath. Meritocracies lead to bad outcomes and perverse incentives that privilege the few over the many. When it comes to video games, widespread meritocratic norms lead the successful to believe their victories are solely accountable to their skill and effort, which can preempt efforts to help other people. The impact of a meritocratic ideology is a consistent thread throughout this project. Chapter 1 provides an extended background on meritocracy, including its history, its impacts, and several implications for video games.

A second key piece to my argument is recognizing how various parts of video games and game culture can be seen as rhetorical constructions. Working from the premise that words and concepts are both arbitrary and based on actual interactions, rhetorical analysis helps critically examine symbol systems, with a focus on what they mean and how they affect our worldview. Quite simply, the words we choose and the symbols we select matter. They tell us something about what we value, how we think, the environment in which we exist, and who we aspire to be. In this case, concepts like "video game," "gamer," "player," and "videogame culture" all shape the terrain in which games are developed and on whom they do their work. Recognizing these concepts as social constructions, while also thinking through how they affect game development, is a key step in unraveling meritocratic norms in gaming.[69]

The final element that underscores this argument is acknowledging the special role that video games play when it comes to meritocratic norms. There are two steps to this process. First, chapter 2 features a discussion of relevant research in game studies, as well as a deeper discussion of contemporary videogame culture. Second, it is important to examine the two crucial ways meritocracy comes into play in video games, in both meritocratic videogame design and narratives. I contend that most games, especially most big-budget, AAA titles, are predicated on what I call meritocratic game design. Meritocratic game design can be seen in almost any instance where a person might respond to a problem or a lack of skill with the response that he or she "learn to play." This approach to design applies in situations where video games are perceived as battles of skill in which the best player should win. Two key premises that support meritocratic game design are the belief that games should be properly balanced to benefit the most skilled players and that success in video games is something that is properly earned by players through their effort and labor. In addition to design, meritocratic game narratives are also infused in many mainstream games, as players set out to rise from being a relative no one to an all-powerful being. Achieving success is not exclusively a hallmark of meritocracy, but when that success is all but assured within the context of video games—where you can often restart as much as necessary, when that success seems determined by skill, and when there isn't room for reflection about what made a player successful—video games advance meritocratic norms within their narratives.

Games are filled with rags-to-riches stories—they form the center of everything from *Kim Kardashian: Hollywood* to the *Final Fantasy* games; even sports video games typically contain a "My Player" mode where players progress from a minor role to eventually become a star. In *Kim Kardashian: Hollywood* players are discovered by the socialite in the opening moments, and the narrative of the game is based on moving up from a retail employee to a leader of the celebrity A-list. The *Final Fantasy* games are typically based around stories where a central character is ostracized from society at large only to become the savior by the end of the game. The "My Player" option in almost all major sports releases allows players to create their own avatar, an athlete who typically begins his or her career pinned to the bench, but through the ongoing intervention of the player behind the controller the avatar can become a superstar.

The overarching narrative in the career mode of sports games is all about rising from a lowly beginning, a trend that is being actualized more completely in recent entries to the series. *FIFA 17* added a mode called "The Journey," where players play as the seventeen-year-old Alex Hunter, aiding his development from a children's league to the professional ranks. The path is predetermined to feature adversity, as players must succeed at exit trials to be picked up by a team, will invariably get loaned out when their chosen team favors a high-priced signing, and face a former best friend as a rival, yet Alex will almost always overcome those challenges to become a highly successful, decorated player. Alex's path is set up for him to outperform the efforts of his grandfather and father, both professional soccer players in their own right, and the narrative is specifically designed to help Alex achieve things his family never did—because of the interventions of the person with the controller. The narrative pinnacle of the game is the FA Cup Championship, the one trophy that Alex's grandfather never won; to the best of my knowledge and reporting about the mode, Alex never gets injured for an extended period of time, which was his father's downfall. Narratively, "The Journey" is a tidy arc, where the game player begins creating soccer stars from the moment they are pushed out of the professional ranks into a rapid, one-season ascension that typically ends with trophies and a call-up to England's national team. Even though there are off-ramps in the game, places where Alex can be stymied, the mode is built on the premise that hard work and skill are sufficient to overcome any structural barriers or obstacles, including the persistent injuries that can end the most promising athletic careers.[70]

There are also tropes in games where meritocratic design and narrative elements intersect. Leveling is a typical videogame convention, where players grow from a powerless level one into a much more powerful, more skilled, and more able level more than one. Leveling in video games is a clear process of progress, as players typically know what they need to do and how much they need to do it to move forward. Working as both a design and narrative element, leveling is often constructed in a manner that encourages players to buy into a meritocratic world, where those with more levels are more deserving than those who have not yet progressed as far in the game—because, after all, the powerful have displayed more skill and invested more effort. Meritocratic game design and narrative will feature throughout the project, as the concepts are developed in chapter 3 and case studies detailing how they appear are provided in chapter 4.

One of the possible paths out of the dependence on meritocracy in video games requires looking outside of games to other fields. In chapter 5, I use examples from sports and higher education in the United States to give a different perspective on how meritocracies can work and how they can be disrupted. The potential for new kinds of video games is more fully explored in the conclusion, which offers examples of games that break with the standard expectations of contemporary games and begin to chart a path out of where games have been stuck for years.

The central, animating premise of this book is that people in positions where they can do something about problematic situations have an obligation to do something. One of the core problems in game culture is the dependence on meritocratic norms, which have the terrible impact of magnifying and excusing any structural inequalities among those playing video games. I hope this book helps fulfill my obligation to make things better by focusing attention on current problems and how they can be addressed. I hope it helps you recognize what your own obligations are and helps point you toward a path of making good on them.

1

Leveling Up in Life
How Meritocracy Works in Society

The idea of meritocracy has been so completely woven into contemporary Western society that it seems ahistorical, like this is how things have always been, but it is actually a far more recent phenomenon. Blending analysis of the history of the concept with contemporary examples of how meritocratic ideals inevitably evolve to be based on things that have little to do with merit demonstrates how the overdependence of meritocratic norms in video games creates a warped, twisted, and negative culture.

A starting place for grounding an analysis of meritocracy is to look to ancient China, where attempts at "meritocracy" were tried even though they predate the term itself. More recently, Michael Young's book popularized the term, so discussing it provides a framework for understanding the more contemporary debates about the use of the ideology and how a focus on merit has produced the society many of us live in today. An earnest look at the perspective of defenders of the term offers a chance to make the case for merit and better demonstrate why the ideas behind meritocracy are so seductive, particularly in the countries that most closely aspire to meritocracy as a system of social order: the United States and the United Kingdom. Given a more complete understanding of meritocracy, it is possible to turn to the effects of meritocracy and what kind of implications a meritocratic system of order has for videogame design, narrative, and culture.

Understanding meritocracy is crucially important to comprehend contemporary society, especially how some things are working well and how others are broken. We are living through the widespread application of a meritocratic approach to distributing resources and allocating positions without much sensitivity to or awareness of its failures. An underlying part of an appeal to recapture the past, with manufacturing jobs and an American dream, is the belief that we have lost our meritocratic way and need to recapture it. The reality of things is quite different, though, as growing inequality leads to a situation where meritocracy cannot work, where it is structurally broken and undermined. Meritocracy is blind to context, a feature that contemporary identity politics movements like Black Lives Matter and some pro-immigrant groups attempt to put in the foreground. As the political scientist Henry Farrell observes, "Meritocracy is blind to the fact that some people face structural disadvantages and others do not."[1] Meritocracy shelters us, individualizes us, and strips out the larger context in which we exist. For people who have been lucky enough to overcome structural disadvantages or those who were gifted head starts, meritocracy instructs us that we have earned our place and deserve to have more than those lesser people who are unable to reach our heights. Meritocracy is deeply integrated into contemporary culture, and although video games are special and can offer an escape to a different world, they are part and parcel of the culture in which they are made. Knowing why meritocracy is important sets the stage for better understanding how we got here and how meritocracy is integrated into contemporary video games.

An Old Yet Rising Meritocracy

Although popularized throughout the twentieth century in the United Kingdom and the United States, the concept of meritocracy can be found in a variety of historical societies and texts. Plato's case for philosopher kings is effectively an argument for the best, most talented people to run society in a meritocratic order. However, I find China's experience with meritocracy to be more instructive for our contemporary experience with the ideology. Chinese references to meritocratic principles were first seen in the Guodian Chu Slips, which are dated to approximately 300 BCE.[2] The primary mentions of merit and skill in the texts are in reference to the moral balance between humanity and righteousness. According to the historian Kenneth Holloway, considerations of humanity were linked to the family "and when expanded to a government perspective emphasizes the aristocratic inheritance of bureaucratic positions. In contrast, righteousness is the promoting of the most skilled individual and can be seen as government by meritocracy." The invocation of the actual term "meritocracy" is a modern translation of an ancient text, but the principle is quite similar to contemporary assertions of meritocratic rule given the importance of considering skill and effort in the decision-making process. Writing about the original Guodian texts, Holloway holds that "the fascinating contribution of the text is that it does not really see a difference between aristocracy and meritocracy, since both similarly contain strengths and weaknesses that must be balanced to create unity. In that the text is specific, it focuses on the application and not the cultivation of harmony." In this case, Chinese philosophy was focused on balancing considerations of birthright and skill in moral decisions. This is the fundamental problem meritocracy seeks to solve. Awarding privilege and power based on merit certainly makes for good appearances, but aristocracy ensures your own family's success. Merit is considered righteous, but it also may cause a person to make a decision in conflict with his or her own family. Eventually governance changed, and Holloway notes that "meritocracy in early China was quickly replaced by a system where the right to rule was passed from father to son." Considerations of family eventually trumped moral guidance based on righteousness; meritocracy was made unworkable by familial concerns and the inequality of opportunity they brought with them. In the end, Holloway observes, "there was no monumental shift from meritocracy to aristocracy from the perspective of Guodian, since both sides were simply focused on the same goal, harmonizing the state and family."[3] Meritocracy and aristocracy are two different ways to make decisions about how to allocate resources and who to put in leadership positions, yet aristocracies quickly sprout out of hierarchical meritocratic orders before people are forced to demote those they know because of their lack of skill or effort. In the case of China, meritocracy begets aristocracy and vice versa. Meritocratic norms become more prominent in a rebellion against the aristocracy, but those meritocratic practices eventually end up producing their own aristocracy.

Well after the era detailed in the Guodian Chu Slips, China revisited the process of decision making based on merit. Late imperial China focused on education and examinations for its civil service, which the historian Benjamin Elman describes as "approximating the world's first political meritocracy in political, social, and intellectual life."[4] First reappearing in a systemized manner during the T'ang dynasty, the recruiting of bureaucrats through civil service exams was a focal part of Chinese governments during multiple eras.[5] Elman found that during the Ming and Qing dynasties, Chinese citizens traveled throughout the empire to take civil service exams with "the hope that they might move from the bottom up to share political power with the ruler as civil servants. The dynasty legitimated those who successfully passed the examinations to hold office and wield political, cultural and legal power. Once holding office, they became meritocratically appointed authorities."[6] Somewhat different from the case with the Guodian Chu Slips, meritocracy in late imperial China was focused on levels well below the ruling class. However, by integrating extensive exams that were widely taken by the citizenry, the masses of Chinese were offered the opportunity to demonstrate skill and join the dynasty as government officials. Without disrupting imperial rule, civil servants became co-opted into the system, and many of the most able (at least according to the test) became far more powerful than they would have been had they stayed where they were born. In this case, the imprimatur of the ruling class in combination with a national exam established meritocratic consideration in governance. Eventually these exams ended, as those promoted into administrative positions via exams began to use the jobs for patronage rather than the promotion of meritocracy.

China's background with meritocracy offers two key lessons for video games. First, meritocratic systems fall apart when they stop measuring merit and focus on elements tied to inheritance. For video games, this can be seen in limited game offerings and a desire to produce more of the same, rather than games that are new and different, as success is determined by prior experience rather than the results of a fresh examination. As Robin Potanin argues about the practices of game developers, games are made for preexisting audiences, not wholly new ones.[7] This rewards those currently part of game culture and raises barriers for outsiders. Inheritance of a place at the table is a huge issue that limits the ability to accurately assess merit. Second, meritocracy is a powerfully attractive idea that quickly co-opts those who are successful into defending the status quo; finding a position from which to critique the system is exceptionally difficult. Even for those who see deep-seated problems in game culture's current state, tracing the cause to the design of games is difficult because it implicates everyone involved in the production and consumption of video games. Players who find success at games are more likely to keep playing, and the developers and publishers catering to that audience are more likely to find funding for their next title. China shows how a putative meritocracy quickly becomes an aristocracy where success hinges on initial access and status, rather than skill or effort. China's use of meritocracy also provides a blueprint for where the application of meritocracy may be headed. Although it may seem that meritocracy is an unavoidable, singular approach to society, how it is applied now is a relatively new occurrence; the historical context in China can help show that there are ways out of where we may find ourselves now. Tracing the contemporary context for meritocracy in the West requires assessing Michael Young's book, as the text is a crucial part of how we got to where we are.

The popular mythology surrounding the term "meritocracy" originated with Michael Young's 1958 book *The Rise of the Meritocracy*.[8] Young argues that judging people solely based on their ability plus their effort will lead to a society that falls apart in a bloody revolution. His book is a satirical novel written as a PhD thesis from the future. The narrator reflects on how much society has changed for the better, but that ends abruptly as the masses rise up, kill the author, and overthrow the meritocratic elite. The primary takeaway is that meritocracies beget broken systems when structural advantages compound over time. The effect of meritocracy is to make the inequality among people seem fair and just. The argument that the most talented, hardest-working people deserve the greatest rewards is much easier to make in contemporary, industrial society than it is to claim that people deserve their power solely through the social class into which they are born. Meritocracy seems like the answer to aristocracy, until the inequality inherent to the system inevitably creates a new aristocratic order.

In Young's book meritocracy is a bad thing, a system so riddled with conflicts and inherent limitations that no one should ever choose to pursue it. However, meritocracies are exceptionally well suited for technological systems, because, as Young notes, a meritocracy can "only exist in any full form if there were such a narrowing down of values that people could be put into rank order of worth."[9] Computers make these kinds of rankings easy, and with innovations ranging from a high-score list to achievements to Gamerscores or gear scores, video games are almost perfectly designed to provide a seemingly objective rank ordering of the worth of players. Borrowing from the tendency for meritocracy as outlined in *MUD1* and executed on computers, video games are uniquely placed to make a meritocratic approach seem natural and normal.

Beyond the broad strokes of high scores, Blizzard's first-person shooter *Overwatch* is an example of how an ideology celebrating merit is consistently reinforced in video games. Each match of *Overwatch* consists of two teams of six players battling it out, and after each round the game "spends a couple of minutes handing out kudos to star players."[10] Patricia Hernandez breaks the process down in her review of the game, noting that, upon launch, *Overwatch* first awards a "play of the game" and displays the player who executed the maneuver along with a video clip; then it shows a bunch of statistics from the match and highlights four of the twelve players in the match for their contributions; players are then prompted "to 'like' their favorite match contributors, and everyone gets to see who got voted the most."[11] This is an incredibly meritocratic approach to assessing what happened in the game, ultimately terminating in a popularity contest.

The feature that received substantial scorn upon *Overwatch*'s release was the play of the game, largely because it takes one moment out of context and then chooses to only celebrate one of twelve players when the efforts of the other members of the team often made the moment possible.[12] For several reviewers of the game, the effective result of the focus on showy moves and the overarching design of *Overwatch* is that praise and attention is more regularly focused on frontline fighters, rather than the sustained, less flashy support players who often play an outsized role in determining who wins and loses the match.[13] This leads to a small group of characters routinely showing up as player-of-the-game winners, while others languish in crucial but uncelebrated support work.[14] Articles reviewing the game frequently suggest alternatives yet note that a more dynamic, holistic system would likely be harder to judge and code, which is a problem at the heart of meritocracy. Actually judging skill or effort is ridiculously difficult to do, as it necessarily also assesses relative starting points and social advantages. The algorithm built into selecting what is the play of the game and which statistics will be highlighted rewards only what it can count and judge, stripping out situation and context, leading to a decision biased by what it cannot or does not choose to measure; however, meritocratic norms obscure the final judgment under a shroud of skill, effort, and talented execution. Even as Blizzard seeks to change the feature to adjust the weighting of contribution or to include multiple players, the key flaw of play of the game remains unaddressed. Selecting a play of the game is a fundamentally meritocratic act, as it boils the game down to a single moment and isolates what happened from the larger, holistic context of play. The whole point of the *Overwatch* postgame is to enact Young's fear of a system that puts players in a rank order of worth, but the lack of context makes those rankings both celebrated for their assessment of merit and partial for their lack of context.

Both players and developers drive the focus on skill in *Overwatch*. In an interview with the gaming site *Kotaku*, the game's director, Jeff Kaplan, notes that an early version of the game prioritized effort over skill. Although both elements are components of meritocracy, skill is a more traditionally praised metric within games. Instead of a system that enabled players to grind to a high rank and then have things sorted out based on skill, Kaplan states that he heard players telling the developers that "we just want this to be skill based and I want to be able to compare my skill against one other person," adding that one-on-one skill comparisons are a "very tricky problem to solve in a team based game. It's really, really hard."[15] Emphasizing the focus on skill in games, later in the interview, in response to a question about the hit boxes for shooting in the game, Kaplan argues that "our intention was never to make the game feel low skill. I think skill means a tremendous amount in *Overwatch*, but we're trying to make a game that feels great to play."[16] Video games are often manically focused on the role of skill and how it sorts out the better from the best, so that the most talented can ascend to their proper, meritocratic heights.

The role of skill leapt to the forefront a few months after launch when *Overwatch* debuted its competitive mode. In the words of the developer, Blizzard, this new mode was "designed for those who truly want to put their skills to the test, and offers a more serious experience than our Quick Play or Weekly Brawl! Modes."[17] *Kotaku* introduced the mode by telling readers, "If you're too dang skilled for the mortal riffraff in *Overwatch*'s regular modes, you'll be excited to hear that the PC version just got a competitive alternative (it's coming to console next week). It's got rankings, golden guns, golden balls—all that good stuff."[18] The mode was largely hyped as a place for players to show off their ability and prove their worth to others. Unlike the other modes of the game, where anyone could join games, competitive mode was designed to assess the true talent level of players, dividing players by rating and offering rewards for success that made an individual player's accomplishments apparent to everyone around them in the form of unique icons and markers. Shortly after the release of the mode the game's forums and subreddit lit up with complaints, many of which focused on flaws with the game design in the mode, but several of which pointed to the way the mode changed how players interacted with one another. Patricia Hernandez wrote, "More than other multiplayer games out there, the *Overwatch* community is so sweet, that the recent addition of a competitive mode almost feels out of place."[19] Nathan Grayson further explored how competitive mode was changing the community in an essay for *Kotaku*:

> Similarly, high-stakes competition and toxicity tend to go hand-in-hand, and *Overwatch*'s competitive mode already has an ugly toxic stain. Don't get me wrong: *Overwatch* is absolutely not bereft of toxic players even in quick play, but it's a game whose developer and community have at least tried to avoid the pitfalls of other online gaming communities. It's a game about having fun and being a team player, one that thrives when players feel unafraid to experiment with heroes and strategies. That spirit pervades much of the game, and it shows in the way tense situations unfold.[20]

Grayson goes on to argue that when players act poorly in other modes, they are dismissed because of the lack of importance of any one match, but in competitive mode losses and mistakes are "a big deal, and I've already watched/listened to some players absolutely go for the throat after matches gone awry. Insults, threats, slurs—you name it."[21] Another player announced in a post that he or she was "stopping competitive play from now on, since 50% of the matches have at least one or two toxic guys who *refuse* to play tank or heal," and that the overwhelming toxicity of the mode makes it something to avoid.[22] After competitive play had been out for two weeks, Grayson revisited the issue, writing that competitive play drives toxicity and that "even with some pretty high highs, the lows were so very, very low."[23] Recounting an interview with *Overwatch* director Jeff Kaplan, Grayson notes that Blizzard flags toxicity as a substantial problem and something that must be addressed, but concludes by wondering, "With toxicity levels rising, though, can they [Blizzard] keep pace and stem the tide?"[24] In the language of meritocracy, competitive mode is absolutely designed in a manner that ensures toxicity as an inevitable by-product because it is based on a system where players are boiled down to their net worth through the creation of a set of numbers that are supposed to represent their true skill. Skill is seductive and enticing. The mode will likely draw players to the game, but the attempt to clearly convey the merit of a player puts people in a situation where they are going to lash out and engage in antisocial behavior. Studying critiques of meritocratic systems shows why fixing these problems is an issue of design and intent, rather than one of management of a community headed off the rails. Much like Whitney Phillips argues that the systems and structures are at least as big of a problem as people trolling, meritocracies encourage norms and behaviors that lead to a toxic environment for their subjects and have to be addressed at the level of design.[25]

Beyond *Overwatch*, meritocracy is also tightly integrated into modern Western business culture, where "stack ranking" employees became all the rage at General Electric and then spread throughout the business world. Although the practice is waning in popularity, it still has advocates, including prominent technology companies like Amazon.[26] The logic of ranking employees is predicated on the belief that businesses can readily identify their best and worst workers and that keeping the worst workers inhibits the productivity and creativity of the best, a system that would seem familiar to many high-level raiding guilds. Ranking systems, from games to businesses, tend to obscure the logic of their judgments and become self-insulating under the premise that those at the top are the best and most talented, and have earned their rewards, including both the knowledge that they are better than others and, often, the ability to pass judgment on their lessers.

For Young, the result of ranking systems is to assign value such that we reach a point where "the eminent know that success is just reward for their own capacity, for their own efforts, and for their own undeniable achievement. They deserve to belong to a superior class."[27] In the wake of British prime minister Tony Blair openly embracing the term and the concept, Young updated his warning in 2001 to observe that "if meritocrats believe, as more and more of them are encouraged to, that their advancement comes from their own merits, they can feel they deserve whatever they can get . . . the newcomers can actually believe they have morality on their side."[28] Meritocracies are beautifully self-reinforcing, self-sustaining systems until they fall apart in crisis because they tell successful people that they earned their rewards, and the people at the bottom of the rankings are instructed that they must do more, do better in order to succeed. This is clearly seen in *Overwatch*, where a player seeking to get the lowest possible skill rating in the competitive mode of the game noticed something interesting: the most toxic environment for play was found among lower-rated players who thought they should be doing better at the game.[29] Instead of focusing on enjoying the game, the meritocratic system in which competitive *Overwatch* players are placed changes the context of play; according to a profile of the player seeking a 0 rating, at the lower reaches of the ratings "players shared precisely two qualities: they were astonishingly bad, and—because they were playing competitive—they were astonishingly *serious* about it," which led to plenty of cursing and yelling.[30] The system strips out systemic critique as a possibility because the whole point is evaluating the individual; when you are assessed as an individual, it is hard to engage with feedback when meritocratic ranking systems consistently remind you of your failures. Even in this player profile, much more attention is placed on individual players and their relative skill and effort than on an overarching critique of the meritocratic system structuring these reactions. The end of the article mentions that players should focus on enjoying their play, rather than winning or losing, but the framework of a rating system and competitive play makes that outcome highly unlikely. In a world where the noted game scholar Jesper Juul contends that skill-based video games can be described as "a meritocracy that rewards according to skill and accepts the subsequent inequalities among players," there is plenty of room for rot to set in and for players to forget about the structural advantages that help them succeed.[31] Juul starts his book about failure and video games by discussing how his personal failure at a game is something to talk about with trepidation and chooses to immediately contextualize his shortcoming with an example where he beat a game on the first try.[32] Under the logic of a meritocracy, the individualization of play personalizes failure. In this case, pairing failure and success adds a positive chaser to a negative story, and the combination retains emphasis on what Jesper Juul, as a game player, is capable of doing. Readers are encouraged to empathize with his loss, content in the knowledge that Juul is skillful enough to beat a game in a single try. When people finally stop thinking about individuals and start thinking about how the scales are tilted on a structural level is the point where the façade of being judged solely based on skill and effort is revealed as an illusion and meritocracy is acknowledged as a system that simply cannot work.

The move toward meritocracy is driven by social dynamics ranging from neoliberalism to technology and was developed in contrast to previous modes of social order based on birth and lineage.[33] These kinds of changes can be read as opening opportunity, but they also drive a critique against meritocracy, as Michael Young puts it: "Underpinning my argument [against meritocracy] was a non-controversial historical analysis of what had been happening to society for more than a century before 1958, and most emphatically since the 1870s, when schooling was made compulsory and competitive entry to the civil service became the rule. Until that time status was generally ascribed by birth." However, under meritocracy, birth matters less than skill, and "status has gradually become more achievable." Skill is certainly a good reason to select people for various positions; however, meritocracies tend to solidify into systems, Young notes, where "those who are judged to have merit of a particular kind harden into a new social class without room in it for others."[34] Put differently by Christopher Hayes, "Where the Establishment emphasized humility, prudence, and lineage, the meritocracy celebrates ambition, achievement, brains, and self-betterment."[35] Meritocracy is a system that rejects the birthrights that previously regulated social interaction; however, it creates new problems when society calcifies into social structures just as rigid as ones based on birth, while teaching those at the top of the social hierarchy that their ascent is based on skill and ability, rather than the luck of being born to a specific family at a certain point in history and in a place that facilitates their success. Aristocracy may seem like an odd fit for games, largely because one is not really born a player. However, when considering the traits necessary to play video games, certain learned behaviors can be passed from game to game, enabling frequent players to benefit from their inherited advantages. Those who were lucky enough to be hailed into games early are the nobility of video games, as their inherited position makes them more likely to succeed in each game they pick up.

Similar logic easily extends into free-to-play games, where players with means can often buy their way into persistent advantages over those who do not spend. There are plenty of examples of what is casually derided as pay-to-win, but particularly interesting are the prison servers of *Minecraft*. Detailed in a lengthy article by Robert Guthrie, prison servers are described as a "dystopian experience unlike anything I've ever experienced in a video game."[36] Prison servers, which are run outside the bounds and rules of the primary version of *Minecraft*, work differently than most other instantiations of the game. Instead of jumping into an open world, on a prison server players start out with just a pick and perhaps some basic gear and must then set out to do hard labor, repeatedly working in stone mines to ascend to greater status on the server. Working hard enough eventually awards players with special titles, privileges, resources, and maybe even a place on the leaderboard. These servers are funded by donations, so a way to move up more quickly is to spend money to skip out on the grind, which offers an aristocratic approach for players with means. Guthrie was surprised to find that players did not object to other players being able to buy their way ahead; instead, they stuck around, "hoping for handouts or an opportunity down the road to make their way into the upper echelons. Occasional generosity from wealthy players and lottery-style games seems to be what keeps these players engaged, but there really isn't a path to the highest ranks without paying real money."[37] Structural advantages matter, as they shape how we engage life. In the case of prison servers those advantages are laid bare, but that is not necessarily a bad thing for the game design, as it is at least clear what is needed to get ahead at the game and rise up the hierarchy, a process that is obscured in many other video games.

Young understood just how important luck and circumstance are, a theme emphasized by how his book came to be published and the idea of a meritocracy subsequently entered the public vernacular. Young writes that "for some years I thought the book was doomed never to appear. I hawked it around from one publisher to another—eleven of them—and was always turned down."[38] The only reason the book was finally published was because Young "happened to meet an old friend, Walter Neurath, on a beach in North Wales," and Neurath eventually released the book "out of friendship."[39] Subsequently picked up by Penguin, the book ended up selling hundreds of thousands of copies and was translated into several languages. The foundational tome on meritocracy only came to light after a chance encounter on a beach vacation, something that tells less about Young's ability and effort, and far more about his social connections and means. The popularization of the idea of meritocracy began with one friend doing a favor for another.

Meritocracy: Its Defense and Evolution

Young's book was a satirical critique in which the author is eventually murdered in the uprising against meritocracy, but in subsequent decades the ideology he presented was twisted and altered; a handful of scholars, among them Daniel Bell, R. J. Herrnstein, and Peter Saunders, emerged as leading cheerleaders for the meritocratic cause. A central theme in defense of meritocracy is that post-industrial society necessitates inequality and that pursuing a merit-based allocation of resources is the fairest way to make decisions about who should be at the top of the social order. Bell welcomes this change, stating that "the post-industrial society, in its logic, is a meritocracy. Differential status and differential income are based on technical skills and higher education, and few high places are open to those without such qualifications."[40] Herrnstein argues that "the biological stratification of society looms whether we have tests to gauge it or not, but with them a more humane and tolerant grasp of human differences is possible."[41] This relative comfort with inequality as a basic fact of contemporary life is an ongoing theme in early defenses of meritocracy, Bell writes: "In social fact, the meritocracy is thus the displacement of one principle of stratification by another, of achievement for ascription. In the past— and this was the progressive meaning of liberalism—this new principle was considered just. Men were to be judged—and rewarded—not by attributes of birth or primordial ties but on individual merit."[42] For Bell and the men about whom he writes, meritocracy is something people yearned for, as it is grounded in a historical appreciation of individual production instead of birthright.[43] Achievement is celebrated, and those talented enough to get rewards in a meritocracy earned them. Through testing and examination, IQ research proponents like Herrnstein held that intelligence measurement was a key part of establishing a meritocratic order by facilitating people freely taking "their natural level in society."[44] Saunders stresses that "a meritocracy does not reward individuals simply for being born bright. As in the parable of the three talents, ability is only rewarded when it is put to good social use. . . . Occupational positions are earned. They are not allocated like sweets as rewards for doing well in IQ tests."[45] For Bell, the allocation of rewards among those who are both bright and producing social good is something to be celebrated, since under "the logic of a meritocracy, these high-scoring individuals, no matter where they are in the society, should be brought to the top in order to make the best use of their talents."[46] Meritocracy is about both resource allocation in considerations of who gets what rewards and the social maximization of talent. Video games make the process of assessing merit straightforward while heaping rewards and achievements on those who prove themselves worthy. If you can actually identify the most talented people, why would you resist putting them in the most crucial positions?

Beyond a general focus on skill and effort, there are two key considerations for backers of meritocracy: equality and open movement. Questions of equality focus on what society should try to equalize: opportunities or results? Bell focuses extensively on this question, coming down firmly on the side of equality of opportunity and expressing disdain for those who think otherwise. Bell sees meritocracy as the culmination of a positive social movement and feels that "what is at stake today is the redefinition of equality. A principle which was the weapon for changing a vast social system, the principle of equality of opportunity, is now seen as leading to a new hierarchy, and the current demand" is for "the creation of *equality of results*." Instead of pursuing what he believed to be folly, Bell emphasizes the status of individuals "as the basic unit of society" with the understanding that "individuals will differ—in their natural endowments, in their energy, drive, and motivation, in their conception of what is desirable—and that the institutions of society should establish procedures for regulating fairly the competition and exchanges necessary to fulfill these diverse desires and competences."[47] Believing in a meritocracy requires that one focus on the role of the individual in ensuring his or her own success. When a person struggles or fails it is his or her individual responsibility to do better. The government's role is limited, constrained to rule keeping and regulating with the intent of establishing and maintaining a level playing field. Not every player will finish or win a game; if they do, developers can simply unleash more difficult modes to ensure both an inequality of results and a proper challenge. Video games ostensibly ascribe to a commitment to equality of opportunity, as players typically start a game from the same relative level of status. Within the game these core design trends are almost perfectly structured to produce the kind of meritocracy proponents seek.

Given this competition for unequal rewards, proponents of meritocracy were quick to note that there must be open movement among the social classes. As Bell puts it, "The principles of merit, achievement, and universalism are, it seems to me, the necessary foundations for a productive—and cultivated—society. What is important is that the society, to the fullest extent possible, be a genuinely open one."[48] Openness is crucial to ensure the proper assessment of merit. For each structural barrier, like racism, sexism, classism, or any other sort of institutionalized bias, it becomes less possible to actually measure merit. Should a test be culturally biased, it ceases to measure skill and ability and begins to assess other inputs, inhibiting the establishment of the equality of opportunity that meritocracy's proponents typically find so critical. Writing decades after Bell, in an attempt to defend meritocracy as a concept, Peter Saunders admits that the system is not perfect, as "of course, some bright and hardworking children from lower-class origins still do not achieve as high a position as they 'should,' but the main 'problem' with meritocracy today appears to be the continuing success of the 'undeserving' children of the middle classes."[49] This becomes an obvious problem for video games as sequels and franchises dominate sales, but it also shows up in genre standards where common norms, like health systems and inventory management, are found in title after title. Skill transfer ensures that certain players will have advantages they do not have to think about as they move from one game to the next. Developers also have a vested interest in including features that keep players buying new versions of games, like a leveling system in the *FIFA* series that allows players of the previous edition to start the new one with perks that a new player does not get. As meritocratic norms have been further integrated into society since Bell and Herrnstein were writing largely in the 1970s, one of the biggest problems a contemporary defender of a meritocratic order can see is the fact that parents of means are not willing to let their children fail, even if, by the logic of merit, they should. At the point that parents can prop up future generations, skill and effort become less relevant than birthright and inherited position, subverting the meritocracy with the very aristocratic dynamics that skill plus effort was designed to reject and continuing the cycle seen throughout China's history with meritocracy.

In sum, the defense of meritocracy is based on the idea that "the meritocracy, in the best meaning of that word, is made up of those worthy of praise. They are the men who are the best in their fields, as judged by their fellows."[50] The focus on men and fellows is especially notable in Daniel Bell's words here. Writing in 1973, he focuses on a world where the best men reap the greatest rewards, yet he does not consider the impacts of key issues like structural sexism and racism in his writing about meritocracy, which is a trait he shares with many of the most vocal proponents of GamerGate. These omissions are focal points for those who have written about the problems of meritocracy, even as they chronicle the ideology's rise to widespread social acceptance.

The idea underpinning meritocracy, rewarding the most able, has been around for an exceptionally long time, but the word itself is relatively new, which increases the importance of its shifts in meaning. The term has changed largely in step with those who choose to use it for their own ends. Societies have long had to justify inequality. Hierarchy can be rationalized for all kinds of reasons—from divine right to innate superiority of one group of people over another to how reincarnation worked in Indian caste societies to legitimize one's place based on performance in past lives.[51] According to Stephen McNamee and Robert Miller, meritocracy is accepted by its subjects because it "is predicated not on what 'is' but on the *belief* that the system of inequality is 'fair' and it 'works.' . . . The most virtuous *get* and *should get* the most rewards."[52] Meritocracy has become understood as a great liberator, freeing citizens from an aristocratic past based on inheritance and lineage.[53]

Daniel Bell's intervention changed the trajectory of meritocracy's meaning. As referenced liberally in the defense of meritocracy, Bell's writing "neutralise[d] and erase[d] those more problematic (or 'dystopian') aspects of the term present in Young's work."[54] Meritocracy's meaning continued to shift after Bell's writing, but it was his work that portrayed meritocracy as a clear social good.[55] Meritocracy runs from China to Young to Bell and beyond, developing from a system that collapses on itself to a term of insult to a path that should not be taken to a prime way to celebrate the individual and resist the dual tyrannies of hereditary aristocracy and creeping socialism.[56] In the most constructive case, meritocracy enables individuals to be judged based on the quality of their contributions to society. However, that case is overly optimistic and deliberately ignores the structural constraints that ensure the inequality of opportunity routinely faced by marginalized groups.

The Effects of Meritocracy

Defenders of meritocracy argue that it is the optimal way to make decisions about how to organize society. Perfected, it puts the best people in the best position to have the greatest impact. However, that dream relies on an idealized meritocracy with no leakage for advantages based on social class, family connections, or other considerations that confuse calculations of skill and effort. Christopher L. Hayes produced perhaps the most excoriating recent evaluation of meritocracy, contending that "meritocracy offered liberation from the unjust hierarchies of race, gender, and sexual orientation, but swapped in their place a new hierarchy based on the notion that people are deeply unequal in ability and drive."[57] Meritocracy focuses on the individual, as Shannon McCoy and Brenda Major contend that "locating the responsibility for social status within the efforts and abilities of individuals, the belief in meritocracy legitimizes existing status differences among individuals and groups and helps to justify the status quo"—after all, if the system is working, "those who have higher status must also be more talented, valuable, hardworking, or in other ways more meritorious than those who have lower status."[58] Meritocracy creates a situation, John Beck argues, where "those at the top seem to feel increasingly entitled to the rewards and privileges they enjoy. Some can even, apparently, feel resentful that their true worth is still not sufficiently recognized," a phenomenon Beck calls "'because I'm worth it' syndrome."[59] Meritocracy places focus on what a person has done or perceptions about what they are able to do, even to the extent that meritocratic systems are linked to causing poor health outcomes for those at the bottom.[60] Furthermore, Richard Breen and John Goldthorpe argue that "the rewards that accrue to merit themselves vary depending on the class origins of those who possess it," which enables those already at the top to reap greater rewards than those at the bottom, even with similar levels of performance.[61] Instead of paying attention to systems and structures, meritocracy emphasizes each person and what they have done or not, which leaves the privileged left to enjoy their earned status and the unfortunate to blame themselves for what they lack.

A clear place to see this dynamic in video games is to explore the case of Geguri and her skills at Blizzard's first-person shooter *Overwatch*. Rapidly ascending into the top ten players in the world, Geguri was extraordinarily successful in tournament play but was accused of cheating because other players thought her aiming was too good to be done without some sort of assistance.[62] Part of the reason for questioning her skill may be tied to the fact that she was not established as a premier player in a game before *Overwatch*, but as Aja Romano notes, "As a predominant female gamer in a culture traditionally dominated by men, Geguri's success is both impressive and inspirational. Naturally, it's also the reason some of her rivals have accused her of cheating."[63] Two of her opponents in a high-profile match accused her of cheating, one of whom threatened to visit her house with a knife were the allegations proven.[64] As Romano summarizes, the two players "were so absolutely, totally, without-a-doubt sure that Geguri couldn't attain stats as high as she did, they bet their entire careers on their assertion that she must be cheating, agreeing to quit their jobs if they turned out to be wrong."[65] Geguri was cleared by Blizzard and engaged in a public display that validated her skills. However, when prominent male players were accused of cheating, they did not need to put on a similar exhibition to evidence their ability.[66] Geguri did not get the same benefit of the doubt as other players because, based on her point of origin as a woman, she was considered to be lesser before she ever sat down in front of her mouse and keyboard. Players, in their pursuit of hierarchy, excuse those they expect or can believe to be exceptional, while those on the margins must do more than others, thereby placing barriers in front of nontraditional communities in games, most notably women and people of color.[67] Further, those players do not have the same social encouragement to play, making Geguri's version of *Overwatch* harder than those of her opponents. She has to fight both the players in the game and the perceptions they hold coming into it, since she is presumed to be lesser before she even begins and her exceptional talent has to be proven to a level that far exceeds that of any man playing the same game. In emphasizing the individual, Geguri's performance is taken out of the context in which it occurs and she has to both display her talent in the game and justify that she is not cheating outside of it.

Contending that "the most fundamental problem with meritocracy is how difficult it is to maintain in its pure and noble form," Hayes argues that "our near-religious fidelity to the meritocratic model comes with huge costs. We overestimate the advantages of meritocracy and underappreciate its costs, because we don't think hard enough about the consequences of the inequality it produces," as "those at the top can use their relative power to alter and manipulate existing institutions so as to further consolidate their gains and press their advantage."[68] These problems are compounded by the fact that inequality also makes people terrible judges of their own relative social status. People routinely underestimate their own place in the social ranking, which inhibits their desire to develop policies to help the less fortunate.[69] The structures of meritocracy are fundamentally flawed, as the process of calculating merit is tremendously important yet frequently obscured. Meritocracy is the product, a system of decisions where Craig Haney and Aida Hurtado observe that "what we define as performance, how we go about measuring it, what social value we attach to which specific measures, and our organized response as a society (or as an employer) to apparent differences in performance are all part of a socially constructed belief system. Yet, the mythology of meritocracy masks these contingencies and obscures the ways in which the assumptions of this system are 'built into' the workplace."[70] From Robin Potanin's observation that an overwhelmingly white and male game development community makes games that they want to play and that feature characters that look like them, to the frank statement by developer Ready at Dawn's Ru Weerasuriya that he develops games because he's a gamer and wants to "see cool things on the platforms I play." Video games are constructed by people who are already part of the community and are invested in making games for the people who already play video games.[71] Instead of developers branching out in new directions, a risk-averse approach to game development and a lack of diversity in the community of people making games creates an echo chamber where recycling content and ideas ensures that those who are part of the community already are rewarded and their success is justified under the guise of merit. Weerasuriya's position that as a gamer he is interested in making "cool things" is not necessarily wrong, but it does elide key dynamics of videogame consumption and production. Producing the kinds of games he wants to play means that he is increasingly speaking to an audience of people like him, which undercuts any idea of a true meritocracy by building key assumptions into the "workplace" of games. In her history of videogame arcades, Carly Kocurek states the issue quite directly: "An industry of men imagines a consumer base that is like them and so makes games that reflect their own interests and experiences; with games serving as a point of entry into the industry, this production cycle helps maintain the status quo."[72] The CEO of Lockwood Publishing, a company targeting young women interested in 3-D virtual worlds, argues that underserved users are key to success; however, he holds that standard industry practice gave him the idea to develop for underserved groups because "predominantly male teams at games studios, free to build the game they always wanted to play, were in fact releasing games that would attract and monetize an audience of their peers. Young males over the age of 18 were making games for—you guessed it—young males over the age of 18."[73] From schools to experiences, many different kinds of resources can be brought to bear to tip the scales toward obscuring a pure calculation of merit. The process of producing meritocracy confounds inborn skill with the effects of structural inequity, which then continues in a circular, self-reinforcing pattern. These inequalities permeate discussions about video games, as traces of sexism, racism, homophobia, ageism, or any other barrier ensures that some players benefit from advantages while others must overcome obstacles.[74]

The point of the meritocratic critique is that the system seems like it is properly balanced and only enforcing values that are readily understandable and defensible. However, meritocracy imbues ongoing structural advantages in those lucky enough to reach positions of power. In a graduation speech at Princeton University, former United States Federal Reserve chair Ben Bernanke presents a positive review of meritocracy, but one that encourages listeners to acknowledge the crucial importance of luck:

> A meritocracy is a system in which the people who are the luckiest in their health and genetic endowment; luckiest in terms of family support, encouragement, and, probably, income; luckiest in their educational and career opportunities; and luckiest in so many other ways difficult to enumerate—these are the folks who reap the largest rewards. The only way for even a putative meritocracy to hope to pass ethical muster, to be considered fair, is if those who are the luckiest in all those respects also have the greatest responsibility to work hard, to contribute to the world, and to share their luck with others.[75]

Bernanke is receptive to a meritocracy, but his words also undercut its foundational premise. Instead of simply measuring skill, meritocracies also inherently assess a person's good fortune and relative success in the genetic lottery. Fellow economist Robert H. Frank stresses the role of luck in meritocratic systems throughout a book-length exploration of meritocracy, arguing that even when luck is only a minor factor in an outcome, it is often the determining one. Frank argues that as modern economic trends ensure a greater number of participants in most contests, and in an atmosphere where those competitions are more frequently winner-take-all, "even when luck has only a minor influence on performance, the most talented and hardworking of all contestants will usually be outdone by a rival who is almost as talented and hardworking but also considerably luckier."[76] Frank specifically applies his analysis to the music industry and book publishing, where success hinges on getting the first few good reviews to generate buzz for your work. The chance event of the first reviewer liking a specific song or book is tremendously important to its future—were it assigned to a less friendly reviewer the same output could be far less successful.

For Frank, the role of meritocracy is to camouflage "the extent to which success and failure often hinge decisively on events completely beyond any individual's control."[77] Where you are born, to whom you are born, and so many other factors frame the success you are most likely to achieve. When considering personal economics on a global scale, studies have found that how much you will earn in your life is set by where you happen to be born, a fact that has nothing to do with your individual skill or effort. Recent economic analysis in the United States shows that "even poor kids who do everything right don't do much better than rich kids who do everything wrong."[78] As a different critique observes, "The truth is that the meritocracy was never more than partial," and it goes on to argue that selective admissions systems at elite colleges ensure some kinds of diversity, but rarely in terms of economic class or parental occupation.[79] Colleges in the United States also fail at social status equalization, as getting into and succeeding in college still leads to lesser life outcomes for graduates who happen to be black, Hispanic, or raised poor compared to their classmates.[80] For Jo Littler, meritocracy "functions as an ideological myth to *obscure* economic and social inequalities and the role it plays in curtailing social equality."[81] Skill, talent, and ability become means by which to mask the value judgments, norms, and exclusions that are happening under the auspices of decisions made solely based on objective measures. The myth that meritocracy is based on skill and talent is exceptionally important, because the myth of merit presumes that the good and bad are sorted properly, but McNamee and Miller argue that in practice the ideology "provides an incomplete explanation for success and failure, mistakenly exalting the rich and unjustly condemning the poor. We may always have the rich and poor among us, but we need neither exalt the former nor condemn the latter."[82] The process of producing a meritocracy has substantial side effects. Meritocracy exalts and punishes individuals based on where they end up, which is heavily influenced by where they started. Meritocracy negatively affects physical health for those at the bottom and teaches those at the top that they have earned their plaudits. The myth of meritocracy is stultifying, as people throughout the spectrum are led to believe that they deserve where they end up and ignore structural explanations for the inequality inherent to a meritocratic ideology. Although these concerns may not initially seem to apply to the study of video games, echoes of Richard Bartle's statements about *MUD1* and the lack of diversity found in many aspects of videogame design linger alongside meritocratic norms that produce similar kinds of problems and assure a game culture that is rotting from the inside out.

Game Design and Meritocracy

Those studying game design and play do not always think through the consequences of having a system where some are put into a position to be far superior to others, and one where barriers to entry are routinely and consistently raised over time. We do not often talk about how being good at one game promises a skill transfer likely to carry over to other, similar games. There is rarely an investigation or mention of how players can arrive at the starting line of learning to play a game with vastly different competencies, giving some players a potentially massive advantage over others.[83] Certain players sit down and know how to move in 3-D spaces, how to hold a controller, how to manage an inventory, where to find save points, how to find and navigate a mini-map, where the default action button is likely located, and how to dive into a game menu. Some players know that checking all the crates in a room will yield treasure, while others will follow the path that is clearly offered by a game. Some players know to look online for optimal build guides for a character or where they can search for advice when they get stuck; without that knowledge, other players are left struggling and may give up when they cannot solve a puzzle or do not realize that the choices they made in character customization are making the game much harder, as these things are generally only discussed in reviews about or forums for a game. All this knowledge gives some players a head start compared to those who know little about games and their attendant systems, making success more tied to inheritance than to skill or effort.

One way to reflect on how meritocracy affects games is to look at key writing from a pair of game designers with different career paths and perspectives. Anna Anthropy is an independent game designer and writer who champions easy-to-use tools to create a world where everyone can make games. Raph Koster, lead designer on *Ultima Online* and creative director of *Star Wars Galaxies*, has written extensively about the role of fun in games. Where these two designers agree provides a fertile area for reflecting on trouble spots in game design and culture. Both have written about the effects of limited diversity of design in mainstream video games and how that interrelates with a heavy dependence on skill transfer. Anna Anthropy notes that "most games are copies of existing successful games. They play like other games, resemble their contemporaries in shape and structure, have the same buttons that interact with the world in the same way (mouse to aim, left click to shoot), and have the same shortcomings."[84] Raph Koster adds that "the historical trend in games has shown that when a new genre of game is invented, it follows a trajectory where increasing complexity is added to it, until eventually the games on the market are so complex and advanced that newcomers can't get into them—the barrier to entry is too high."[85] As games build on one another, the tower of knowledge needed for access into video games keeps getting higher and in a way that frequent players may not even notice. However, skill transfer is far from the only obstacle circumscribing the gaming audience.

Beyond general issues in game design, we rarely think through how the interrelationships among designers, players, journalists, and academics mean that games are often targeted to an insular community with relatively consistent expectations and standards. As the balance of resources tilts, expertise and success in video games is based less on merit and more on the inheritance of structures that let certain players circumvent examinations of ability or skill. Playing a video game is far from a straightforward test of skill. Game tutorials, which are increasingly integrated into the first few minutes of game play, only exacerbate these issues, as they typically require a player to have a basic level of competency in moving around virtual space and knowing where buttons on the controller or keyboard are located in order to navigate a set of tasks that are rudimentary for veteran players yet may be completely foreign to new ones. Merit in video games is assessed by the time a person has been able to invest in learning this game and all the similar games a player has played before. Being successful in a game depends on the economic ability to pay for games and systems, the cultural permission or encouragement to play games, and the good fortune to find game narratives, characters, and genres that are at least somewhat relatable or interesting. As Adrienne Shaw established, the representations chosen in media matter, as what is selected for representation "provides evidence of what could be and who can be possible."[86] Much like Bernanke concludes that the broader culture measures luck in addition to skill, meritocratic norms in games are influenced by all the social factors that affect the ability to actually assess skill and effort in game play. In the end, those most able to rally against the prevailing order are cognitively captured by it, as they gather benefits from a system that render them less interested in fighting against inherent imbalances that work in their favor. Much like a standardized test can be hard to see as a problem if you score well on it, video games that cater to one's own skills, abilities, and habits can be hard to see as a systemic problem. Hardcore gamers can often be seen calling for more video games that suit them, rather than for diverse games that draw in more players or test new kinds of skills. The creative director at Ubisoft argues that this predictability and consistency in video games is "less about familiarity than it's just enjoying the content. That's the misunderstanding. I think players honestly like it, because if they didn't it's still $60 or $70. It's still a lot of money."[87] To Ubisoft, the reuse of common tropes and the prominence of sequels is a player-driven development. This recycling of known intellectual property and design practices is driven by industry dynamics and a general aversion to risk taking, which caters to established players over attempts to reach new ones.[88] When players pick up video games, having played the same games or genres for years, the video games measure not just their natural abilities but also all the inherited advantages that let certain players start well ahead of others. Meritocracies are designed to seem balanced and fair, even as structural inequality stifles any semblance of a level playing field. As we think through our roles as critics, designers, players, or whatever else we may be, we must guard against a tendency to become compromised by what we study/make/play, especially when many of us are often getting a head start on the possible competition.

In considering the broader cultural factors surrounding meritocracy, Hayes observes that "the playing field may be level, but certain kids get to spend nights and weekends practicing on it in advance of the competition."[89] Although he is talking about standardized testing and the role of external coaching and studying, similar concerns relate to video games. Time and money are huge factors in shaping how good someone can be and how likely they are to realize their maximum skill at any given game. As Carly Kocurek found in her analysis of videogame arcades, the population of people currently playing games is shaped by the early discussion around video games, putting young men in a position where they are far more likely to be encouraged to play games and find games related to their interests.[90] Considering additional factors, from speed of internet access to social support, the external factors that shape play cannot be forgotten in considerations of merit and who deserves the advantages they "earn." Supposed skill at games is also heavily dependent on the distribution and kind of luck from which a player has also benefited. Merit is not something that is simply out there to be found and discovered; it is produced through a system largely developed and chosen by those already in positions of power.

Even seemingly unbiased arbiters of merit carry judgments about what is best, further replicating the status quo. In a social system like video games with the regular intermixing of game players with developers, the culture is routinely developed and designed to reward those already there. As Anna Anthropy puts it, "The problem with videogames is that they're created by a small, insular group of people. Digital games largely come from within a single culture."[91] Raph Koster takes a slightly milder tack to the issue, observing, "By making gaming their hobby, game designers are making an echo chamber of their own work."[92] Being invested in games for longer and learning how systems are likely to work enables frequent players to reap rewards from all kinds of external factors that can benefit them, and then designers, who are also players, make more of the same.[93] From being readily accepted into a community because you share social traits to having the time and money in the first place to invest in games, the meritocracy produced by games considers many factors that have little to do with skill. The perceived level playing field is further subverted by access to video games in the first place. Anna Anthropy lists several core issues with access in her critique of console games:

The amount of both manual dexterity and game-playing experience required to operate a game designed for the Xbox 360 makes play inaccessible to those who aren't already grounded in the technique of playing games. And to attain that level of familiarity with games requires a huge and continuous investment of time (and money—keeping up with new games costs bucks). This means that older people—people with families and obligations, people trying to raise kids, or any people with a lack of free time to invest—have a harder time gaining access to games.[94]

Some of the obstacles Anthropy lists are related to skill or arguably to effort, but many are also structural; as these barriers rise, the supposed meritocracy of games evaluates far more in its players than just merit. When subject to meritocracy, part of the function of the ideology is to obscure that it is a practice and a series of choices that deliberately rewards some things and not others. This has huge implications for games, and it is absolutely necessary to think critically about how the meritocracy within video games is built, what traits and factors are rewarded alongside skill and effort, and which are punished.

Another area for thinking about how video games intersect with meritocratic norms is to take a step back and examine how meritocratic systems are supposed to work and how they end up affecting the subjects within them. A first key tenet of meritocracy is that it depends on downward mobility. Because there is a limited amount of room at the top of the meritocratic pyramid, the less able in the upper classes must fall to make room for the more able in the lower classes.[95] For thinking about games, this means that all players must have a risk of falling backward or otherwise losing the advantages they have spent a playing career building. It is often the subtle parts of playing games— the knowledge that comes with playing game after game and learning which buttons to press when and how to navigate the various systems that have become genre standards—that simply will not let frequent players drop to the bottom when they move to a new game. Although it seems like this would only apply to multiplayer games with a single spot at the top of the ladder to award, aspects of it also sneak into single-player games. Such games cannot be so easy that anyone can beat them, and yet the skill transfer veteran players take with them ensures a head start.

Video games often feature iterative design that is used to tune the difficulty so that players feel challenged, engaged, and mad at themselves instead of the game when they fail. Popularized by Shigeru Miyamoto and Nintendo, such design is predicated on taking the knowledge learned in one game and deploying it in the next game, but with a twist.[96] Many people can win single-player games, but badges, achievements, leaderboards, and speed runs all push single-player games into meritocratic contexts. Athletes face issues with age or injury to force them downward, but outside the top end of eSports, players of video games tend to get more sophisticated over time, rather than less. Instead of an inheritance of resources passed down through generations, games feature skill and knowledge transfers that, combined with limited genres and plentiful sequels, ensure that frequent players never slip too far down the social hierarchy. As players rarely, if ever, truly fall downward in the avatar and social capital they have acquired, an actual meritocracy in games is subverted as those at the top reap outsized rewards, which means the distribution of awards and places is even less likely to be based on skill and effort, and more likely to judge the less noticeable traits players bring with them into games.

A common issue in actually addressing problems within a meritocracy is the paradox that attempts to reduce discrimination in meritocratic systems actually end up in a loop where, according to Emilio Castilla and Stephen Benard, "bias can be triggered by attempts to reduce it, particularly in organizational contexts that emphasize meritocratic values."[97] This type of prompting is similar to research about addressing discrimination, as both accusations of racism or the mere presence of more people of color lead to white people demonstrating higher levels of racial resentment.[98] I contend that games are predicated on a generally meritocratic organizational structure, which makes them particularly resistant to efforts to reduce discrimination because of the cues presented in the course of video games. Priming for meritocracy through playing games is likely to make players less prone to be critically reflective about structural bias and more likely to uncritically accept the ideology of meritocracy. One explanation for why this happens is the concept of psychological cues and prompting. Shannon K. McCoy and Brenda Major argue that "subtle meritocratic cues in the immediate environment can induce system justifying responses among individuals who are aware of this worldview, irrespective of personal endorsement."[99] By being prompted about meritocracy a person's individual beliefs matter less than the cue, and even the people who are aware of the arguments against the ideology are more prone to defend it as proper and just. McCoy and Major conclude with the argument that "subtle cues to meritocracy in the cultural environment may encourage members of low status groups to construe personal and group disadvantage as deserved and to minimize the perception that such disadvantage is due to discrimination. These system justifying responses to meritocracy cues may be most likely precisely when individuals would least like them to occur: in the presence of clear, meritocracy-violating inequality."[100] This dynamic encourages and propagates meritocratic systems, as those who have the best case to demonstrate how the system is broken end up defending the system as fair and just. I believe games readily work as a meritocratic cue and, based on McCoy and Major's research, the prompting of playing games that contain meritocratic elements leads players to be more accepting and defensive of meritocracy. The economist Robert H. Frank has found similar results in his experiments concerning sharing. When participants believe they are more skilled than others, they divide resources less fairly, keeping more for themselves. Participants' false beliefs about their skills "apparently induced a powerful sense of entitlement to claim the lion's share, while falsely believing themselves to be less skillful had much less of an effect."[101] Getting out of a meritocratic loop is incredibly difficult, and if games function as a meritocratic prompt, dismantling the dominant ideology within game culture will require great effort and reflection. This may be a key reason why certain people opt out of games in general, as players are quickly trained to individualize their failure instead of critiquing the system that is stifling their chance at success.

An additional harm of meritocracy within games is that the ideology brings discrimination with it. In a legal context, appeals to merit have actually made it harder to address claims of discrimination in the workplace.[102] In attempts to remedy discrimination claims meritocracy is deployed to support the powerful and ends up ensuring that organizations maintain an ability to discriminate on the basis of factors like race and gender.[103] Meritocracy is all about judging people, and it works on those at the top and the bottom, quickly teaching the less successful that their failures are their own.[104] Meritocracy causes discrimination and encourages people operating under the ideology to justify the exclusion or marginalization of those who are less successful because they are considered naturally lesser. Meritocratic systems are exclusionary and marginalizing, which offers a fine corollary to arguments about the relative lack of diversity among players of core games and in game design more broadly. By appropriating the logic of merit, video games limit their audience, as those who are not initially advantaged are pushed away by those who judge them as poorer players, and by their own adherence to a skill-based ideology that teaches them that they simply are not as good as others. Reflecting on this trend in U.S. society more broadly, McNamee and Miller write, "If merit were the sole cause of achievement, one would wonder why the vast amount of raw talent is found in white males, who clearly dominate leadership positions in key institutions in society."[105] Games create the perception that we can find the most qualified quite easily, as that can be determined by playing the games themselves. However, the lack of diversity among players should prompt questions about whether games are actually meritocratic.

Beyond the broad understanding that core games are often a heavily white male space, another area to see structural privilege within the world of video games is eSports. The dominance of Korean players in games like *Starcraft* and *League of Legends* is due in part to the large systems of support to back them, from state-run organizations like the Korean eSports Association (KeSPA), the large infrastructure and rewards enabling players to improve, wide broadcasts and support for tournaments, and financial rewards that enable players to focus on play.[106] All of these elements produce a system where some are led to believe they are better than others and those who struggle are led to the conclusion that it is their own personal failing, rather than potential systematic issues that ensure the deck is stacked. Structural factors are occasionally acknowledged—Todd Harper finds that some fighting game players justify certain players' performance based on their "Asian hands"—but these elements are tied to creating an environment where a particular kind of skill is praised.[107] It may be easier to see these dynamics at work in a clear case like eSports, but the homogeneity of game designers and core players should prompt deep questions about how video games are designed. The pool of players in video games is limited, and part of the reason why is likely the inherent inequality and discrimination that comes with following a meritocratic ideology.

A huge part of the reason for the inability to reach out and diversify a group under conditions of meritocracy is the focus on individuals and what is seen as their proper behavior. As Jo Littler writes, under meritocracy "the act of addressing inequality becomes 'responsibilised' as an individual's moral meritocratic task. This process devolves onto the individual personal responsibility not just for their success in the meritocratic competition, but for the very will to compete and expectation of victory which are now figured as moral imperatives in themselves. Not investing in aspiration, in *expectation*, is aggressively positioned as an abdication of responsibility which condemns yourself—and even worse, your child—to the social scrapheap."[108] Subjects under meritocracy are expected to get better, to drive themselves to attain a higher position. Even if the competition may be rigged, participants are asked to jump on the treadmill and work themselves forward for fear that if they opt out they are not only failing themselves, but all those they support. The context of games carries less immediate or lasting stakes than meritocracy does as a government program, but the expectation that players should get better is woven throughout the dominant culture around games.

From particular kinds of games players are supposed to like to a skill they are expected to demonstrate, players of video games expect things of one another, and showing vulnerability or demonstrating a lack of merit is a huge risk. This individualized personal drive expected of meritocratic subjects is succinctly displayed in the gaming phrase "lrn2play n00b." It is an individual responsibility to learn, not a communal expectation to teach. Players compare what they have done, what they can do, and are expected to work to continue to climb the ladder of skill, without regard for social circumstances and structural barriers, many of which are clear choices made by game developers and game companies, rather than objective standards. There are occasions where players help one another out, like EVE University, which is a group dedicated to helping new players assimilate into the notoriously difficult game *EVE Online*.[109] However, individual skill is a key concern for many. In an article for *Gameranx*, Nick Monroe distills this position, beginning by stating plainly, "Most games require some skill. Without that requirement, they are not really games." Monroe goes on to note that games are special and valuable because "the instinct of wanting to *be the best like no one ever was* is a healthy pursuit. . . . Gamers with proficiency will naturally have more educated opinions than those without, by sheer virtue of having actual experience and familiarity with the subject." Monroe contends that games are played to be beaten, "and the only way to do that is to get good, and that's what gaming is all about."[110] Norms celebrating skill and effort are encouraged by meritocratic design and narrative, which limits the population of people likely to play games, continuing the circle of limited options and a limited audience for games. Monroe's perspective is typical of many, but distilling games into examinations that assess skill strictly limits what video games can be and who they are likely to attract as potential players.

There are games, interactions, and studies that have explicitly sought to assess concepts like meritocracy or social inequality in action. *StarPower*, an educational game designed in the 1960s to encourage reflection on social status in a classroom setting, is typically used to address racial and social inequality.[111] The game starts with players on a relatively equal playing field, but they are quickly divided into three groups, where the most powerful get to make the rules for the game going forward and the least powerful quickly find themselves disaffected and removed from the process of playing the game. Those in positions of power are given the option to consult others on new rules, but they rarely do and proceed to rig the game to favor their group.[112] In the typical debrief conducted after the game, the most powerful players also tend to insist that the game was fair and fail to observe the systematic oppression they orchestrated. More recently, the psychologist Paul Piff has conducted research on a modified *Monopoly* game where one player is given substantial advantages over the other as determined by a coin flip at the beginning of the game.[113] This experiment, in conjunction with other experimental research, leads Piff to an argument that being wealthy affects behavior in profound ways.[114] Across multiple measures, his research has found that being in a powerful position leads a person to be less empathetic, less supportive of others, and more likely to ignore structural inequality. This dovetails nicely with the research on meritocracy, as the work overwhelmingly holds that people in a position to make rules will set out to create situations that benefit them, ignoring those who are less fortunate and have less influence. This structural inequality is routinely part of video games, where the already invested and talented seek out more of the same, which systematically disenfranchises those who start with less.

These are clear points at which metrics that seemed to be measures of skill or ability are actually indicators of previous structural positions. However, games can help both diagnose and challenge these problems when designed accordingly.

The final key piece of how meritocracy works is to look at how it shapes the terms of interaction in game culture. As detailed more thoroughly in the following chapters, video games are rife with examples of meritocratic game design and narratives. Players are routinely taught, through both the things they do in play and the stories in which they participate, that they earn their success because they started from the bottom and have risen to the top through the quality of their efforts, effectively making this a question of ideology and orientation.[115] Players are consistently given the message that if they try hard enough, work more, and push the buttons better, they will succeed. These experiences are at the heart of many of the games we play. They also have a noxious effect, as they foreclose critical thought about the problems with this kind of approach or about whom games may leave behind. They limit the audience for games. They teach the skilled at games to revile those who are not as good as they are, and instruct the less talented that it is their own fault they are struggling. Meritocracy in games teaches players that the only way to succeed is based on their own talent and effort, eliminating concerns about the structural issues surrounding access. The lack of ability to empathize or think beyond one's circumstance is a hallmark of the problems with meritocratic discourse and a key driver of the toxicity of game culture. Better understanding the status quo is a key step in breaking the toxic culture in and around games, which requires examining relevant work in game studies and analyzing the culture around video games, particularly its most virulent aspects.

2

A Toxic Culture
Studying Gaming's Jerks

One way to start to see additional connections between meritocracy and video games is to look at how games have been studied and how they are being talked about. Within the field of game studies, scholars have examined topics like game culture and gamers, and advocated for changes in how video games need to be developed and considered, occasionally while employing the tools of rhetorical analysis.[1] Also, in light of the deeper discussion of meritocracy, rhetoric, and how to study games, it is relevant to circle back and examine the culture around video games, making a more thorough examination of the current state of game culture a crucial part of raising awareness about how important it is to change. A deeper investigation of game culture also ties into how meritocratic norms are feeding problematic behavior through a dependence on appeals to balance, player skill, and the notion that players earn their victories on a level playing field. I begin with a brief explanation of rhetoric as a critical tool.

A key to rhetorical criticism is understanding the relationship between the reality we perceive and the symbol systems we use to describe it.[2] The words and expressions we have shape how we see the world, and how we see the world constructs the words and expressions we have. As a small example of this, by introducing the idea that people have an obligation to help make the world a better place early in this book, I am framing how readers engage with what is written and laying out a framework for how I sought to write the book. Past videogame conventions and norms set expectations for future games, as successful formulas are regurgitated time and again; the symbol systems create a reality of what video games can and should be, as well as who should be playing them. Particular words, like "terrorism" or "freedom," can help foreclose debate and discussion or enable them. The way we see colors in the world, and which colors we can see (or not), are likely tied to the words we have available to us, as research has indicated that lacking a word for a color or shade makes it more difficult to discern.[3] As we think about how games work, it is important to remember that the existing symbol systems of games set the terms on which people engage. A limited, meritocratic culture will provoke a certain kind of response, and changing that symbol system will require the development of new, different modes of interaction. However, the job of a rhetorician is to examine the various influences we face in society in an effort to help people better understand how symbols do work on us.[4] There are many different ways to understand any given set of symbols, and rhetorical analysis articulates how we are influenced and how symbols frame how we think. Rhetorical critics can explore how video games work as symbols through the words within and around them, the design of games, the community of people who play games, and the modes in which we play games. Rhetorical analysis, when done well, helps people understand the subtle factors that influence them. In the case of video games and meritocracy, rhetorical analysis can explore how a series of seemingly small advances over time can create a situation where norms and expectations around skill and effort shaped the culture that grew up out of those systems, and how that affects contemporary games.

Meritocracy is a complicated symbol system that includes preferred appeals and lines of argument. Thinking about meritocracy as a set of symbols, rather than an all-enveloping culture, helps achieve the critical distance to assess how the ideology forecloses debate and reflection. Rhetoric can help articulate the links between meritocratic norms in games and game design and how they overlap with the culture created in and around games. Of particular interest in the course of analyzing how meritocracy relates to games are the symbol systems surrounding the mechanics and design of key games and the narratives that regularly set players on a path to value power, overcoming obstacles, and victory over one's opponents. Rhetorical analysis explores how decisions repeated in game after game normalize certain belief systems, while others are neglected. Audiences who are routinely subjected to certain kinds of appeals are more likely to internalize them, but perhaps even more important, the kinds of symbol systems deployed set the terms for engagement with video games. The consistent use of one kind of appeal connected to meritocracy sets the terms of the vocabulary and imagination that all those who play video games are subject to and limited by.

Part of the impact of any discourse is to frame the boundaries for what kinds of ideas and imagination are possible. Symbols help shape how we live and interact with other people. The rhetoric of meritocracy consistently advances certain ideas as natural and normal while dissuading people from thinking about other ways of structuring cultures. Meritocracy encourages thought about how people earn their success, how if they work hard enough and are talented enough they, too, can make it to the top. Meritocracy leads to rewards being heaped on the most talented people and requires rigorous testing systems to determine exactly who is worthy of those rewards. In tandem with these principles encouraging judgment about the worth of individuals, meritocracy also leads to a lack of thought about structural inequality and situations where not all people start from the same point. Further, an overarching principle that the successful "earn" their rewards leads to a lack of critical analysis about how initial success in a meritocracy compounds in value and makes additional rewards even more likely. Rhetorical analysis provides a subject position to reflect critically on the situation in which we find ourselves. Reappropriating the classic line from Marshall McLuhan that "I don't know who discovered water, but I'm pretty sure it wasn't a fish," rhetorical analysis separates us from the meritocratic soup and enables a critical look at how discourse does work on us.

As a dominant and important media form, games have been subject to increasing analysis in an effort to better understand how they work and what they can do. Game studies, a rapidly expanding field, comprises researchers from almost every discipline, and that wealth of perspectives adds a heterogeneity to the research perspectives one can find about games. Summarizing the whole field is not necessary for this book, but three areas deserve extended mention: rhetoric and games, assemblage and co-creativity, and game culture and gamers.

Rhetorical analysis has been a primary mode of analysis for games. Ian Bogost developed the concept of procedural rhetoric to analyze how games work as a practice of "using processes persuasively." Todd Harper and Gerald Voorhees have used rhetoric to analyze character representations and game genres. Ken McAllister broadens the application of rhetoric, analyzing games, players, and the industry surrounding them in an effort to understand the meaning-making processes at stake in and around video games.[5] Rhetoric's flexibility and focus on analyzing symbol systems makes it a good fit for analyzing media, a theme that can be seen throughout the work that has already been done in game studies. There is one piece of rhetorical analysis that deserves extended mention in this project, however: a deconstruction of the notion of "real games."

A key rhetorical construction in video games is that some games and "gamers" are more "real" than others.[6] Concerns along these lines are almost always implicit comparisons between an idealized vision of what video games should look like and what particular instantiations of video games actually are. Real games are typically played by real gamers in a circular discourse that marginalizes new and different approaches. In so doing, a broad, diverse discussion is shut down in favor of an insular, narrow one. A general belief among some that games with meritocratic norms are more authentic than others sets the framework for toxicity in games; it normalizes meritocratic discourse and implicitly contends that non-meritocratic games are necessarily lesser and should be marginalized.

A second crucial idea that can be borrowed from game studies is the understanding that games are a product of assemblage and co-creativity. The central idea of the assemblage is that everything needs to be analyzed when it comes to games, from the environment of play to the means of play to the person playing.[7] Assessing and understanding games requires looking well beyond any individual piece of video games and often benefits from analyzing how multiple elements work in tandem to create specific situations for play and interaction. Part of the reason why games cannot be isolated into neatly compartmentalized parts is that the co-creative relationship of players and producers of games is crucial to their production. Co-creativity is the belief that media products are constructed in the interactions between producers and consumers of content.[8] The concept of co-creativity has substantial effects on games, from situations where prominent members of fan communities get hired as designers to active solicitation of players' opinions through beta testing. However, combining the notions of assemblage and co-creativity facilitates an understanding that there is a clear feedback loop in game design. A key part of what video games are and what they can be depends on the active participation of and feedback from players. This interdependent relationship facilitates a conservative game-design process that gives those who are already in the community an upper hand in determining what comes next, what is acceptable, and what should be designed. The meritocratic norms of games are a key part of the production of games, and they comprise a worldview that is advanced and furthered through the co-creative process where players advocate for systems that further their own interests, routinely giving themselves a head start.

The final relevant piece of game studies to this project is the research that has been conducted on game culture and "gamers." Adrienne Shaw argues that the foundational idea of videogame culture is problematic, as it defines a culture around the study of a particular kind of media and makes it more difficult to obtain the distance necessary for critique.[9] This dominant approach, of seeing a culture defined entirely by the play and consumption of games, encourages those within it to focus solely on games, largely from a noncritical perspective. Placing games at the center of a subject position leads to attempts to understand everything through games, rather than seeking multiple, diverse perspectives or looking at other fields, cultures, and activities for inspiration and context. This places those within the culture in a limited position, where it becomes difficult to think of things outside the frame of games and defines all things in terms of how they fit games—like protests in Ferguson, Missouri, or the death of a United States Supreme Court Justice—regardless of how tenuous or relevant the connections may be.[10] This is an important lesson to keep in mind, as the culture around video games has a history and is a subset of a much larger whole that has little to do with games. In this case, the dominance of meritocracy in countries that are crucial to the development of games affects the ideology those games are likely to advance. In others cases, the deep history of games and how they are produced is crucially important, as Carly Kocurek evidences in her analysis of videogame arcades.[11] Beyond a critical assessment of game culture, Shaw also critiques the notion of "gamer" and contends that the term itself is laden with assumptions; blithely using the term strips the context out of many people's play experiences. The social construction of a category called "gamers" puts certain people in a position where their role is to consume a particular kind of media, and only analyzing "gamers" means that we leave out large sections of game players.[12] "Gamer" is a term that focuses on consumption, and part of thinking critically about how games work requires reassessing the baseline assumptions frequently made about games and those who play them.

Finally, it is also necessary to consider how elements of labor are intertwined with game play. A key aspect of many games, particularly role-playing games, is ongoing and incessant small tasks that must be repeated over and over again to reach a goal. Often referred to as "the grind," this repetitive play can be soothing and relaxing, but it is also inextricably linked to considerations of effort in games.[13] Video games tend to depend on and reward repetitive "hard" work. Players are frequently cast in a position where clicking, tapping, or pressing similar buttons time and again will help them transcend their initial paltry state on a journey to become powerful and/or wealthy within the game. Player efforts are generally also rewarded with the ability to perform more, and different, moves and skills. This effectively become a means by which to continue the labor in a new way or in a different situation. Although games are often described with words like "play" and "fun," they are also integrated into larger structures of work and productivity on which the relative merits of player effort and skill are judged. This idea of celebrating effort and skill makes contemporary games well suited for meritocratic norms, as success is typically judged by a player's effort plus skill.

Rhetoric and the use of rhetorical analysis to study games offer a way to look at and think about games differently in order to obtain the critical distance Shaw seeks. It is crucial to remember that designing and playing video games is the product of a co-creative relationship between players and designers, and that interaction with games is tied to a complex assemblage of many different factors that construct play in specific, situated contexts. Finally, all the questions we ask are subject to understanding the larger context of who is playing games and how they play. Concepts like "gamer" and contexts like "labor" help shape how we think about who plays and why. The next step is more completely addressing discussions about games, gamers, and game culture.

Toxicity and Games

Appropriating the title of an article written by Adrienne Shaw, one reason why video games are full of jerks is because the world is full of jerks.[14] Games are certainly not an exception to the problems found elsewhere in the world, but, as Leigh Alexander argues, games seem somehow, somewhat different, even worse than other elements of society, media, or the internet. Part of the problem of toxicity in games can certainly be explained by the fact that there are elements of any culture that are troubling, antagonistic, or repugnant. Understanding what accounts for the specific situation in video games and discussion about them can be partially accomplished by examining some of the problems that have crept up in and around games.

Popularization of the blanket term "toxicity" largely comes from the work of the *League of Legends* developer Riot Games, which has worked for years in an effort to stamp out particularly offensive behavior. *League of Legends* (or *LoL*) may be the most played PC game in history, debuting in 2009 and featuring billions of cumulative hours played.[15] The game is a multiplayer online battle arena (or MOBA) where two teams, typically of five players, try to destroy an object protected by defensive structures in the other team's base. Games generally last from about twenty minutes to an hour, and players need to both cooperate with their teammates and compete against the other team. Early stages of the game focus on leveling up your team's characters and gaining resources while stopping the other team from doing the same, all in an effort to eventually overpower the other team and their defenses. When players kill opponents on the other team they benefit from substantial experience and resource gains, so if your team is particularly good (or bad) at killing the other team it will likely shift the game's balance.

In MOBAs, one team leveling up substantially faster than the other often leads to a situation where it is clear which team is going to win and the losing team cannot do much but wait several minutes to lose, often while being repeatedly slaughtered. The waiting, combined with the advantages gained by the other team for killing other players, means there is plenty of time for blaming other people for what went wrong in a losing game of *LoL*. Relatively early in the game's life cycle, the developers identified that their "vicious player community" had the effect of "hurting the game's reputation and hemming in its potential to grow," as "toxic players are among the top 2 reasons players quit the game and never come back."[16] Riot Games established a Player Behavior team that created a tribunal system to mete out punishments, including temporary or permanent bans and full posting of relevant chat logs on appeal.[17] The developer also started a policy of telling players they were acting in a problematic manner, which led to some players self-policing and reducing their own troublesome behavior. As of this writing, the efforts of the team were reported to have decreased toxic behavior in the game as a whole, but the *LoL* environment remains toxic enough that the company is still experimenting with new efforts, including instant bans and bans of professional players.[18] Each round of new policies receives substantial attention in videogame media, but I contend that the continued need to increase policing and punishment of behavior points to deeper problems. A squad of people reprimanding players for offensive language or disruptive play is addressing symptoms, not the root causes of the problem that lead people to behave in troublesome ways in the first place. Riot's attempts are also clearly linked to a desire to attract and retain players for their game, rather than addressing the structure of videogame culture as a whole. They are a starting point for thinking about toxicity in a particular game, but a problem with behavior in any single game is a symptom of deeper problems in the culture around video games as a whole.

Taking a broad look at videogame culture requires taking a step backward and thinking about how the design of particular games crafts the interaction of player communities within them.[19] The terms on which a game is played and the tasks players are seeking to accomplish have a tremendous impact on the culture found within any given title. With this in mind, it is crucial to look at individual instances in a given game and also at the design choices made in specific games, with an eye to the broad culture around games as a whole. The interactions among design elements of given games and the biases of those making and playing games are at the core of why videogame culture is the worst. As cultural problems, these issues must be addressed by better understanding the issues that are widely apparent in and around games.

Critiques of the culture surrounding video games are abundant, and many of them make the argument that the culture of games is different, worse than the culture around other media. Although the world is full of jerks and the internet is full of jerks, one can certainly make a strong argument that some of the jerkiest are found circulating around video games. As the gaming editor of *Badass Digest* Andrew Todd observes:

> The Video Gaming Internet can be a horrible place. Hiding behind infinite fake Twitter accounts and message-board anonymity are some of the worst examples of humanity. The abuse gushes forth in such torrents that reporting tweets becomes almost useless. You block or report one anonymous, anime-avatared account, and then fifteen more take its place: fifteen more slackly flapping mouthpieces for cowardly, whining crybaby manchildren. (Because they are always, always men.) It's so bad that hacker groups like Lizard Square have gone so far as to commit real, actual acts of terrorism, like calling in bomb threats to a plane carrying Sony Online Entertainment chief John Smedly. The internet lit up with shock that gamers had sunk to the level of real, actual terrorism, but the sad truth of the matter is that terrorism had been going on for far longer. Terrorism is terrorism regardless of whether the target is a nation, an institution, a vehicle or an individual. . . . This is a problem endemic to gaming, and everyone is part of that problem. There is a culture of harassment, abuse, and bigotry in the rotten core of multiplayer gaming; it has been allowed or even encouraged to fester by developers, and it has created some of the most toxic individuals on the internet.[20]

This quote is excerpted at length because it does a sound job of illustrating the breadth and depth of activity that characterizes online discussions about video games. From bomb threats inspired by feelings about video games to a culture that makes multiplayer gaming inhospitable, the author voices some of the harassment he faces because he writes about video games online. Todd presents a case for how bad things have become, and he points out that this is a long-standing issue specific to video games aided and abetted by those who play and develop them. There are many things that both enable and prop up hateful behavior, and there are plenty of blameworthy actors, but the common discourse and actions that have become a normal, routine part of the environment around video games is troubling.

A way to measure the depth of the problem is simply to look at the women who have been harassed for simply inhabiting a space within video games. Shortly after Anita Sarkeesian published an episode of the video series *Tropes vs. Women in Games*, she was forced out of her house because of specific, detailed threats against her and her family.[21] The game designer Zoë Quinn was the target of harassment after her ex published details about her personal life online because he could count "on the most reviled hubs of our community to live up to their sordid reputations."[22] Based on what she experienced firsthand, Quinn wrote that she was motivated "to continue trying to break down barriers and disrupt the culture that enabled the abuse I've endured for the last two weeks from ever happening to anyone ever again."[23] The award-winning game journalist Jenn Frank suffered such harassment after writing an article for *The Guardian* that she quit game journalism.[24] The game developer Brianna Wu spoke out against harassment in game culture and promptly received a number of terrifying threats, which caused her to flee her home and also precipitated her withdrawing her company's exhibition at a major industry conference.[25] Beyond these highly visible cases, Wu argues that "if you are a woman working in the games industry, especially in a public way, you're going to experience harassment," and that women in games are subject to an "emotional and even physical minefield they're signing themselves up for" simply by being a part of a community surrounding video games.[26] Putting the blame on women and contending that they should simply toughen up is not a remotely viable answer; as one aspiring woman in the game industry puts it, "Having a thick skin beneath such magnified attacks—not criticism—is nearly impossible when your entire being is being mangled."[27]

One place to start detailing the culture surrounding video games is to examine game conventions as well as presentations by large game companies. One would think these would be places where people would be on their best behavior, as they know they are being watched and documented by the various reporters and bloggers present. However, examining what has actually happened at recent events is just one more way to recognize how bad things are. The single biggest videogame industry event is the Electronic Entertainment Expo (E3), which takes place in late spring and is a showcase for new developments in the industry and specific, notable games. E3 news routinely reaches outside the videogame community and into mainstream coverage of culture, which makes it a great place to locate disconnections between videogame culture and the broader society. At an E3 presentation for Microsoft's Xbox One a man (a producer on the game) and a woman (a community manager) were brought out to demonstrate a fighting game called *Killer Instinct*. Unsurprisingly, the person who worked on building the game was more skilled at it than the person who did not.[28] Choosing stereotypically coded gender roles was a problem, but it went further, as the producer said, "Just let it happen. It will be over soon," to which a journalist added the unspoken conclusion: "You know, like a rape."[29] Since the presentation was at a major event, the press coverage reached well beyond game-focused journalists and into the mainstream media. The NBC News account of the comment included the poignant statement, "We're talking about a press conference for a company that's directly involved in the production of a sizeable portion of video games worldwide. The representations they incorporate into their advertising suggest the types of customers they think are worth seeking out."[30] E3 is far from the only conference with a troubled track record. In 2013, at the International Game Developers Association party at the Game Developers Conference, one of the largest industry events for those who make games, was marked by what one journalist described as a mixed group of attendees, including "industry leaders, industry hopefuls . . . and scantily clad female dancers," that made "IGDA look more like a frat house than the voice of an industry. How very disappointing, IGDA."[31] The party occurred a day after the widely praised #1ReasonToBe panel, where women listed their reasons for being part of the industry and made suggestions about how to fix gender imbalances and increase diversity in video games.[32] The good news of the panel was rapidly undercut by the party, which led to several IGDA officials resigning from their positions with the organization.[33]

The Penny Arcade Expo (PAX) presents more troubling cases for video games. *Penny Arcade* is one of the largest consumer-driven web-sites dedicated to video games, with a web comic and commentary that has positioned its two creators as leading tastemakers for discussing issues from a gamer perspective. Unhappy with the conference options for game consumers, particularly E3, and its lack of focus on players, Penny Arcade launched its own conference in 2004; it has grown from the initial event in Seattle to add PAX East, PAX Dev, PAX Australia, and PAX South to the list of annual conferences. Penny Arcade is a key rallying point for gamers, offering a chance for ideologically similar people to gather both online and off. The first major issue surrounding Penny Arcade was the criticism its creators faced for releasing a comic strip that featured a rape joke. They then released additional comics making fun of their critics, eventually selling merchandise to celebrate their initial strip, which centered on a fictional character called a Dickwolf.[34] In a self-accounting of why one former PAX regular no longer considers attending, Rachel Edidin explains that when asked in a PAX question-and-answer session about what they learned from the incident, the cartoonist for the site, Mike Krahulik, contended that his regret three years after the Dickwolves comic was "pulling the Dick-wolves merchandise from the *Penny Arcade* store—merchandise that he had created as a 'screw you' to rape survivors who had the temerity to complain about a comic strip. When the audience burst into applause, [Robert] Khoo nodded sagely and said that now they knew better; now they would just leave it [the Dickwolves merchandise in their online store] and not engage."[35] PAX has also seen trouble in its ranks of volunteers, called Enforcers; in a critique of PAX, Elizabeth Sampat writes that one Enforcer "was accused of sexually assaulting a woman using the Enforcer network as a way to get closer to her, and Penny Arcade covered it up and did not address it publicly. When asked, [cofounder] Mike [Krahulik] said he would not have done anything differently, and that not releasing the name of the assaulter or the fact that the assault took place was the right call."[36] Conventions are a public face for the game industry. They are a place where products are promoted and networking connections are made. They are also a space in which there is constant policing of who "belongs," as dominant norms are reinscribed to make women feel less welcome. This shapes game culture and becomes the terrain from which judgments about merit will be made. These events are illustrations of the ground on which gaming's meritocracy is based and offer a perspective on just how hard some categories of people have to fight just to reach other people's starting line.

Culture also reaches directly into the play and design of games. High-level eSports, from *Counter-Strike* to fighting games, demonstrate how players actively participate in policing game culture. eSports come in a variety of forms and are typically tied to playing a video game as a competitive activity. A number of scholars have investigated competitive gaming from a variety of different perspectives, with particularly good work being done by T. L. Taylor, Emma Witkowski, and Nicholas T. Taylor.[37] eSports often appropriate tropes from other sporting competitions—for instance, the use of trash talk suffuses much of the culture. Although different games typically have norms that are specific to their competition—real-time strategy and fighting games draw from different communities of players, much like soccer and baseball do—eSports typically present themselves as meritocratic spaces open to the best players on the basis of their skill. However, competitions and the discourse surrounding them are often noxious places to those who are not male and white. In an analysis of the fighting game community, Todd Harper found that, to his dismay, "players who object to this treatment [harassing speech] aren't really true players, and that if they were true players they would understand that these are 'just jokes' that are inherently *and inseparably* part of the game."[38] Harper extends his analysis to address the community's perception that the women who play are often lesser players than men and benefit from a different kind of standard, which often includes hedges like "she's good for a girl." Similar instances of harassment often occur to prominent black eSports players as well, with racist sentiment expressed when they compete in prominent games or win tournaments.[39] Visible players who do not fit the norms of what a frequently sexist and racist audience expects are subjected to harassment they must overcome in order to participate on the same terms as those gifted a far less hostile starting position. One of the clearest places in which to see toxicity at the root of competitive games is the case of Cross Assault.

Cross Assault was a promotional vehicle for a new Capcom fighting game, *Street Fighter X Tekken*, which combined characters from two leading fighting game series, *Street Fighter* and *Tekken*. Pulling top fighting gamers into teams and placing them into a tournament, the event featured prizes, promotion by IGN, and broadcasting by Twitch.tv. Set up as a reality show produced by Capcom, IGN billed the event as "a social experiment with fighting game players as much as it was a fighting game competition[;] Cross Assault mixed up the standard competitive format and put players in new and unique situations, with unprecedented amounts of stress."[40] The competition's context was shaped largely by the fact that the game was new, so players were learning strategies and approaches on the fly, rather than using well-practiced techniques developed over years. Uniting the teams were experts who served in roles akin to coaches; each roster comprised four men and one woman who were particularly well-known in the fighting game community.[41] The official IGN recap states that "it was the responsibility of the coaches to strategize on their team's behalf, and each took a drastically different approach on how to manage their team."[42] By day 5 of the competition, the leader of Team Tekken, Aris Bakhtanians, had engaged in sustained harassment of the female player on his team, Miranda Pakozdi. From asking her bra size to directing the webcam to parts of her anatomy to smelling her as part of a display of dominance on camera, Bakhtanians harassed Pakozdi to the point that she refused to actively fight in her final matches, effectively throwing the games to her opponents. When asked about the harassing behavior by Twitch.tv community manager Jared Rea, Bakhtanians contended that sexual harassment was a fundamental part of the fighting game community, that "they're one and the same thing. This is a community that's, you know, 15 or 20 years old, and the sexual harassment is part of a culture, and if you remove that [sexual harassment] from the fighting game community, it's not the fighting game community."[43] Bakhtanians then continued into an analogy where he argued that taking the sexual harassment out of fighting games would be like trying to get the National Basketball Association to play with an American football rather than a basketball; in Bakhtanians's mind, advocating to remove sexual harassment from fighting games is "ethically wrong."[44] Additional reporting indicated that the "team leader sat at the center of a number of comments made during livestreams that made her [Pakozdi] feel uncomfortable, and he had refused to show any concern when the issue was brought up."[45] Months after the incident, the story of harassment at Cross Assault led to a *New York Times* article about harassment of women in videogame culture.[46]

The events of Cross Assault are a single case that is years old at the time of this writing. However, they are a near perfect distillation of many of the problems with game culture and representative of the experience and harassment that many of those playing games have to face. As a small example of this, Todd Harper's book transitions from a discussion of Cross Assault into Maddy Myers's experience with harassment while playing video games in her local community.[47] This event and other cases of harassment often are about policing the boundaries of an imagined community, fueled by a strong desire to retain what already exists. Typically, the cases are carefully swaddled in appeals to skill, to being good enough, and to working hard enough to make it. All these tropes are at the center of any sort of meritocratic appeal. If the harassed were tough enough to take it, then they would be able to reap the rewards of success. Systemic harassment sets the terms on which players engage, giving stark advantage to those who are not targeted and retaining power for those who have already climbed the ladder. This level of harassment also short-circuits any appeal to skill, as an initial test for some is putting up with jerks, not playing video games. These problems are carefully rooted in the meritocratic discourse of video games and illustrate how meritocracy in games is a sham because it cannot account for context. Another case can clearly show how this way of conceiving of video games as skill-based enterprises reaches deeply into game design.

Cooperative play is often a tricky thing for video games to master, as players who are differentially skilled are often frustrated by their partner's lack of or excess of ability. As many people have difficulty finding a person perfectly matched for them, some games, particularly those made by Nintendo, come with settings or adjustments that help to make the partnership or competition between players more pleasurable. Gearbox Software sought to do this by adding a fifth character, the Mechromancer, to its game *Borderlands 2*. One of the skill trees for the character was a set of abilities that softened the learning curve for the game, giving poor shots a better chance to hit enemies and otherwise improving the play of people who were learning the game. Officially dubbed "Best Friends Forever" as a skill tree, the feature was referred to as "girlfriend mode" in an interview by the lead designer of the game, John Hemingway.[48] Quickly denounced as a personal anecdote by the president of Gearbox, the original story included the rationale behind the feature, where the lead designer states, "The design team was looking at the concept art and thought, you know what, this is actually the cutest character we've ever had. I want to make, for the lack of a better term, the girlfriend skill tree. This is, I love Borderlands and I want to share it with someone, but they suck at first-person shooters. Can we make a skill tree that actually allows them to understand the game and to play the game?"[49] Commentary about the feature quickly sprang up after the story, with sharp analysis focusing on the flip use of the term "girlfriend mode" and the casual sexism it conveyed. A feature that was designed to get more new people playing a game ran the risk of alienating them through the sexism lurking behind it. As one essay argued, "Their use of the term [girlfriend mode] should be treated as a symptom and not a cause—and a reason for us to ask bigger questions and tackle sexism on a larger scale."[50] For another, the core contention was about the fact that "girlfriend mode" rolled off the tongue quite easily, which would not likely be the case for "boyfriend mode," and that "people simply don't think about women that much in the triple-A game industry, and when they do, it's often as an afterthought, as we see here."[51] There was also a side of the discussion that contended that attacking a designer for uttering the phrase "girlfriend mode" was political correctness run amuck and stood to create a chilling effect whereby developers would feel less free to talk with the press.[52] After about a month of reflection Leigh Alexander wrote that she delayed her essay about the issue for two reasons: she doesn't like that "as a woman writer on games, . . . I am conscripted to act as an authority on every gender-oriented debate," and "because I privately felt it was a case of some problematic wording of an otherwise-good idea."[53] The additional time also gave Alexander a chance to cite a marketing survey that showed how calling the feature "girlfriend mode" actually may increase sales and attention.

For my purposes, there are two key issues at stake in this controversy. First, the whole intent of the design feature was to upset the traditional meritocratic design of games and give newer players a chance to play with their more practiced compatriots. For several of the writers covering this game, this innovation was the key, exciting takeaway: a company structuring a game in a manner that subverts the traditional meritocratic order. Second, women are assumed to be of lesser skill by default. Although many claims were made about tremendously talented women game players, the informal title of the feature makes a certain set of assumptions about how men and women play games. The inferential leap about the feature is that those who are going to need it are more likely to be interested in the game's cutest character, as the Mechromancer was clearly designed to be, and that women are far more likely than men to be in a position to need to learn how to play a first-person shooter. A feature like Best Friends Forever mode has the potential to change meritocratic norms in games by altering the terms on which players interact, but its presentation with such polarizing terms offers a vantage point to see the bias threaded throughout game culture.

Although issues of sexual harassment and sex-based discrimination have been covered to some degree in the gaming press and academic literature, issues surrounding assumptions about race are present, but far less attention has been paid to them. However, what is there provides a complementary perspective on the problems inherent within game culture. *Gamers against Bigotry*, founded in 2012, asks game players to sign a pledge acknowledging that they "contribute to an incredibly diverse social network of gamers around the world, and that [their] actions have the ability to impact others," and requests they not use bigoted language, including slurs "based on race, ethnicity, gender, religion, sexual orientation, and disability."[54] Within a week of launch the site was defaced with racial slurs and eventually brought down entirely; shortly thereafter, the site's database of pledges was erased.[55] Even a basic, nonbinding effort like signing a pledge against hate speech is a target for those who seek to retain a toxic videogame community. Organizing for a more harmonious, less spiteful environment is likely to incur the wrath of those who benefit from the current order or at least do not see a problem with it.

Academic analyses about race and ethnicity in video games have also found a deep set of problems.[56] Playable avatars of color are found almost exclusively in sports games (which have the veneer of representing real life) and fighting games.[57] The handful of representations of minority characters in games like *Grand Theft Auto* are likely to rationalize fears about people of color and how they live and/or exoticize the characters as others in an effort to rationalize and excuse the graphic narrative of the game, which is likely quite foreign to the average player's life.[58] In online, interactive play, Kishonna Gray has found that minority gamers face substantial amounts of hate speech based on the way they sound, much like women are harassed based on the simple act of speaking aloud in an online game.[59] Being found out as something other than a straight, white male in a videogame community is likely an invitation to harassment and derision, a situation for which a meritocratic order cannot account. These processes are inextricably tied to masculinity and, as Derek Burrill argues, link to how video games have expanded boyhood, offering a safe space "to engage in violent and aggressive play without the threat of real bodily injury found in sports and other real-world activities and conflicts."[60] Technology and class have altered what masculinity means over time, and R. W. Connell argues that masculinity is a social process with historical and cultural contexts. This process can be seen in computing and gaming, as working with a keyboard has been transformed from secretarial work that should be done by women into a techno-cultural geek masculinity dominated by middle- and upper-class white men.[61] For spaces of play to be safe, one must fit proper expectations of the digital boy, which are tied to being white, male, and of means. Perhaps the most poignant recent example of the perils of being something other than a white male in game culture is the movement dubbed GamerGate.

GamerGate

There are many essays written about the beginnings of GamerGate and how it originated, but the earliest moments of the movement can be traced to the initial reaction to Anita Sarkeesian's efforts to Kickstart her video series.[62] With toxic energy waxing and waning over the two years since Sarkeesian's public funding request, Zoë Quinn's release of *Depression Quest* led to a brief spark of venom as a portion of the game community sought to get the game removed from cloud-gaming platform Steam's Greenlight program.[63] The game, a text-based adventure about what it is like to live with depression, was distributed for free, with any donations going to the National Suicide Prevention Lifeline. The game was pulled from and then put back on Greenlight and eventually made it onto the Steam platform, which ensured wide availability, after which it seemed as if the ire was dying down. But then Eron Gjoni, an ex-boyfriend of Quinn's, posted a nine-thousand-word screed about their relationship and how it ended, and accused her of sleeping with a game journalist to get positive coverage for her game.

Gjoni's post had been deleted from forums like Something Awful and Penny Arcade but found traction on 4Chan, which adapted the message into a story about "an indie game developer who used sex to get ahead professionally."[64] Quinn responded that personal matters were personal and should not be discussed as news, the *Kotaku* editor-in-chief investigated and cleared the journalist of any wrongdoing, and things seemed like they might die down.[65] However, when Sarkeesian posted her latest episode of *Tropes vs. Women* everything fired up again, and Sarkeesian was driven out of her home because of death threats. Two days later, the actor Adam Baldwin coined #GamerGate and the hashtag took off. Eventually, three women fled their homes because of death threats and several others, including the award-winning freelance journalist Jenn Frank, pledged to quit writing about games because of unyielding harassment. Twitter analysis showed how pernicious the commentary was, and Quinn infiltrated the 4Chan message board that was organizing the harassment and posted the chat logs.[66] Quinn eventually wrote a piece titled "5 Things I Learned as the Internet's Most Hated Person" for *Cracked*, who "were bombarded with demands we cover something called the 'GamerGate Scandal'" and deemed it "an Internet harassment campaign against a random indie game developer who, like many such targets, was a female and feminist."[67] Far more people not mentioned in this brief recap were attacked and harassed as part of GamerGate, including academics like Katherine Cross, Adrienne Shaw, and Mia Consalvo. The movement is interesting for a number of reasons, but perhaps most notable for this work is how much it shows the blind spots of segments of videogame culture and how the events represent video games in broader society.

One crucial element of GamerGate is that it is a decentralized, largely unorganized movement. Surely there were pockets of people working together with similar interests, but one of the notable points of criticism was the lack of a clear agenda. Each individual seemed to have his or her own personal mission of change, which enabled all participants to disavow whatever they found displeasing and made discussing issues with proponents of the movement frustrating, as talking with one person had no bearing on the next. Ostensibly, the most charitable read of the movement was that it was about concerns surrounding journalistic ethics and corruption. However, for those on the outside, Frank Lantz's experience was common: "I have not been able to find a single explanation of a coherent GamerGate position. It remains completely unclear what is being called for or denounced. As far as I can tell there are no useful ideas with which to engage here— only an inarticulate mess of confused feelings, uninformed opinions, and second- and third-order meta-arguments."[68] Or, more simply, in the words of Film Crit Hulk, "the end result is that you can't even get to the nugget of disagreement on the world view. there is no world view. there is only the attack and the response."[69] Finding common ground among GamerGaters ceased to be practical, but there were a couple of themes in the discourse that are largely indicative of what was going on: concerns about a lack of control and the harassment of women.

The most frequently cited touch point for GamerGaters was the insistence that a key part of their movement was about journalism ethics.[70] The most constructive read of the group is as a consumer boycott of people concerned about journalistic coverage that insulted their target audience instead of providing objective coverage of relevant news.[71] The most common flashpoint in this regard was a flurry of articles that appeared shortly after the #GamerGate hashtag was born that decried the death of the gamer. The two most widely circulated and referenced essays were those by Leigh Alexander and Dan Golding.[72] The argument about the end of gamers had three key claims. First, video games were reaching a broader audience than ever before and, as such, game publishers need not focus on the classic gamer stereotypes as their primary audience. This argument largely followed in a tradition of cultural criticism that proclaimed the death of the author or a variety of other subject positions, and was backed up by data that clearly indicate the audience of videogame players is far more diverse a group than the white males of means who match the typical stereotype of a group of gamers.[73] Second, the term "gamer" was at one point a key reclamation of space that reframed people away from being a nerd or some other insulting label into something more positive. However useful "gamer" had been, all progress was now being compromised by fractures in the community that led to some subsets of people advocating against and silencing others. This line of thought is akin to loving an idea so much that you smother it, promoting a gamer-above-all identity so vigorously that the very idea of a "gamer" is conflated with "jerk."[74] Finally, Casey Johnston, among others, argued that the hostility shown toward women engaging in cultural criticism demonstrated that the label "gamer" was becoming irretrievable, as each silenced and harassed woman "advances the goals of the most poisonous 'gamers,' while regressing everything else."[75] For those who self-identified as gamers these articles were likely hard to read, as they questioned a thing that was core to who gamers were and wanted to be. That this tumult happens around video games is one element that makes them a different kind of media form, as there are people who care about identifying as a gamer so deeply that they can get lost in something like GamerGate. It is hard to imagine something happening on such a wide, sustained scale in many other communities of media enthusiasts (e.g., those passionate about literature, film, or music).[76]

In the wake of these articles and as the number of posts behind GamerGate grew, supporters of the movement launched Operation Disrespectful Nod, which targeted advertisers and outlets that published what they deemed anti-gamer articles. There were rallying cries for journalists to be fired and for companies to cease their affiliation with certain publications. Intel was the first to cave, prematurely terminating an advertising campaign with *Gamasutra*, the publisher of Alexander's article.[77] Intel later released a statement explaining that it was not seeking to take sides in the matter and that it valued diversity as a company; later it established a $300 million fund to advance diversity in the tech industry.[78] Adobe was targeted after a flurry of tweets by a *Gawker* writer, and the company asked that its logo be removed from a page on the site.[79] Adobe later clarified that it wished to take a stance against bullying and that it was "not and [has] never been aligned with Gamergate."[80] GamerGate claimed victory in both cases, but these were also points where additional attention was brought to the movement and how its members were choosing to conduct their business. Max Read of *Gawker* chose to sum up the events of Disrespectful Nod as a story about how the blog got "rolled by the dishonest fascists of Gamergate."[81]

Beyond focusing on those in the videogame industry, GamerGate also targeted academics, largely tied to a session at the Digital Games Research Association (DiGRA) conference in 2014. In a fishbowl panel titled "The Playful Is Political," game researchers were brought into conversation about issues surrounding diversity, representation, and video games. Notes were communally taken on a Google Doc set up by the organizers, Shira Chess and Adrienne Shaw.[82] As GamerGate was roiling through the internet, GamerGaters found a link Shaw had posted on Twitter to the Google Doc, which would subsequently be defaced and used as the origin point of a campaign to attempt to discredit an academic organization and its members.[83] Ranging from theories of a covert connection to the United States defense-department agency DARPA to decrying members of the board as feminists, GamerGaters rallied against academics who allegedly set out to censor their favorite games. Primarily focusing on women academics, DiGRA president Mia Consalvo, organizer Adrienne Shaw, and scholars Katherine Cross and Torill Mortensen, among others, were harassed and/or doxxed.[84] Members of GamerGate set out on Operation Digging DiGRA in an effort to "fact-check" academic essays in the DiGRA Online Library, which led conference organizer Jose Zagal to note that this was one of the first times a substantial portion of academic research had "come under [broad public] question, scrutiny, and comment."[85] Chess and Shaw argued that a key point of divergence in having nonacademics review structures that are part of academe is that "academia simply does not make sense from the outside. More than that it is perceived as threatening."[86] Like many cultural products, academia comes with titles and rituals, obscure practices and judgments that may seem invisible for those in the system yet are inscrutable for those outside it. Within academia, those who choose to focus on issues of diversity, difference, and issues affecting marginalized groups have always had to walk a harder road than those who study less radical topics.[87] GamerGate's move to address academia is a chance to see the connections that run throughout the whole of the culture surrounding video games, as well as a notable point that women were overwhelmingly more likely to be harassed than men and that the communities and cultures surrounding games reach far beyond their initial platforms.[88]

Gamers rallying under the banner of GamerGate were effectively a conservative force within games. As Adrienne Shaw argues, the label "gamer" is fundamentally consumerist, as it is defining a group of people by their media consumption habits.[89] In seeking to limit the kinds of games that should be published and how those games should be discussed, the movement sought to reframe video games and those who played them in a particular way. The impact on videogame culture and its relationship to meritocracy can be best seen in the differential treatment of women and in the reception of GamerGate in the mainstream media.

Plenty of disturbing things happened within the context of the movement, which had the result of scaring every woman in the game industry, and any of a number of different situations could be isolated and analyzed.[90] However, I think there are two particularly illustrative moments that show how deeply the problems in game culture run. It would be easy to pick the instances of people being run out of their homes or opting out of the industry in response to harassment, but I would hope anyone reading this book would reject those things as obviously terrible. Looking more deeply at what could initially seem to be small issues makes it possible to see just how slanted and insidious the bias in harassment can be. First, one of the cofounders of the gaming site *Kongregate*, Emily Greer, posted about the harassment she has received for her participation in the game industry. Prompted by GamerGate to reflect on the difference between messages sent to her and her brother, she wrote that she had assumed the harassment she received was "normal for a co-founder of a game site" and was surprised to hear that her brother and fellow cofounder did not have the same experience. Counting up their messages, she found that she receives about four times as much harassment as her male sibling.[91] Greer viewed her experience as normal, typical, just the way things were. However, that kind of belief is precisely what ensures differential access to games and subverts any hope for an actual meritocratic order within them, as it guarantees structural inequality for some. Greer's experience is different from her brother's—it is harder, which is not an unusual position for many people who are not white, male, and straight in videogame culture, as they are judged by the intersections of many different factors that have nothing to do with their skill plus their effort. Greer has been successful and achieved status as a cofounder, but the sexism she faced made her journey more difficult than her brother's. In a meritocracy, structural obstacles like this should not exist, as they interfere with proper assessments of merit by denying equal opportunity of starting positions. Unfortunately, situations like this are all too common.

A second test of difference in a similar circumstance directly related to GamerGate is the response to Chris Kluwe and Felicia Day.
Kluwe, a self-proclaimed gamer and former punter in the National
Football League, wrote a scathing piece about GamerGate with fascinating use of profanity and name-calling, and then conducted an
"Ask Me Anything" on reddit targeted at proponents of GamerGate.[92]
Felicia Day, an actor and frequent media personality within the videogame community, wrote a piece about how GamerGate scared her
and how she had remained silent on the issue due to concerns about
"self-protection and fear."[93] Day's piece was far more sympathetic
and worlds less offensive than Kluwe's. Nonetheless, Day was immediately doxxed in the comments, as "Gaimer8" published her address
and e-mail, yet nothing of a similar magnitude happened to Kluwe.[94]
Kluwe subsequently noted that the reason no one had come after him
was evidence of a societal misogyny, and that "until we get to the root
causes of it, similar things are just going to happen over and over in
different arenas."[95] Day and Kluwe received different treatment because one conforms to certain aspects of what is expected and one does
not. Although sexism is not unique to gaming, the way external media
covered GamerGate further illustrates what videogame culture is like.

The mainstream media reception of GamerGate only occurred
after events had been roiling in the videogame community for weeks.
There are two key elements to consider in the reaction: the tone of
the pieces and whom the media targeted as experts to either quote
or to have write editorials. The *New York Times* came out against
GamerGate, arguing that the movement "made it impossible to over-
look an ugly truth about the culture that surrounds" video games, and
subsequently turned to Anita Sarkeesian for an editorial that argued
"the term 'gamer' is no longer useful as an identity because games
are for everyone."[96] *Vox* noted that "#GamerGate's most prominent
targets are all women," *Newsweek* analyzed the discussion to argue
that women were harassed more than men, *Time* had Leigh Alexander write an essay, CNN and the *Washington Post* went to Brianna
Wu, and Zoë Quinn was the subject of an extended interview for the
BBC.[97] Perhaps the harshest reception for GamerGaters was from
Stephen Colbert, who used an episode of his late-night talk show *The
Colbert Report* to criticize GamerGate and then turned to Anita Sarkeesian for an interview.[98] In the wake of the Colbert interview, one

journalist summed up the situation as follows: "Gamergate died ironically from what it wanted most: mainstream exposure."[99] Attention to GamerGate may have reached its mass-media peak with the airing of an episode of *Law & Order: Special Victims Unit* that dramatized "a virtual carbon copy of [GamerGate's] darker fantasies."[100] By gaining attention, the ideas and actions of GamerGate were exposed to a different kind of audience, and people less intimately tied to the videogame community had a difficult time understanding what was going on. I know I found the events hard to explain to anyone who was not immersed in it; however, in addition to widespread social problems with misogyny and sexism, one of the best explanations for what was happening was a desperate effort to hold on to meritocratic norms in video games.

The worst part was that the additional exposure did not kill GamerGate: the movement just became more concentrated and, in many ways, more extreme. GamerGate "is not over, and some of the wounds it opened . . . are as fresh as ever."[101] Reflecting on what will come out of GamerGate, Natalie Zina Walschots contends that it will "take years to sort out the impact on the industry, on the community, on the way games are made and played. Years before we figure out what game journalism can possibly look like in a post-Gamergate world. Years before we can even begin to get a grip on the personal trauma suffered by so many after such a massive campaign of harassment and violence. And before any of that work can be done, Gamergate has to end first. It's an inevitable victory, perhaps, but one that's going to leave deep, presently unfathomable scars."[102] Summaries of the GamerGate movement dominated end-of-year reflections in 2014; as an example, Ben Kuchera wrote that "GamerGate's lasting legacy will likely be the fact that they've made harassment of women in the video game industry impossible to ignore," and that "it's become a completely insular network of paranoid, reactionary gamers who just want things to go back to the way things were, before they had to exist in a world where women played games and outlets wrote about more than just 'fun factor.'"[103] GamerGate also managed to become *NeoGAF*'s Fail of the Year and *The Vine*'s biggest nerd story of 2014, and was named in the Electronic Frontier Foundation's statement about the challenge of online harassment.[104] Legal implications also began to surface, with women harassed by GamerGate speaking in front of Congress, members of Congress calling for prosecution in cases of online harassment, the United States Department of Justice announcing an intent to pursue cases of online harassment, and frequent GamerGate target Brianna Wu publishing essays calling for involvement by the FBI and prosecutors representing districts from which she has received death threats.[105] GamerGate is unlikely to end quietly, and while it still simmers its targets will continue to feel the brunt of the harassment and rage, which ends up silencing many and, at the very least, guaranteeing unequal access to video games.

Contemporary society is riddled with sexism, and this is certainly part of the problem in GamerGate. However, videogame culture is particularly impacted because of the desperate effort of some to cling to the ideals of a meritocracy. Meritocracy in video games tells players that they are special, that they are uniquely gifted; if you were a gamer who defined a large part of yourself around video games, why wouldn't you fight tooth and nail to hold on to that feeling? Meritocracies generally function to insulate those who get ahead, a dynamic that occurs throughout society. Meritocracy amplifies the real-world effects and harms of social biases. To enact the ideology in practice requires equal opportunity. Structural inequality undercuts its functioning by confounding attempts to assess merit, while the prevalence of the ideology reassures the most successful that they earned their position because they are the most skilled and hardest working. Video games actualize meritocracy, as they teach players judging people based on their relative merit is right, normal, and something that should be encouraged. As one Twitter user put it in the wake of Intel's decision to pull advertising from *Gamasutra*, "I support meritocracy, I support equality, I support #gamergate, I support @intel."[106]

GamerGate is about many things, but one crucial lesson it can teach concerns how meritocracies fall apart. In his disassembling of meritocracy, Christopher L. Hayes argues that one of the first casualties of the ideology's failings is a growing lack of faith in our institutions, "since people cannot bring themselves to disbelieve in the central premise of the American dream, they focus their ire and skepticism instead on the broken institutions it has formed."[107] Game journalism is far from perfect, but it is arguably one of the most prominent institutions in video games. Short of critiquing the people who produce the games that gamers love, game journalism is the structure that shapes what gamers want, how they think, and what should be happening in the industry. Game journalism is a key component of game culture, and the academic study of games, targeted through attacks on DiGRA, is tied to prominent universities and key elements of institutional power. If Hayes is right, it is also reasonable to expect that these are the elements of videogame culture that will be vilified well before players question their skills or the overall role of meritocracy in videogame design.

Within the general critique of game journalism, a specific request of many GamerGaters was that reviews should be objective evaluations of a game.[108] Cultural criticism holds that an objective review is impossible, as merely describing features is imposing ideological values on a game review, but it is striking that to strive for objectivity in game reviews is consistent with a meritocratic position. A different way of describing this position would be to say that it is about evaluating games based on their merits and what they offer to players. An objective review would strip out context and subjective claims, building a foundation for equality of opportunity in reviewing, where all games are judged based on externally verifiable elements like their frame rates and length. In large part, the problem is not just that videogame culture, like our culture more broadly, is a white, straight, wealthy, male space, but that it is an especially meritocratic space. GamerGate is a preview of the kind of thing that happens when meritocracies fall apart, as those in relative positions of power scramble to hold on to what they have. GamerGate was also a forerunner of what happened in politics throughout the United States and United Kingdom in 2016, as Matt Lees wrote for *The Guardian*: "This hashtag was the canary in the coalmine, and we [broader society and the media] ignored it."[109] We must stop ignoring moments like this, and deconstructing the meritocratic appeals in video games is a key part of disassembling a movement like GamerGate. Video games offer a particular route into understanding broader culture and, right now, that requires focusing on the underanalyzed aspects of those games and the culture surrounding them. Defining games and gamers in a specific manner rewards the investment that a certain subgroup of players has made over years. Seeing that cultural capital eroded is hard, making the status quo something worth desperately fighting for. Unfortunately, certain aspects of game design and production are a base from which these problems arise in the first place.

Moving Forward

Video games and game culture are symbol systems rife with implications and assumptions. Meaning swirls within games, the way they are played, and the discussion around them. Game culture is currently a toxic place that excludes and ridicules those who are presumed to not fit. Critique of what exists is not welcome, and dissent is frequently shut down in comments or campaigns to harass those who dare to speak out. Rhetorical analysis and critical thought about meritocracy offer a chance to examine what works, how it works, what it does, and what can be learned from it.

In the case of video games, the meritocratic order is borrowed from broad technological culture and most thoroughly applied in the case of digital games, where it forecloses reflection about how broken that assumed meritocracy is. Rather than acting as a test of skills, being good at games is about a complex assembly of sociotechnical factors that benefit certain people more than others. Being encouraged to play games, growing up with them, having the money and time to play them, and being born with the physical capabilities to excel all help give certain people structural advantages that outweigh individual skills or effort. Understanding how meritocracy pairs up with video games requires a deeper dive into meritocratic game design and meritocratic game narratives, with a particular focus on how prominent both are and why that matters.

3
Coding Meritocracy
Norms of Game Design and Narrative

Video games can represent anything, a trait that can be used to put players into unfamiliar and challenging subject positions. Video games can also be seen as glorified rule systems, where fictional worlds are laid over obscure axioms and algorithms governed by a computer.[1] Much like any mode of communication, video games are part of a larger culture and rely on certain tropes that get recycled time and again in a way that makes them seem normal, natural, like doing things in a particular manner is simply "the way things are." Though far from the only realm in which meritocratic appeals are used, in videogame culture meritocratic norms dominate communication and permeate both game design and game narratives.

Video games came into prominence alongside the coining and proliferation of the concept of a meritocracy. As Michael Young's idea transformed from the basis for a satirical novel into a dominant philosophy about structuring society, video games were invented and transformed into a primary pillar of contemporary entertainment and media consumption. In video games, meritocracy becomes an actualized practice, and they are one of the few places where the ideology runs rampant, unchecked and celebrated while slipping into the background and becoming part of the perceived natural order.

Within video games, meritocratic norms appear in both game design and game narratives. Game mechanics and approaches are designed to offload computational processes onto a computer, which becomes a seemingly perfect, objective arbiter of skills in play. Videogame design typically revolves around providing a platform where luck is limited and talent is praised. This is a historically situated set of practices that are highly influenced by the technologies and communities of people playing. However, from the arcade to the console to personal computers, video games have often focused on providing frameworks for players to develop and showcase their skills. In the arcade, players needed to keep winning to hold the machine, while contemporary console and PC games challenge players to battle others online in a test of ability or to overcome challenging puzzles and boss fights in both single- and multiplayer games. Mobile games, especially those produced for iOS and Android, are a possible exception with the prominence of luck-influenced card and casino games, but there are also of skill- and effort-driven games released for mobile devices. Games are often balanced with an eye toward creating a level playing field—one where multiple approaches are possible and, when we win, we praise our skill, but when we lose we blame poor game design or inferior teammates. Contemporary game design revolves around limiting risk and giving players what they already know they like, which means limiting the role of luck and building out ways for them to prove their merit.[2] Beyond the way games work in game play, meritocracy is also furthered through game narratives. The story lines of many video games teach players that if they work hard enough, if they try long enough, if they are good enough, they will be victorious. These preconceptions—central tenets of meritocracies—are included in game after game after game. In addition, there are spaces in which design and narrative come together, like the nearly ubiquitous levels players can gain, as they give a quick view on where a player stands in a hierarchy and teach players to strive to be just a bit better. Beyond helping players quickly identify who merits the most, or least, attention, levels also craft a narrative structure in which we all start from the same place and we can all make it to the top. The systematic integration of leveling systems throughout games helps leveling as a process recede into the background, thereby making it hard to notice that leveling up is part of a widespread message that meritocracy is a default mode of the social organization in and around video games.

Understanding the history of meritocracy and rhetoric facilitates analysis of meritocratic design and narrative in two key areas. First, rhetorical analysis is a way of seeing the impact of symbol systems and how they work to structure interactions among people. By repeating meritocratic elements over and over, video games normalize those kinds of appeals and make them seem natural. Thinking deeply about the structures of games, both how they are built and the stories they tell, articulates the terms on which players play games. The symbols we use structure the ways we think and how we play. Better understanding those symbols can help us develop something new and different by disrupting what has been there. Second, by relying on meritocratic appeals, video games fall into the same traps widely discussed in analyses of meritocratic systems. Meritocratic systems ossify and become aristocratic, measuring inherited advantage rather than merit, while justifying their existence by teaching those at the top that they have earned their spot and those at the bottom that they deserve their lower status.[3] Meritocracies quickly become mythical, as they seem like they are judging skill and effort, but they actually judge social situation, circumstance, good fortune, and starting points.[4] Videogame culture has developed with merit placed as a key, praiseworthy element of play. Meritocracies cognitively capture those within them and stymie attempts to break away and build something new. Systems that reward those at the top are hard to disrupt precisely because the successful are getting seductive messages confirming the quality of their abilities and character. Splitting away from a reliance on meritocracy and averting the crumbling demise that Young predicts for meritocratic systems requires explaining meritocratic game design and meritocratic game narratives.

Meritocratic Game Design

Games are artificial systems that could be designed in any of a broad number of ways, but most video games are designed around a consistent set of expectations and approaches. Designing contemporary video games for consoles or PCs typically means focusing on balance, fairness, skill, and rewarding a talent or time investment over spending money to advance. Many of these things may seem innocuous at first thought or like a genuinely praiseworthy aspect of design, but further exploration demonstrates how they work in tandem to create a certain, specific way of thinking about symbol systems in games.

In his book *The Art of Failure* Jesper Juul articulates that there are three different approaches to success or distributive fairness in games: skill, chance, and labor. Games of skill are meritocratic, where talent is clearly rewarded and the resulting distribution of players is rife with inequality because of differential levels of ability. For Juul, skill is "the least controversial of the three paths." Chance, which is primarily about luck, "is the most controversial, mostly for its association with gambling."[5] Finally, games of labor are relatively newer and generally tied to sustained effort over time. Often actions within these games are trivial, with a cost for failure; Juul cites *FarmVille* and *World of Warcraft* as examples to demonstrate how games of labor revolve around the ongoing effort, or grind, made by players. Two of these models of game design—skill and labor—port quite clearly onto meritocratic systems. They are also the most common design approaches for video games. None of the games of chance listed by Juul are video games; instead, they are traditional gambling games, like roulette, or card and dice games, like solitaire and *Yahtzee*. All games are designed around some kind of fairness in approach, and mass-market, nonmobile video games have typically chosen to adhere to choices that most clearly represent a meritocratic balance in game design based on skill, effort, or a combination of the two.

"Balance" is a seemingly neutral term. All games and activities are balanced; it is simply a question of how. In most Western video games the kind of balance sought is actually one of equality in approach and potential outcome for similarly talented players, which ports directly on to the equality of opportunity expected in meritocratic systems. Western video games are typically designed in a manner where multiple factions or characters can fight things out and should be able to count on various approaches being relatively similar in potential power. Although there are occasionally rock, paper, scissors elements, where an approach is highly successful against one potential opponent yet highly vulnerable to another, multiplayer games are typically designed to minimize variability among in-game choices. Formal and informal rules are often developed and enforced to limit the role of certain outside agents, like a computer program that optimized play in Blizzard's card game *Hearthstone*, which ceased development after the company asked the programmer to stop the project because of the threat to game play and balance.[6] The program, which automated and systematized decisions about which cards to play, eliminated the human element of choice, which Blizzard decided violated expectations of fair play. Competitive matchmaking typically works to pair up similarly skilled players—and in the case of a game like *FIFA*, similarly matched teams—in a battle that should tend toward the most even playing field within the bounds of the game itself. Unlike contests between older and younger siblings or between sports teams with radically different talent levels, videogame balance is an appeal to meritocratic ideals. In trying to set the terms of engagement as balanced, these video games seek to create a framework within which skill is paramount and prior status or luck is minimized. Players and developers often work together to further norms around balanced play by developing phases in tournaments where particular characters (*League of Legends*, *Street Fighter*), teams (*Madden NFL*), or maps/stages (*Super Smash Bros.*) are banned or restricted from play. Meritocratic game design is predicated on creating environments that focus on skill (i.e., merit) to ensure that the most talented are most likely to win, which further advances the ability to ignore structural inequalities.

Balance in video games rarely stops with the initial release of a game, however. The advent of online play and the relative ease of updating games means that most video games are in a constant state of flux, in which designers release a game, players play it, and then designers rebalance the game to account for trends in the player base. Players and designers now frequently refer to "the meta" in video games ranging from card games like *Hearthstone* to character-driven match-three games like *Marvel Puzzle Quest*. Although not unique to video games, metagaming is a process of working out the rules of the game to find the optimal approach at any given time. Where video games differ from other types of games is in how quickly the game designers can adjust and adapt the rules of play to account for how players behave in practice. Supercell's *Clash Royale* is a textbook example of this process. A mobile game that blends elements of collectible card games and multiplayer online battle arenas, set in the universe originally developed for the smash hit game *Clash of Clans*, *Clash Royale* built regular game-play balancing into both the plan for the game and its business model. In *Clash Royale* players develop decks of eight cards and then use the characters, spells, and buildings on the cards in an effort to defeat their opponent by destroying opposition towers and defending their own. Cards can be leveled up to be more powerful and, like in a collectible card game, a better deck makes it easier to win. However, building on the balancing norms inherent to contemporary video games, Supercell regularly adjusts the power of each card based on player behavior. Cards that are not being used are made stronger and cards that are being used most often are made weaker. This then incentivizes players to continue to develop new cards to take advantage of the current state of the game, driving spending and attention across the entire group of cards, rather than just the subset of eight each player can use at a time. In my experience from playing the game and reading the forums, players rarely object to the process of balancing and even make suggestions about how cards should be adjusted in the next round of balancing. By appealing to a core norm of balance, Supercell has built a free-to-play model that fits nicely into broadly accepted practices in video games. Processes of rebalancing and the requisite agonizing over "nerfs," which make something weaker, and "buffs," which make something stronger, are further testament to a widespread dependence on balance in video games. Balance is not something that is inherent to video games; it is an iterative practice constantly reinscribed into them. The circular process of game balance is widely accepted, and players routinely appeal to balance in order to get changes made in the games they play. Although this practice is far more common in multiplayer games than in single-player ones, even single-player games are occasionally rebalanced to either help players overcome particularly difficult moments or present a greater challenge if things are too easy.

This notion of balancing and rebalancing video games and the hyperfocus on sustaining and advancing a balanced mode of play is particular to video games, particularly competitive play in video games. Other games and sports may advance discussions about competitive balance or means by which to match up players of similar skill, but balance is rarely as central to discussion as it is within videogame design. Video games without proper balance are criticized for being broken, for being less than games where skill wins out. This is often summed up in objections to free-to-play games that are monetized in a way that leads to complaints about how the game is pay-to-win, where success is determined more by the size of one's wallet than one's skill and effort at the game. It can also be seen in objections to cheap tactics, where players use a technically possible maneuver that the community finds objectionable. From the *Clash Royale* player building his or her deck around the mortar to the fighting game player who relies on characters that are commonly banned in tournament play to the sports gamer who insists on only using the most powerful teams, the online community of players typically expects others to behave in a manner that fits norms of fair play.[7] Even cheating in video games is socially negotiated, with many players arguing that cheating is abhorrent in multiplayer games even if it may be acceptable in single-player titles.[8] Although this may seem like a basic, sensible kind of appeal to many of the people who play video games, it is a meaningful one and a key bias in videogame design and play. This particular notion of balance is also a perfect starting point for advancing a meritocratic agenda within video games, as balance is deployed to ensure that skill and effort win out.

There is a substantial hedge to the routine focus on balance in video games. Although many games, designed in many different countries, appeal to a meritocratic kind of balance, there are occasional exceptions. Two of the most prominent are the *Mario Kart* and *Mario Party* series of games. Both are designed and published by Nintendo for a variety of its game systems, targeted at wide audiences. Both games also have a decidedly different approach to balance, as they typically punish the most successful person and reward those who are struggling. The "best" player can often win these games, but to do so he or she will have to overcome substantial additional obstacles not presented to other players. *Mario Kart* is quite contentious among hardcore gamers, largely because of item boxes that generally reward players with an item of a quality inversely proportionate to their place in the race. Perhaps the most infamous is the "blue shell," also known as the "spiny shell." First appearing in *Mario Kart 64*, this targets the leader of the race to rapidly stop his or her progress and drop back in the pack. However, the blue shell is only given to those who are losing at the time they reach the box. Writing for *Wired*, Chris Kohler distills the meritocratic stance on the blue shell: "It is widely known that the worst, stupidest item in the *Mario Kart* series is the Blue Shell. When you launch it, it flies above the course, homing in on the racer in first place, then lands directly on top of them, causing them to explode and be slowed down considerably. This is no help to the person who threw the shell since they are still in last place. This is a great help to the person in *second place*, as it allows them to get into first."[9] Much of Kohler's objection centers on the idea that items like the blue shell enable players who are not the most skilled to punish those at the front of the race. One list of complaints about *Mario Kart* highlights the blue shell as the single most objectionable part of the game, referencing it as "socialism in action," "evil," and "what made *Mario Kart Wii* luck based."[10] However, *Mario Kart* is designed with a different approach to skill and merit. A prominent designer on the *Mario Kart* series, Hideki Konno, notes that he is routinely asked about a version of the game without items, but contends that the game is defined by them and the blue shell functions to keep everyone in the race until the end.[11] Konno appeals to a different kind of balance, one based on keeping the game competitive and interesting for all, rather than on ensuring that the most meritorious player wins. *Mario Party 8* has a similar feature, where Chump Charity is awarded to the player in last place as the game nears its end; the board is then filled with coins to maximize the importance of the end of the game, rather than what came before. Although the games have been quite successful, players complain with comments like the series relies too much "on luck, it sucks all the fun out of the experience," and request a skill-based mode where luck is minimized and the most talented player would win the game.[12] In both cases, the typical meritocratic underpinnings of videogame balance are challenged, which is likely why Konno gets so many requests to produce a game mode without items. Similar dynamics can be seen in *Super Smash Bros.*, where the stages with the most variance and opportunity for luck to play a role are typically banned in competitive play.[13] The negative reaction to Nintendo's different form of balance is simply more evidence of how deeply meritocratic game design is woven into contemporary Western videogame culture.

The maniacal focus on balance feeds into several other norms of meritocratic videogame design. The first is that games are generally expected to be fair and that players will quickly decry those that are not fair as "cheap" or "abusive." The fairness of games is typically judged against something akin to a reasonable person—perhaps a reasonable gamer—standard where the player making the argument judges reasonableness based on his or her own abilities. These contentions of fairness rarely consider infrequent or lesser-trained players, as fairness needs only to be ensured for the game's perceived target audience. Effectively, fairness is a subset of balance; balance is a prerequisite for a game to be fair. Fairness as a game-design trope feeds into the idea of meritocracy by setting a baseline expectation that the game does not discriminate against potential players. In fact, if the game is adjudged as fair, then failure is the responsibility of the player rather than the game. Fairness, when combined with balance, works to isolate and individualize gaming, placing the player in a position of responsibility to perform at a certain level. If players fail in a fair, balanced game, then it was because they have not demonstrated sufficient merit to warrant success.

Video games are often expected to reward skill. Unlike activities like reading or watching television or film to decode additional meanings or story lines, meritocratic game design advances the idea that games should be tests of skill. Unlike in games that can be conquered through a sheer investment of time or repetitive tapping, players in "real" games have to show off their talents. Questionable games, like *FarmVille*, are ridiculed in efforts like *Cow Clicker*, where repeated simple actions are the only necessary and sufficient conditions for success. Skill in "proper" video games requires more than simple button mashing, as meritocratic game design encourages games to be built around timing, careful judgment, strategic decision making, and other techniques that can be put to the test against the computer or other players. Social and mobile games can often require skill or effort, but the kind of skills and effort in social and mobile games reward traits that are not incentivized by contemporary console and PC games.[14] Patience and planning are far more common on platforms other than consoles and PCs, and the balance between effort and skill typically places more focus on effort, while console and PC games emphasize fast-twitch reflexes, hand–eye coordination, and mastery of spatial geography. When it comes to consideration of merit, core video games not only require players to show merit but also to show socially approved kinds of merit, which often runs counter to what is found in mobile and social games. This kind of appeal anchors neatly into the notion that videogame players earn their successes, that victory in a game is proof of talent and skill, rather than a gift of presence or an inheritance of birthright. The idea that players earn their victories is a seductive appropriation of meritocratic norms, since it valorizes players and gives them reason to savor their successes. Earning rewards through skilled play is at the center of game design, as players claim to seek proper challenges to overcome and designers advance a meritocratic conception of games through the repeated use of these tropes.

Finally, Western PC and console video games are expected to reward talent and time investment—or in meritocracy's terms, effort—instead of money spent on the game. Somewhat different than design predicated on skill, designing in favor of talent and time further focuses game play on the individual and his or her relative abilities. It also creates a situation where it seems like anyone could be successful at video games if they were good enough and simply chose to invest enough time. These notions are central to meritocratic norms, as they focus on individuals and their efforts, not the larger system around them. This may feel like a good, reassuring thing, but it ignores how prior time, skill, and cultural investment helped put a player in a position to be successful. Previous time spent playing one video game rolls into the next one, as part of a knowledge scaffolding of everything from how to move in a 3-D environment to how to use a controller or mouse–keyboard setup to the intricacies of inventory management. All that work is easily erased and rapidly forgotten as it fades into the background for experienced players while building additional barriers for anyone new to video games. By also adding in the expectation that players should not be able to pay their way forward, hurdles are erected for those who could pay to skip steps while meritocratic expectations are maintained. Free-to-play games only get a pass from these concerns when the advantages are largely cosmetic, as in *League of Legends*, rather than central to the game, as in games with energy timers or purchasable weapons. The fear of a player being able to buy progress is substantial enough that the monetization structure for *Halo Online* led one commenter to write, "So far this is like *Halo* from hell, where combat is just abysmally skewed towards players who are willing to shell out cash for victory."[15] A system where players could buy their way ahead could be quickly dominated by those with deeper pockets, which is the central criticism of free-to-play games deemed pay-to-win. In the case of meritocratic game design, investing money is taboo, as it represents an external structural inequity; however, investing time to develop, hone, and deploy talent is expected, showing how much work a player did to earn the accolades he or she accrues, even if those elements also carry structural biases with them.

Specific applications of meritocratic game design will be unpacked in the next chapter's case studies, but two examples provide context for how video games are more dependent on meritocratic norms than the category of games more broadly is. In reflecting on playing a live-action game called *StreetWars*—where players are given a dossier and tasked with shooting a target with a water gun while avoiding someone trying to do the same to them—the noted videogames journalist Leigh Alexander writes, "That's the thing about games. When luck is a factor, it's just one within a generally-predictable ecosystem. In a video game there are only so many things that your enemy can do. You can learn what those are. You can, through practice and repetition, gain complete control over an environment where there is only so much that can go wrong."[16] Video games typically exist in a space that is different from life outside them. Unlike the luck required to have things go right when people can act in unpredictable ways, video games are subject to a rule set that can be exhausted and memorized. The boss will always move in a certain pattern; opposing players are limited to a certain set of choices. The focus on this kind of predictability is specific to, and possibly unique to, video games. In an article about his frustration with the distance tracking in the augmented reality mobile game *Pokémon Go*, Stephen Totilo argues that video games comprise systems that can be understood, and that the point of playing them is to learn those rules and how to exploit flaws in them. He sums up his argument with the contention that "the logic of a well-structured game promises the predictability that regular life doesn't have. If we understand how a game works and input something into its system, we assume we'll get a fair output. Players of *Diablo* know this as they kill enemies and pick up loot. Players of *Candy Crush* know this as they plot their moves. Players of *Super Mario Bros.* know this as they time their jumps. Know the system, then take advantage of it."[17] Totilo claims to address the general category of games, but he is really only addressing how many video games currently work. Designing video games in this manner is a choice reinforced by the community of designers and players that continue making and playing titles built around the general premise of a fair, predictable game. Systems with greater human interaction are subject to much more social interaction and can be far more unfair in their design, especially if they are based on the unpredictability of people, like Alexander's example of *StreetWars*. Although culture binds us in other interactions, we could act radically differently than expected. The eventual lack of options in video games puts a particular focus on skill and practice while limiting the role of luck as a design consideration, which feeds directly into meritocratic norms. Alexander continues, "The beauty in video games, in all designed interaction, is that they offer you the delusion of grandeur, the intoxicating misconception that all challenge in life is simply a matter of systems thinking . . . Video games will always protect us from the truth: how smart we are not."[18] Video games are typically designed to make players feel like they earned their victories, that it is to their own credit that they won. Video games are made to be conquered and, outside of competitive forms of video games where players are directly pitted against one another, players are generally supposed to win. Meritocratic game design creates a situation where players are led to believe they are attributable for their successes and discouraged from thinking about how the game is set up for them to win. Although these are comforting thoughts, they also set up terms and expectations that quickly turn sour when players do not encounter the success they have been taught to expect.

A second example of how the broader category of games parts ways from video games is in the case of collectible card games (CCGs) like *Magic: The Gathering*. In a collectible card game, the options and resources available to a player are dependent on the cards a player has available. In many cases, the cards one has are directly related to the amount of money a person has spent buying cards with which to play the game.[19] As one player notes, "Typically, in the CCG world new cards are released as an entire set that you need to chase down by opening up packs of cards. In the world of *Magic*, this makes for an awkward couple of weeks as people without the time, money, and desire to track down all the new best cards are at a significant disadvantage."[20] In effect, the balance in the typical collectible card game runs counter to the balance in video games. Instead of focusing only on time investment or skill, these games add financial resources to the equation, as a lesser player with a better deck will more readily beat the most skilled player. Money may not be the best way to subvert meritocracy, but the reliance on amassing a card collection makes CCGs lean toward an aristocratic mode of order. Skill and time investment still factor in, but they are far less pure concerns, and it is widely understood that investing in the game increases one's chances at success. Players who buy the occasional pack without focusing on trading or purchasing specific cards are effectively playing a more difficult, limited game than those who invest more money, time, and energy into the game.[21] There are game types and specific tournaments that limit a player's prior investment, from restricted modes to drafts that limit access to a certain set of cards, and games like *Ascension* and *Dominion* are based around a common set of cards. However, the addition of financial resources into consideration upsets any sort of appeal to pure meritocratic expectation and changes the terms on which certain games are played, potentially opening the door for one example of how to subvert a consistent reliance on one approach to designing games.

Meritocratic game design is a key thread throughout many contemporary video games that frames the culture that develops around them. The tropes advanced by this mode of approaching and designing games leads to a reciprocal relationship between designers and players that continually reinforces the importance of merit in games. This process limits and constrains the kinds of appeals players and designers make while shaping our expectations about what makes something a good video game. Buying into the notion of meritocracy also sets the terms for our interaction with one another. We think about video games as a proper test of skill and effort, rather than as something more contingent. Meritocracy is even more thoroughly integrated into video games, however, as it is repeatedly used as a key narrative trope.

Meritocratic Game Narratives

It is easy to find meritocratic narrative elements in games. One of the most consistent examples is how games typically begin from a position where the central character is a weak, relatively powerless individual who then transforms over the course of the game into something quite different. The most recent version of the *Tomb Raider* franchise set out to tell Lara Croft's origin story, putting her on an island, which gives a narrative setting for a series of events that, according to one reflection on the game, takes "her from player surrogate to toughened survivor in a believable manner" in which "the player relationship with Lara shifts dynamically from start to end."[22] Part of the point of rebooting the game was to alter perceptions about Lara Croft and to change her from a rich kid of great means into a vulnerable character with whom players were likely to identify. Effectively, this recast the *Tomb Raider* series from being centered around a person of privilege to a person who suffered and worked her way through great obstacles to become successful. According to one critic, rebooting Lara Croft and *Tomb Raider* was about "making Lara into a survivor, both inside the game and out on real-world store shelves."[23] This redescription of Lara Croft fits clearly within a meritocratic narrative, where the player is given a chance to grow and develop alongside the character that represents them within the game. As the player becomes more powerful, the character is also, reflecting processes carefully wrapped in a narrative where those who are talented and who work hard become powerful and successful through their own, individualized actions.

Meritocratic game narratives can be found in other, similar series, like *Uncharted*, in which *Uncharted 3: Drake's Deception* tells of protagonist Nathan Drake's origin. Although allegedly related to the famed explorer Francis Drake in the lore of the game, care is taken to highlight all the obstacles Nathan Drake overcame to get to a place of fame, fortune, and adventure. Released into the custody of the state after his mother committed suicide and his father gave him up, Drake is clearly cast as someone who overcame substantial obstacles through his craftiness and hard work. Nathan Drake started with nothing, but through the player's efforts and the character's canny repartee Drake ascends to capture relics all over the world and overcome both natural and supernatural enemies. His mentor, Victor "Sully" Sullivan, selects Drake because of his skills rather than because of his birthright, presently a true meritocratic tale. The tie to Francis Drake is even more interesting considered in light of meritocracy and player identification. The clear implication of the narrative arc in the series is that if Nathan had easily proven his lineage under any sort of aristocratic norms he likely would not have become a highly capable explorer and adventurer, because he would have been gifted status instead of earning it through the player's efforts. Nathan's fight to prove his identity also gives him a much easier route to identification with players. Instead of being a clear heir to an explorer's legacy, Nathan is someone the world has aligned against, giving the player far more agency to help him establish his merit and reason to work on his behalf.[24]

There are also plenty of spaces in which to find tales of merit outside the realm of action games. The casual game sector also relies on meritocratic tropes, as players are cast as settlers of the wild west in Zynga's *The Pioneer Trail*, while Glu Mobile's pair of *Stardom* games and *Kim Kardashian: Hollywood* (*KKH*) are all about ascending to the status of superstar from nothing. These three games are based on a similar game engine and all possess the same basic narrative structure: players are tasked with becoming famous by climbing the celebrity ladder from E-list to A-list and, ideally, holding the number-one spot as the most famous person in their version of the game. Different editions of the games start the player in different positions: *Stardom: Hollywood* sets the player out as a "Starbeans" barista, and players in *Kim Kardashian: Hollywood* are working in clothing retail when they have a chance encounter with Kim Kardashian while closing the store. Seemingly chance encounters and substantial effort at tapping dots are wrapped in a narrative of straightforward success, as long as the player keeps showing up, working hard, and making good choices. Backsliding is all too easy if the game is ignored, as players are required to labor attentively to accrue four or five stars on missions to gain fans and climb the social ladder. Further, if players fail to check in daily, they will quickly find that many of their in-game fans have left them, pushing them down the A-list and back toward being forgotten. *Stardom* and *KKH* offer worlds where the path to fortune and fame are clear because there are no structural barriers to success. Anyone can make it, but one must prove oneself appropriately meritorious to get there.

Building narratives around meritocratic character arcs gives players an easy access point by which to identify with the avatar that embodies them in the game. Basing the story around skill and success is also a way of seducing the player, as we are shown just how much we matter. These story choices pair well with meritocratic game design, helping to solidify a position where video games can frequently be seen as empowerment fantasies, where players are allowed to do and become things we simply cannot imagine trying outside the framework of a game. These narrative choices also establish worlds where all players are asked to play by the same rules, which sorts the skilled from the unskilled. Rarely encouraging reflection about access issues or structural impediments, a focus on meritocracy in the narrative of the game partners with meritocratic game design to focus on the individuals playing games, on their skill, and on their responsibility to work harder and get better. The story is something all players experience, putting everyone in a similar position and on common ground so that we can be sorted out based on our relative ability in a seemingly sensible, balanced, and fair way. We must work to overcome the obstacles in front of us in order to reach the end of the game or the top of the ladder, but that journey requests that we prove our merit. The story reassures us that if we work hard enough, if we are persistent enough, if we are skilled enough, we will meet with success. As we may find less and less of that in our real lives, the seductiveness of games with stories predicated on being able to make it big will likely become more irresistible. Beyond points where there are clear game-design or narrative elements that advance meritocratic norms in games, however, there are also parts of games that have both design and narrative function. One of the most interesting features to consider is the ubiquitous integration of leveling into games.

Leveling: You Just Keep Getting Better

Originating in role-playing games, player levels have become a widely used mechanic across almost all types of games. On its face, leveling appears to be a design concern, as it relates to how players interact in the world of the game and to what options and abilities they are likely to have access. However, leveling also drives an underlying narrative of forward progress in games, as player effort is quantified into experience points and character growth. Leveling has been integrated across a variety of genres, including first-person shooter games like *Borderlands* and *Destiny*, sports games released by both Electronic Arts and 2K Sports, and throughout the casual gaming sector. *Borderlands* was praised for the integration of role-playing elements, like leveling and loot, in a genre where players typically only became more powerful by getting new weapons. Leveling allows the integration of different skills, abilities, and options over time, which allows players the opportunity to further specialize into the kind of roles they wish to play and better show off their talent and ability. Leveling in sports games enables EA Sports to create incentives to play repeatedly under a given account by earning experience and gaining access to the various perks that are locked behind level barriers, thereby transforming the process of playing sports games into an ongoing, potentially endless experience with plenty of rewards along the way. Leveling systems also offer players a visible marker of their merit and a compelling reason to keep upgrading to the newest version of a series (i.e., to avoid losing their progress). Leveling and other role-playing and CCG-like elements in various versions of EA's "Ultimate Team" features are powerful enough that prominent online power-leveling sites, like IGXE, offer *FIFA* and *Madden NFL* coins alongside *World of Warcraft* gold. In casual games, levels can work as paywalls or as a means by which to encourage continued play and attention. In contemporary game play and design, player leveling is a big deal.

One of the first books in the most recent wave of game criticism, Edward Castronova's *Synthetic Worlds*, focused largely on his experience playing games like *EverQuest* and an early incarnation of *World of Warcraft*. Speaking directly about status gains and player differentiation in online games, he wrote:

> Humans seem to prefer the challenge that inequality represents rather than the security that equality affords—with one very important proviso: everyone's status at the start of the game must be equal. If (and only if) everyone starts with the same opportunities, the same amount of money (usually none), the same ability to choose roles and character types, then the resulting inequality is not taken to be unfair. Rather, status inequality happens because of the choices people make, and so long as everyone starts out with the same opportunities, the inequalities that choices create acquire the character of a fun game rather than a crushing of the spirit.[25]

This brief manifesto for game design, echoing Daniel Bell's calls for a meritocracy based on equality of opportunity, is integrated throughout contemporary video games. Leveling in video games provides the kind of design and narrative function of inequality that Castronova praises here. Leveling gives a quick and easy way for players to compare themselves to others. Leveling provides a clear goal for players to strive for, motivating them to keep playing for the next perk that will make them stronger. Leveling promises a transparent kind of inequality that makes abstract effort at a game concrete and intelligible. Leveling is the kind of game mechanic that drives commentary like the following from Simon Parkin: "There are many reasons that video games are a potent draw to the human mind, but perhaps none more so than the fact that they are endlessly fair and just. They reward you for your efforts with empirical, unflinching fairness. Work hard in a game and you level up. Take the path that's opened to you and persevere with it and you can save the world. Every player is given an equal chance to succeed."[26] These ideas are foundational to the establishment and advancement of meritocratic norms in games. When considered in isolation, video games certainly seem fair (e.g., they are consistent from player to player), but there is enough difference and challenge to them to create inequality among players (and certainly in comparison to those who do not play games). As Parkin continues, this sort of appeal is alluring, "especially to people whose experiences in life have been of injustice and arch unfairness," but the particular notion of fairness embedded in systems like leveling drives the development and adoption of meritocratic norms.[27]

Meritocracy is predicated on inequality of character and effort. The ideological drive behind it is to sort people based on their ability and talents. However, the clear, obvious issue with meritocracy is that it can be hard to measure a person's skills and drive. Certainly, assessments can be developed, interviews can be done, and conclusions can be reached about a person's relative merit; it is attempted all the time. However, the design conceit of leveling in contemporary games is that it makes those judgments automatic, fluid, and so easy that they recede into the background. Leveling ensures the appearance that we all start from the same place and then allows us to see how we stack up against other players, as we know they are going through the same things we are. The status inequality Castronova believes we seek is translated into a number that grows slowly over time and broadcasts our efforts and skill to everyone we encounter. However, the notion that we all start from the same place requires deliberate inattention to the resources players bring to a game in the first place. From skill transfer to economic resources to free time, players rarely start at the same place, much like standardized exams in schools assess far more than just talent and effort.

Leveling is perhaps the single most powerful meritocratic trope in contemporary games, a design and narrative device that is rapidly approaching omnipresence in video games. Fed by the prominence of leveling in such a wide variety of games, levels teach players that there is a preferred approach to play. Engagement is driven by accruing the next level, the next piece of gear, the next win. Effort in the game is readily translated into clear demarcations of skill and ability that fundamentally affect how players interact with one another. It was generally understood at the launch of *World of Warcraft* that hitting the maximum level in a massively multiplayer online game (MMOG) was just the pretext to begin a new game based on the continuous acquisition of newer, better gear. In games like *Destiny*, levels are integrated as a way to gate progress and require players to grind to get to the appropriate spot of progression and then be tested in some new way, all of which is just a fancy way of quantifying player effort and ability. Leveling is a clear game-design element, but it is also tightly anchored into a narrative of progress, advancement, and winning. By integrating leveling into games, designers set up a certain kind of expectation about how the game will work and how players will interact with it. Beyond the primary story of whatever is happening in Azeroth or the NFL, game players are encouraged to think about games in particular kinds of ways, ones where the allegedly central story often recedes and the compulsion to get just one more level or a bit more progress becomes the driving narrative experience. Leveling is often the key way players interact with the game, as it is the feature that lets us believe we are all starting from the same place and establishing our power and status through our own skill and effort.

There are a few examples of games where players could actually lose levels, most notably in MMOGs like *EverQuest* and *Final Fantasy XI Online*. In these games, if players died they faced harsh consequences, from losing experience points to accruing experience debt that would have to be paid off before they could level freely again. Should a character lose enough experience points they would actually drop levels, becoming less powerful and requiring them to earn their way back up to reach the same level of status. In my experience this led to a very risk-averse style of play for most of the game, as players sought to limit their chances of dying in ordinary play and focused on engaging in battles they knew they were likely to win so as not to risk penalties accrued upon death. These design features certainly fit norms of meritocracy, as players who could not prove themselves worthy were the ones being punished, but they have largely faded away—for instance, a successor to these titles, *World of Warcraft*, was hailed for getting rid of harsh penalties for death and facilitating more dynamic, risky play.[28]

The ubiquity of leveling in games shapes the terms on which we interact with them and crafts the environment of what we expect and how things work. Leveling is a key part of the symbol system of video games that translates the abstract efforts of button pushing into a framework of progression, advancement, and skill. Status inequalities become clear, and leveling helps us figure out both who we should be looking up to and who should be looking up to us, based on what players have displayed in the game. Effectively, leveling works to facilitate and adjudicate decisions made based on merit. By infusing both design and narrative, leveling is a primary ordering premise of contemporary video games that frames how we think video games should work while requiring us to operate under the auspices of a meritocratic system, with all its flaws.

Leveling is a starting point for seeing how thoroughly meritocratic elements are integrated into games, one that is particularly powerful because of its prevalence. Perhaps a single example of the meritocratic norms in games is enough for some, but a deeper dive into specific cases of games, game elements, and how they work together to advance a meritocratic ideology demonstrates just how much video games celebrate and depend on a presumed social order based on skill and ability, even though initial access points to video games are riddled with inequality.

4
Judging Skill
From *World of Warcraft* to *Kim Kardashian: Hollywood*

I believe the reason meritocratic elements have become so central to video games is closely linked to what the target audience of video games expects from them. The chance to develop, prove, and show off skill is precisely what draws a certain kind of person to a specific kind of game, which frames the culture, expectations, and terms of engagement surrounding video games. This chapter presents a tour through a variety of examples showing just how integral meritocracy is to the core of video games.

In the early days of modern videogame studies, by far the most frequently studied genre of games was massively multiplayer online games (MMOGs). From *EverQuest* to *World of Warcraft* (*WoW*) with an occasional *Final Fantasy* or *Star Wars* game in between, these on-line role-playing games dominated journal publications and confer-ence proceedings. They also proved quite popular with the larger population of people playing video games, as *EverQuest* and *World of Warcraft* were both huge, high-water-mark games. *WoW* specif-ically, and MMOGs more generally, are easy places in which to see meritocratic elements dominating game design and play. Beyond the dependence on levels as an ordering principle for the game, players at the highest level quickly encounter a gear treadmill, where they are enticed into a system by which they play largely to acquire bet-ter equipment that will surely be made obsolete at some point in the not-too-distant future. As Jesper Juul explains, MMOGs are games

111

of labor that, in meritocratic terms, are largely about testing the effort and personal drive of players.[1] Effectively, the game of almost any MMOG boils down to leveling as high as possible in order to collect better gear, then collect even better gear, and on and on. This does not necessarily make for a meritocracy, but the way things are read and interpreted by the community is clearly meritocratic.

As my play in *World of Warcraft* moved from launch to the first few expansions, I saw players go from judging others based on whether they were of an appropriate level to assessing them based on other, more nuanced factors. Elements like required achievements and gear score, which is a rough calculation of the quality of a player's equipment, evolved to become key parts of how players interacted with one another due to designer decisions and player choice.[2] New measures for sorting and assessing the capabilities of strangers were developed shortly after designers introduced new modes of grouping players. As developers released group- and raid-finding systems, players were placed in situations where they were judging whether they wanted to play with others they may not have previously met. Players were being asked to risk their time and potential repair costs for the chance to play with people they did not know. Judgments of strangers were based exclusively on perceived ability, and the easiest skill-based decisions were made based on what a character had accomplished before. This was a particular interpretation of skill, as it was entirely backward looking, and it drove evaluation based on a snap assessment without any room to judge the context in which those accomplishments were achieved. Meritocratic decisions can be quick and straightforward, but they strip out nuance. When trying to pull a raid group together, the speed at which one fills out a group often takes precedence over judiciousness in the selection process. In the case of *WoW* it is notable that the primary objections to things like gear score were not that they were based only on skill, but that they did not judge skill appropriately since they only looked at what a player had once done and not what a player was likely to do now. In my experience, objections to judging people based on their skill were muted; rather, the central question was about which system was the best at assessing the likely talent, capability, and relative merit of players.

Meritocracy in *World of Warcraft* spreads well beyond putting a group together and assessing which strangers with whom to group up. *WoW*, like many MMOGs, is riddled with multiple ladders and sorting systems for players to show off their accomplishments. Media coverage of players is dominated by reports about highlights and accomplishments, from completing all the achievements at any given point in the game to accomplishing world-firsts in raiding and the far more common realm-firsts.[3] The design and interpretation of *WoW* was fundamentally based on assessing which players and groups of players were the most skilled relative to others at any given point in time. Players who were not on the bleeding edge could still sort themselves against what they perceived to be their peer group to benchmark where they were and where they wanted to be. Focused on skill and effort, *WoW* and other MMOGs tend to be based on design elements that further meritocratic expectations among players; this builds a community where the default expectation is that all will be judged based on their perceived talents and systems will be developed to make judgments quick and automated.

One point where merit is most openly assessed in MMOGs is in competitive raiding, which is typically only engaged in by high-level, frequent players. In the course of raiding, games like *WoW* arguably shift from games of labor into games of skill, as players are required to learn elaborate strategies in order to defeat computer-controlled bosses and acquire new equipment.[4] Because new gear is prized, the groups of people engaging in raiding need a way to distribute rewards. The most commonly accepted method has become the use of dragon kill points (DKP).[5] As detailed by Mark Silverman and Bart Simon, the original form of DKP gave players points for each dragon kill they attended, which could then be converted into opportunities to roll a die to try and win a desired item when it became available, effectively an effort-plus-chance system. However, as Silverman and Simon note, DKP has shifted over time, as the system became more complicated and the allocation of loot changed from being determined by the game of chance inherent to dice rolls to being replaced with "a kind of symbolic currency through which play could be exchanged for DKP, which then could be exchanged for in-game goods."[6] The process turned participation in desired activities into points that could then be spent on rewards. Silverman and Simon discuss how some of the best guilds in the world rejected DKP because it focuses players on rewards, rather than on group accomplishments, and can encourage players to hoard points in order to get a highly prized item, rather than pursuing a handful of incremental upgrades that are in the best interest of the group as a whole. The broad adoption of DKP, along with the process of developing and enforcing it, disciplines players, thereby incentivizing certain kinds of choices, like acting in self-interest on one's individual desire, and discouraging others, like pursuing collaboration and a utilitarian focus on the group, through the development of a personal currency in a group context. In so doing, guilds end up using DKP to enforce standards of meritocracy on players. DKP tracks effort through presence at activities, and rewards skill by awarding points when the group is successful. Silverman and Simon argue that DKP is a form of disciplinary power that "associates a quantifiable measure to the value of each guild member in terms of their level of contribution."[7] As a system wholly developed by players and generally tracked and maintained outside the games themselves, DKP is an artifact of how players can intervene in play and further meritocratic norms by codifying what counts as merit in their own allocation of scarce resources beyond what game developers originally intended.

A second genre of game also relies on meritocratic norms in both design and narrative. Sports games, like the *NBA 2K* and *FIFA* series, integrate single-player modes where the player can engage in a "My Player" or "My Career" mode. The specifics of each experience depend on the particular game, but the basic outline is that the player can create a personal avatar that then tries to make it in the professional sports world the game represents. In setup, the player will typically name his or her avatar and make some key selections, from appearance and measurables like height and weight to position in the game and favorite team. In some games the player can pick the team with whom they are affiliated; in others they are subject to a draft or other sort of team-selection mechanism. In some of the newest versions of sports games, like *NBA 2K16* and *FIFA 17*, the create-a-player mode features an extended scripted component to increase immersion and integrate a meritocratic narrative within the game. Overall, though, the player is placed in a position where his or her avatar starts out relatively unskilled and develops over the course of repeated play. Games like the *NBA 2K* series let the player choose where to spend points to make his or her on-court avatar better. In others, like the *FIFA* series, points are earned and distributed based on achievements accomplished in various games played. The player starts out as a relatively weak, fringe member of the team, but with enough effort, with enough playing time and enough personal success, he or she will rise to become one of the best players in the game. Before the end of my first season of *NBA 2K13*, my much taller version of NBA star Chris Paul had become a beast, leading the league in both points and rebounds, and was clearly established as one of the most dominant players. On the other hand, my *FIFA 14* avatar took more work and was constantly loaned out to lesser teams by my parent club, Juventus. In both worlds, I was a top prospect whose progress was constantly moving forward and who would become a star if I were good enough and played often enough to get my avatar there.

The one thing that might set meritocracy in sports games adrift would be injury. However, after playing many seasons in multiple games I rarely found my player getting injured for any substantial length of time. My experience could certainly be the benefit of short-run luck, but it also would make some sense that the developers decrease the risk of injuries to allow players to enjoy the game more. In any case, the game modes are largely based on the player's ability to elevate his or her avatar's level of play. In so doing they lay out a meritocratic framework where players who work hard enough and play frequently will progress forward in their virtual career. Instead of being derailed by all the kinds of things that can happen to professional athletes, the virtual avatars we create in games will progress as long as we are there to play as them and make them better. This straight path celebrates merit and ignores any structural barriers to life as a professional athlete, as players can achieve far more than most real people ever will. Career modes celebrate skill and achievement, depicting success in virtual life as simply a matter of showing up and playing. The videogame version of a professional sports superstar is never a "could have been" or "never was," because of the skill and effort displayed by the person behind the controller.

Quite different from MMOGs and almost a genre of its own, the *Grand Theft Auto* series shows a different side of meritocracy in games. As a single-player game for most of its existing run, the game is predicated on telling repeated meritocratic narratives. After the game introduced an overarching narrative with *Grand Theft Auto III*, the story is almost always based on a criminal who starts at the bottom and rises to the top of the criminal underworld through the player's deftness at making choices and pushing buttons in a manner that moves the game along. *Grand Theft Auto III* starts with the player being left for dead by his girlfriend, *Vice City* starts one as a hit man who was recently released from prison and who almost immediately falls into a drug deal gone wrong, *San Andreas* tracks a character who returns to his old neighborhood after his mother is murdered, *GTA IV* tracks a survivor of an Eastern European war, and *Chinatown Wars* is based around a character whose father is killed and who himself is then assaulted, kidnapped, and left for dead. *GTA V* deviates from the framework somewhat by introducing three characters as protagonists, but all have their own bottom from which to start the game. Michael is in witness protection after a botched robbery, Franklin bonds with Michael by rebelling against his oppressive boss and getting fired, and Trevor is at war with everyone from motorcycle clubs to the Triads, an Asian crime syndicate. *Grand Theft Auto* games mix up the location and certain elements of the game play, but they invariably start with a character who has fallen from grace and who, through the intervention of the player, will rise to the top.

Grand Theft Auto IV is a high point in the narrative development of the series, and the tale the game chooses to tell is intensely meritocratic. The protagonist in the game, Niko Bellic, is introduced to players in the opening moments of the game as a recent immigrant to Liberty City, which is based on New York City, from Eastern Europe. Niko is a war veteran who was betrayed in a pivotal battle and is setting out to start a new life in Liberty City and to find out more about what happened in the war. His only established connection in this new life is his cousin Roman, who promised to let Niko in on his massively successful business ventures, but Niko quickly learns that Roman is prone to hyperbole and that to be successful Niko will have to make it on his own. Early in the game, Niko starts out by doing grunt work for other people. He delivers packages, metes out justice for those his bosses send him out after, and scrabbles together resources to try to upgrade his clothes and housing. As the game progresses, players unlock new areas of Liberty City, places with more to do and higher-value housing and cars. Through successful play, Niko rises through the underworld, transitioning from doing things for others to accomplishing his own goals. Players see real, tangible benefits, from comedy shows and other features they can access when deeper into the game to a greater variety of romantic partners to seduce and the wider selection of guns available for those who have proved their merit. Niko's arc is incessantly upward, as players move through the story line and Niko establishes himself as a kingpin in Liberty City. Any setback is temporary, as a failed mission can easily be restarted and tried again. Niko's arc is a violent version of the American dream: by the end of the game, in both material wealth and accomplishment of life goals, Niko is far more successful than he was when he arrived in Liberty City. The meritorious intervention of the player behind the controller is what drives his story forward, and the player completes chapters in a meritocratic tale.

Similar to the way MMOGs demonstrate meritocratic norms through their design and game play, *Grand Theft Auto* games integrate a focus on success and the ability to overcome the worst of situations through hard work and the player's ability. Casting the character at the lowest point in his life gives the narrative a clear place from which to rise and also gives players an opportunity to buy in and bond with the character they are going to be controlling. The writers get a straightforward, appealing story to tell, while players get a chance to start at a place that is clearly below their station in life and then make it to a place far above where they likely reside. *GTA*, like *WoW*, is an actualization of a meritocracy, but in a fundamentally different way. Instead of being based on game-play elements that privilege and reward skill, *GTA* games tell a tidy yet bloody story about how one can rise through the world. As low as the characters start in the game, if played in any way resembling what the designers intended, they will rise up and become rich, powerful, and elite. Although players are unlikely to ever follow the life path of the protagonists, the *GTA* series reinscribes a meritocratic world where hard work and skill always win the day.

A fourth genre of game that relies on meritocratic norms are multiplayer online battle arenas (MOBAs), most prominently represented by *League of Legends* (*LoL*), which was first discussed in chapter 2. MOBA games are typically based on dividing players into two teams and having them engage in play with the ultimate goal of destroying something in the opposing team's base. The games typically move in stages, with early time being spent on gaining experience and resources so that players become powerful enough to attack the opponent's base. Players typically level up by either battling non-player characters or trying to surprise or overwhelm opponents, as there are substantial rewards for killing members of the other team. As one team gets more powerful than the other it is easier for them to kill their opponents, compounding their advantage as they press forward to win. Defenders have an advantage because of defensive structures within their own base, but being out-leveled and out-resourced can quickly make a more powerful team's victory inevitable. *LoL* typically revolves around teams of five players, which can either be premade groups or assembled by the game. Matches typically run from twenty to sixty minutes, which means that when one team gains a seemingly insurmountable advantage players may be playing for a fair amount of time simply to see the game out. The most played title in the world at the time of this writing, *LoL* has probably done more outright work to battle problems in gamer culture than any other game. Riot Games has gone on a multiyear campaign in *LoL* to try to "cure toxic behavior."[8] With the premise that negative behavior would never go away on its own, Riot developed "Team Player Behavior" with the intent of trying to solve issues of griefing, trolling, and harassment.[9] The whole point has been to encourage good sportspersonship, and progress has clearly been made through occasionally restricting the chat options of players and nudging them toward good behavior.[10] Developing game structures like "The Tribunal," which lets players review complaints about bad behavior, and being willing to ban professional players for abuse and harassment puts Riot in a position to make strides in combatting negative behavior, but I contend the fight will never be over because of the game's reliance on extreme meritocratic expectations.[11]

Much of the trouble surrounding *LoL* comes from one particular form of play: ranked games. Players in ranked games need to have achieved level 30 and have at least sixteen different champions from which to choose to play the mode. Specifics of ranked games have changed over time, but the general framing dynamic is that players are placed within a ladder system and their wins and losses move them up and down in accordance with an Elo system, like the one used for chess.[12] Elo systems are designed to group players of similar skill together in order to facilitate the most competitive games. Winning and losing changes a player's Elo rating, which moves them up and down the rankings and matches them against somewhat different people. As players win, their Elo ratings go up in an amount determined by the system's prediction of whether they are expected to win. In their next match they will likely be paired with a better opponent, as the system tries to divine their "true" talent. The converse happens in the case of a loss, as a player's rating will be lowered and he or she will likely face an opponent the system sees as weaker. *LoL*'s system, like many other appropriations of Elo, is divided into levels, and players can move between labels like Bronze, Silver, Gold, Platinum, Diamond, Master, and Challenger, along with five different tiers within each category. Being promoted from one tier to the next requires both consistent success and regular activity, as the higher levels have a built-in decay where players lose points if they are not playing frequently enough. These formulas effectively require players to demonstrate both skill and effort, boiling the relative merit of players down to a number and a place in the rankings.

Pitting players against one another in this framework has multiple notable effects. First, matching players of ostensibly similar skill means that players are going to lose roughly as often as they win when they find their appropriate level. Second, ratings like Elo get more accurate as more games are played. The ranking system cannot immediately judge your skill; it needs you to play game after game to finally calibrate and assess where you should be. Third, Elo was originally developed for a single-player game, chess, and porting the concept to multiplayer games means that your rating is dependent in part on the performance of other players. A loss in any Elo system reduces your rating, which is not fun, but in a multiplayer game the quality of the performance offered by other players affects the likelihood of your ability to increase your rating. In a single-player game, save a distraction or other circumstantial obstacle, you are largely accountable and responsible for your own play. However, in a multiplayer game with an Elo system you are accountable for both your play and that of your teammates. A player could be the most skilled yet be paired with partners who opt not to engage, and such a player will be hard-pressed to do anything other than lose. Your teammate's actions have an outsized impact on your individual rating. Individualizing the rating means that Elo marks are personal and the actions of others can negatively affect your score. Although you are losing together, the impact is personalized as the outcome of the game on each player is different and has little to do with how he or she played as an individual. Unless players are playing with a premade group, this kind of relationship has little in common with raiding groups in an MMOG or with pickup sports teams. In those contexts winners and losers are banded together and there is far less focus on the individual in the outcome of a game. The individual impact on your rating within *LoL* fosters the perception among some of an "Elo hell" that is "populated by griefers/trolls and 'bad' players that prevent them from moving up the ranks."[13] A guide to ranked games in *LoL* contends that Elo hell is a figment of players' imaginations, since "a large misconception is that it is always team-mates that is bringing you down [*sic*]," and the answer is that "ratings become more accurate the more games are played [*sic*]. Think 'big picture.' It can take hundreds or thousands of games to be consistently matched with similarly skilled players."[14] Although incredibly rational and likely true, this kind of thinking is much harder to remember in the moment when you believe some other player has cost you something through his or her inactivity or poor performance. At the same time, reports from other games with similar systems, like the competitive mode of *Overwatch*, indicate that there may be sections of the ratings that are more hellish than others, largely based on the gap between players' expectations of their ability and their actual skills.[15]

Elo is an attempt to develop a meritocratic system that sorts players into groups or rankings predicated solely on their skill and effort. Elo aims to provide a framework in which skill is the sole determinant of where you are placed and how you encounter the game. In porting that ideology to *LoL*, Riot inherited a straightforward way to figure out how to put players into matches, but the rankings also inject inequality and toxicity into the system by individualizing group results. Layer on a healthy dose of needing to depend on others in a multiplayer game and it should be no surprise that toxicity in the community is a primary outcome of ranked play. As one commentator notes, Riot is fighting a never-ending war on toxic behavior, where "it often feels that when you aren't playing with four other friends, chances are you're going to run into the scum of the earth. Sure, you can just mute them, but once someone starts to act this way, it's immediately reflected in their play."[16] Ratings decay is an ideal meritocratic companion for Elo's measurement of skill, as *LoL* asks players to both demonstrate ability and do so often or let their hard work slip away. Elo's need for hundreds of matches for proper calibration, in conjunction with the requirement to grind to level 30 to enter ranked play, ensures that *LoL* players must demonstrate plenty of effort in addition to skill.

Riot has pursued a variety of efforts to improve community interaction and the quality of player conduct in games. At one point "Ranked Restrictions" were introduced, which meant negative players faced chat restrictions and were prevented from engaging in ranked play until completing a requisite number of games.[17] Players quickly pointed out that this program essentially "turn[d] draft play [where offenders had to play to lift their restrictions] into a 'prison island' for folks with mile-long mean streaks. That seems like it could hurt non-offenders over time, fill their matches with bad eggs. Meanwhile, reporting tools can be abused, and innocent players could find themselves in the clink because somebody—somewhat ironically—got mad at the game and threw a temper tantrum."[18] Riot contended that the game has seen a precipitous decline in bad behavior, which is now limited to about 2 percent of the player population. However, that explanation does not line up with the experience of players, one of whom writes, "At least half of my matches are overwhelmingly negative, at least in my memory. Perhaps some of this is due to the gruelingly long nature of *League of Legends* matches. Regardless of whether it's a win or a loss, most matches take a decent amount of mental fortitude. It seems rougher when I venture into the Ranked Queue alone, only hoping that all four others on my team won't jump down my throat the first chance they get."[19] Although Riot chalks up matters like this to negativity bias (our tendency to remember bad experiences more vividly than good ones), there's also the matter that when players report about their games with Riot employees "you better believe that everyone is on their best behavior. It's not like that when they're not around."[20] Riot employees are likely to always see a different version of the game, one that is generally less toxic. A frequent player argues that one of the key design elements of MOBAs in general and *LoL* in particular is that "they're a *lot* less fun when you're not on the winning team. Uniquely so, I mean."[21] Games can last for about an hour, and in many matches the advantages accrued by the winning team make that victory highly probable long before the match actually ends. Much like the endgame of *Monopoly* and *Risk* can be arduous as the winner marches to his or her almost assured victory, playing from a perceived losing position is not enjoyable, which leads to the perception that *LoL* can be especially brutal to lose. It is certainly reasonable to concede that Riot has made improvements in the behavior of players playing it game; however, the foundation of the game is built on design underpinnings that weave toxicity into its very fabric.

Beyond the implicit integration of meritocratic norms into the structure of ranked play, Riot's preference for meritocracy can also be seen in how it is developing *League of Legends* as an eSport. Featuring World Championships that have massively grown in size and scope, aided by streaming viewership numbers that rival the totals traditional sports draw on television, *LoL* is one of the most popular competitive games in existence. In Riot's fostering the development of competitive tournaments, however, women have largely been absent. When asked questions about the lack of women in competitive *LoL* in advance of the 2014 World Championships, Riot's spokesperson responded that "it's just a matter of time before there's either all-female teams or very successful female pros," leading an analyst to note that "the company isn't looking at ways to actively facilitate anything on that front, which implies that they want to treat eSports as purely a meritocracy. They're relying on expanding the game's general audience and playerbase to add more women to the pool of potential professional players."[22] The reliance on meritocracy in the competitive version of *LoL* is certainly consistent with the overall design of the game, but in trying to treat everyone the same Riot is overlooking the structural obstacles that certain communities of players face. Getting more people to play *LoL* is likely to add more diversity to the player base, but it is unlikely to prompt a substantial change in the overall trends in player demographics, especially when the game is deliberately designed for the best players, rather than new players or the masses.[23] A lack of diversity in the player community already demonstrates the fact that the game is not a perfect meritocracy and, therefore, simply adding more players to a structurally imbalanced system will not fix the problem. When the platforms and games already require arcane knowledge and players benefit from structural advantages, equality of opportunity is illusory at best and the system that remains assesses far more than merit.

The entire structure of *LoL* is predicated on putting people into competition with one another for status, yet the lead designer of social systems at Riot holds that "every standard in #LeagueofLegends is defined by the community. We (the devs) haven't influenced or contributed at all to the standards."[24] This willful blindness to the impact developers have on the game is notable, particularly coming from the person at the head of battling toxicity. It points to the structural inattention to addressing how design and development issues are a key part of toxicity in *LoL*, not just what is said in a particular game. Although Riot has achieved a landmark in lowering the proportion of games with abuse to 2 percent, that approach overlooks two key points noted by *LoL* players. First, a "toxic culture is more than just using slurs; the machine may be getting very good at preventing players from calling each other offensive names, but is it teaching them not to be massive jerks in other ways?"[25] Second, even if one accepts the 2 percent number as a meaningful metric, "two percent of 67 million *League of Legends* players is still 1.4 million people. Which isn't a small number, let's face it."[26] Structurally, the design of *LoL* ensures that players meet in a meritocratic framework that is most likely to activate any toxic feelings they may be prone to exhibit.

Any individual's efforts are dependent on the actions of others, often people they do not know. Simmering in this cauldron, it should not be a surprise that people act out and push the limits of whatever boundaries are put into place. The critiques of meritocracy hold that systems based on merit get perverted and become corrupt. Further, by setting up a system on which players are assessed based on their perceived skill, a community of people is put in a position to question the decisions being made by their teammates, their opponents, the game logic, and the developer's intent. *LoL* is an enormously successful game that is clearly doing a number of things right, but thinking deeply about how the game is built demonstrates how the toxicity in it can be read as a feature, not a bug. There is sufficient toxicity after years of work that player behavior is still a key focus of the game. Riot has numbers that are trending in a positive direction, but personnel at the company are also insulated from the worst of things, as they do not play the game under the same terms as others and they are only looking at a particular kind of toxicity. Their mere presence in a game as elites warps everything around them, and gathering data from aggregate game logs cannot give a complete picture of the experience for more typical players. Further, by recruiting active gamers and *LoL* players as employees, Riot comprises a homogenous group that does not necessarily have the ideological diversity to address problems with groupthink. Building a game based on perceptions of skill and getting players to buy into the myth of meritocracy is a driving force behind the toxicity in *LoL*. Fixing player behavior in the game will take far more than restricting or banning certain players; the system itself is broken because it is predicated on teaching those at the top that they have earned both their place and the ability to judge others. By focusing on individual players and their relative merit, it should not be a surprise that a team game based on merit and individual rankings has problems with bad behavior.

Dependence on merit in game design also stretches into mobile gaming, with *Marvel Mighty Heroes* representing one of the purest distillations of an attempt to build the appearance of a meritocratic system onto a monetization scheme predicated on inequality. Free-to-play games like *Marvel Mighty Heroes* are an interesting consideration for meritocratic game design, as their monetization structures are typically built in a manner to enable players to spend vast, potentially unlimited, amounts of money in order to buy their way ahead in the game. This necessarily imbues a structural advantage for those players who have more offline resources to invest. Should a game follow the path of monetization too far, it is frequently derided as pay-to-win, so many games in the genre try to design their game play in a manner that lets players progress through their skill and effort, not just their pocketbook.

Marvel Mighty Heroes offers a story mode in which players can send their heroes into battle alongside a computer-controlled partner, and also a mode called "Fury's Files" in which players send their unused heroes out to complete missions for Nick Fury (a major character in the Marvel universe). The main function of these two modes is to incentivize players to keep a larger roster of characters and to develop all of them, which offers more opportunities to spend money on the game. The primary game mode is a multiplayer arena in which players are sent into battle with three other players on a variety of mission types, including defeating bosses, defending supplies, and surviving against waves of computer-controlled opponents. Players pick three of their characters, who are placed into battle with similarly matched teammates based on the level of their characters, with higher-level teams eligible for greater rewards. For a period ranging up to a few minutes, players try to accomplish whatever task they were given by moving around and rotating between basic attacks and special moves. Players can alternate among the three characters they selected, either as they lose health or as one choice might cause more damage than another. Upon successful completion of the event, players are ranked based on the amount of damage they have done and given rewards consummate with their ranking. Those rewards, called event points, then correspond to a player's position on the various leaderboards in the game. All players are sorted into brackets of one hundred based on five tiers ranging from bronze to vibranium (a fictional metal that appears in the Marvel universe). Several times a week the top-ranked group of players in each bracket is promoted to the next tier; at the end of a weeklong event, players are awarded prizes based on their tier and ranking within it. The primary goal of this mode is to collect event points, which means that the ability to do more damage is highly valued and generously rewarded.

On its face, this system appears highly meritocratic. *Marvel Mighty Heroes* rewards skill based on the amount of damage done in each battle. The game rewards effort based on consistent play and placement in the brackets and rankings. Paying one's way forward can be mitigated by earning characters through both skill and effort. However, the game's design and the immense value of inherited position ensure considerable structural inequalities that shape how the game plays out in practice. The first major element of the game that compromises any attempt at meritocracy is the sorting of characters into tiers of value. Characters are rated from one to five stars, with higher-star characters typically being much more powerful than lower-star characters. Players procure additional abilities as they collect multiple copies of a character, so players who spend to buy many characters or get exceptionally lucky are given a huge advantage in battle.[27] Almost without exception players with higher-star characters will dominate those with lower-star characters, which enables those with greater resources to readily earn more event points without demonstrating additional skill or effort.

A second major inequality is guaranteed through the damage multiplier system. Three heroes are selected for each event and given a damage boost. Players who choose to play with one of the selected heroes get a multiplier of three, two heroes grants a multiplier of seven, and if someone plays with all three his or her damage is multiplied by ten. This means that a player can go into battle with an order-of-magnitude advantage against his or her teammates/competitors. Perhaps the most aristocratic part of the arrangement is that the required characters for the upcoming week are typically the awarded characters from the previous week. This locks in a potentially hefty advantage for the winners, as they both get to bolster their team and gain a huge advantage in the upcoming competition, making it far easier to retain their position. It has the effect of holding back new participants who may be highly skilled, as they are unlikely to be successful competing against people who have substantial inherited advantages.

These dynamics shape how players engage in play. In my experience, both at play and from reading the accounts of other players, the vast majority of players are solely focused on increasing their damage output and limiting the damage of others. The play becomes far less about cooperating with others or working as a team and more about trying to boost one's own score as much as possible. Alternately, in a match with superpowered players with built-in damage multipliers, the contest becomes about collecting the meager rewards for finishing at the bottom and hoping for a better shot at competing next time. Loading screens in the game talk about rewarding the "most effective player," but effectiveness is almost entirely circumscribed by the structural advantages brought into a fight, rather than the skill that may be displayed within it. Highly limited chat options and battles that last ninety seconds or less limit the magnitude of toxicity in *Marvel Mighty Heroes*, but for a game that seems on its face to aspire to meritocratic norms it actually has little to do with skill and only nominal links to effort. By dressing aristocratic behaviors up as a putative meritocracy, the game boils down to getting what little you can manage or simply accepting your fate (i.e., lesser rewards) if you don't have a head start in battle. The appeal to merit and effectiveness is likely designed to appeal to a broad category of players, but the trouble the game has in execution points to issues in game design based on a nobility of wallet and inheritance of status. However, there are titles trying to thread the needle between creating a game based on skill and retaining free-to-play mechanics, most notably Supercell's *Clash Royale*.

Based in the fictional world established in Supercell's game *Clash of Clans*, *Clash Royale* is a highly successful hybrid game that blends various genres to attract players. The core of the game is battling against other players in a battle arena reminiscent of MOBAs, all in an effort to destroy more of your opponent's tower than he or she destroys of yours. Combat is simplified, though, in a style reminiscent of *Clash of Clans*, where the primary control players have concerns about what to place on the battlefield and where to put it; once the item is played the game takes over control of the outcome. Players battle with decks of eight cards they have chosen from dozens of options. Cards are divided into three primary categories: creatures, like giants and Valkyries; buildings, like cannons and mortars; and spells that can do things like damage opponents or freeze them in place for a period of time. Games take three minutes, but if players are tied they go to a one-minute overtime. If neither player destroys an opposition tower during the overtime the game ends in a tie. Players' success is defined by a combination of their own skill and the cards they bring to a match. Possessing both a rock, paper, scissors element, where certain decks are highly likely to beat others, and an inheritance of privilege through both the rarity and level of cards, *Clash Royale* is far from purely meritocratic. Influence for the card system comes from collectible card games, where spending more money gets a person rarer and more powerful cards. *Clash Royale* magnifies that dynamic by allowing players to level cards up, with each level making the card about 10 percent more powerful, but the cost of leveling up is exponentially more expensive. The main part of *Clash Royale* is an open battle system where players have a ranking like in *League of Legends* and move up and down in rating based on their success or lack thereof. Higher-rated players get access to more exclusive battle arenas, which can result in obtaining a wider variety of cards. There is also a tournament mode, where players enter a time-limited contest and are subject to restrictions in an effort to level the playing field. In a tournament, all players start at a zero rating and must win to move up the ladder. The rating system is similar to the primary game, but the limited time frame magnifies the importance of effort, as a player who loses often can obtain a higher rating than can a player who never loses but plays far fewer matches.

The hybridized influences for *Clash Royale* place it in an interesting position with regard to meritocracy and toxicity. The elements, from battle arenas to rating systems, are lifted from the meritocratic world of MOBAs, while the card system and free-to-play elements mean that the game has advantages for the aristocrats who choose to spend on the game. Luck also plays a role, as which cards a player gets in a pack can help determine his or her success regardless of whether they are paying for the game.

There are two key pieces of *Clash Royale* that warrant longer discussion: the paywall and the chat function. *Clash Royale* is a free-to-play game where players can pay almost an unlimited amount of money to progress. Although there is no clear way players can buy wins, there are three primary ways to spend money in the game: buying special chests; speeding up the unlocking of chests won in battle; and buying cards that are released in the store. Getting additional copies of a card enables players to pay a steadily escalating fee to upgrade them, with thousands of copies needed to upgrade some cards to the highest level. The monetization system was set up such that a top player spent $12,000 on the game within months of its launch.[28] Play in the primary mode of the game is based on attempting to earn trophies to move from the first arena to the last, with rewards and cards available upon successfully climbing the ladder. Wins earn trophies and losses lose them, which means that a losing streak can drop players down the ladder as quickly as a winning streak can help them climb it. The game is set up so that players accrue trophies until they hit the point where their combination of cards and skills is quickly beaten down by other players, which according to one reviewer can feel "like a pay wall, and maybe it is, as for a lot of people the only way to progress further is to keep plugging away at getting free cards or just spend some money until you get better cards or level up the ones you have."[29] Patience and steady effort can help a player subvert the payment mechanisms in the game, but having lesser cards means a player needs much more skill to ascend the ladder and possible payment always lingers as a way to climb more quickly.[30] This design blends meritocracy and aristocracy, as skill can trump better cards, but better cards magnify the importance of greater skill and effort for those with lesser decks. The lack of traditional videogame balance in the primary mode of the game is constrained somewhat in tournament mode, where players are limited in how powerful their cards can become, which caused one player to argue that tournaments were more fun than ranked mode because players in tournaments do not play at as much of a disadvantage, making the game more meritocratic.[31] Players seek out both inequity and chances to play on a level playing field, making efforts to subvert meritocracy difficult. *Clash Royale* attempts to deal with toxicity in an interesting way, however, by limiting interaction among competing players.

In addition to the short games, which typically are completed in fewer than three minutes, chat options in the game are limited to ten choices with six words or phrases and four emotes. As Eli Hodapp sums it up for *Touch Arcade*: "Communication in the game has been distilled down to ten buttons, and through the miracle that is human nature on the internet, people have figured out how to be total sh*t heads with only these ten emotes at their disposal."[32] Typically, players seeking to harass others spam choices like "Wow!" and a crying emote while winning, leading players to request an option to mute the emotes and play without them. As player calls for a mute button grew, the game's developer, Supercell, released a statement claiming that the core design principle of the game was building cards that players either loved or hated, and that "the same principle—*evoking strong emotions*—is at the heart of why we're not planning to implement a mute option. Emotes are loved by some and hated by others—even within the *Clash Royale* team! We believe these strong emotions are integral to the core of the game."[33] The ability for players to harass one another shines through even with limited options, largely because the stakes of the game are both so high and so low. Moving forward is fun, but moving backward is not, and being harassed with emotes makes it all less enjoyable. As Eli Hodapp concludes his response to the decision by Supercell, "Emote spam is one of the many reasons I don't play *Clash Royale* anywhere near as much as I used to. I play games to have fun, not be frustrated, which I guess puts me in the minority when it comes to *Clash Royale*? This all seems real strange to me."[34] By placing players in zero-sum combat, even a limited number of choices leads some to try to rattle others, leaving the game less fun for many. Supercell eventually reversed the decision and added a mute option to *Clash Royale*; however, the communication between players is shaped by the system, and bad behavior does not go away when you have the option to silence opponents.[35] Meritocratic systems, combined with competition and the ability for players to interact, leads to toxic cultures, especially when developers are focused on unleashing strong emotions among their players. In the wake of examining several game genres in general, the celebration of skill in videogame design deserves specific attention.

Achievement Culture: Proving Your Skill

The dominance of skill and merit in video games reaches well beyond individual games and into the larger framework of video games and how they are perceived. The design of game culture celebrates achievement, and the roots of that commitment to skill date back at least to the Atari systems and the patches that Activision sent out to laud certain achievements in games. Now morphed into things like leaderboards, Gamerscores, and trophies, the effect of these mechanics becoming so solidly integrated into videogame culture is that their gravitational pull changes how games are played and interpreted. Leaderboards are a clear place where players are compared with one another. A former highly competitive *Madden NFL* player writes that leaderboards are "a devilish feature," as they transform "*Madden* from an escapist pastime into another stage on which to prove your self-worth."[36] Gamerscore is a measure that turns abstract effort in a game into concrete results that are intelligible to others at a mere glimpse. Gamerscore bends how games are played, as playing for these meta-points becomes a play style to which some adhere and others push beyond any reasonable bounds or limits and are then celebrated for their exceptional proof of merit. My paltry Gamerscore pales in comparison to Raymond Cox's million-plus points and ten-thousand-person audience on Twitch, but the inclusion and search for points layers a different kind of game over the top of everything else we play. For Cox, having the highest Gamerscore has meant that his efforts are tracked and celebrated by Microsoft, are recorded as Guinness World Records, and have earned him a modest degree of income through his fame.[37] Perhaps first and foremost, though, the quest to acquire impressive amounts of Gamerscore twists play, as Cox plays as many games as possible and with the primary intent of leeching as many points from them as he can.[38] By adding ranking elements like Activision's patches, leaderboards, Gamerscore, and trophies to play, video games are altered as players are encouraged to think about them as part of a larger, meritocratic system. Motives shift, intent changes, and our ability to judge others negatively is magnified; the rhetorical framework in which video games are produced and played shifts to accommodate a specific kind of instrumental play. As Joel Goodwin sums up the balance of achievement versus art in video games, "If you're still looking for the Citizen Kane of Game, you're not going to find it on a leaderboard."[39] Although Cox's single-minded focus on Gamerscore likely seems quite foreign to many game players, it is an edge case of what quantifiable systems can do to how we think about and play games. Players can opt out of Gamerscore or simply choose not to think about it, but Microsoft regularly advertises its premium service, Xbox Live Gold; the games players get for subscribing by mentioning the achievements available and highlighting how many points players can get by paying for the service and playing the games. By opting out, players can ignore this metric, but the inclusion of leaderboards and achievements means that play is made instrumental. In the e-mail missives that encourage me to subscribe to Xbox Live, Microsoft spends less space telling me about the game and more space talking about the achievements I could get from playing it. That advertising decision helps construct the means by which players will engage a game, encouraging them to focus on the shiny points, defining what makes that particular game compelling, and establishing an instrumental relationship with the game. A clear example of how skill is a key part of contemporary games can be seen by looking at advocacy for a different conception of how games should work: the balance between requiring players to read the story in a game and requiring players to play through action sequences, best exemplified by the controversy over the BioWare game *Dragon Age II*.

In 2011, BioWare released *Dragon Age II*, which was "produced under a very tight time budget"; the game was not well received by core fans, potentially because "it went a little lighter on the action mode of playing, as opposed to a strategic, old-school strategy style playing."[40] Commenters on both the BioWare forums and on reddit went back and found a 2006 interview with one of the writers on the game, Jennifer Hepler, in which she said her least favorite part of working in the industry was "playing the games" because she has "awful hand–eye coordination, I don't like tactics, and I can't read a game map to save my life. This makes it very difficult for me to play the myriad games I really should be keeping up on as our competition."[41] Hepler went on to hypothesize that one thing that would make games more engaging for her would be to include a fast-forward that would let players skip through action sequences, just as they are routinely able to skip through story-driven cut scenes. She contends that a feature like this would make games shorter but far more accessible to a wider audience of people, and that it would give players "the same options that we have with books or DVDs—to skim past the parts we don't like and savor the ones we do."[42] A version of story mode actually ended up shipping in BioWare's *Mass Effect 3*, but it did so alongside an action mode as a pair of difficulty settings. In action mode players' dialogue choices were automated, while in story mode combat sequences were quicker and easier.[43] Action mode was an expansion of the oft-used ability to skip cut scenes, as it automated choices for the player, but story mode just made combat easier, not skippable. The centrality of combat and the acceptance for relegating narrative to the background is a prime statement on their relative values in video games. Action and combat (where players prove their merit) matter, while narrative is secondary at best. Something like a story mode that Hepler proposes is a substantial change in what games are and, potentially, what they should be, as it would disrupt some of the skill-based barriers to entry for new players.

A faction of BioWare's audience reacted negatively to the suggestion that games should be changed to be less reliant on player skill. Hepler was called the "cancer that is killing BioWare"; a page appeared on the *Star Wars: The Old Republic* wiki titled Jennifer "The Hamburglar" Hepler; and an image of an alleged forum post made by her laid out a mandatory homosexual story line for players in *Mass Effect 3*, even though she did not work on the game.[44] After Hepler joined Twitter, the situation became offensive enough that she discontinued her account and one of BioWare's cofounders released a statement of support for Hepler.[45] While a verbal assault on a woman who works in video games for voicing her opinion about how they could be designed differently, the vitriol in the reaction points to a desire to hold on to video games as separate from other forms of media, that a special kind of place is expected to be reserved for those who are talented enough to prove their worth. This is precisely the kind of dynamic one would expect to find in a meritocracy, in which the skilled elites believe they have earned their high status and then protect the hierarchy against encroachment by the less-worthy masses.

Hepler laid out a different way of thinking about video games that was predicated on making games accessible. Instead of putting gates and limitations based on skill in a video game, more people could experience the range of experiences in a game if titles were designed differently. Instead of being an actualized meritocratic space where the only ones involved in the subculture were those who "deserve" to be there because they "earned" their place, video games would become a different form of a book, movie, or television show that anyone could play. Some people see this kind of approach as an existential threat to games, a line of argument that often comes up around pieces of interactive fiction, which some argue are not games because they do not have sufficient challenge or particularly rich game-play elements. Hepler got attacked because she was a woman speaking out about games and also because she dared to question the meritocratic conceit of how games should be designed. The toxicity of the response is notable because what Hepler was choosing to advocate was a way of thinking about and designing games for everyone. Meritocracies do not work like that; meritocracies need to exclude some to build the inequality that gives value to status positions at the top. For video games to be meritocratic there needs to be an overriding belief that players earned their victory, they won their success, they deserve their just rewards, and that others cannot just skip over the parts of the game that require skill.

Focusing on completion and winning in single-player games is particularly interesting because of what happens when we think more deeply about how they are designed and how "winning" works within them. In Hepler's case, there was little outcry about differential difficulty modes, although playing on a harder difficulty mode certainly maintains more credibility for players. Variable difficulties are well established in games. Difficulty is even used as a means to reach out to a "hardcore" audience who believe that things like *BioShock Infinite*'s 1999 mode are cool. In a reflection on the design of the exceptionally difficult version of the game, creative director Ken Levine argued that "the average gamer stops playing when they fail. The hardcore gamer says 'That's it, I'm gonna show this game who's boss.'"[46] The mode was designed to evoke nostalgia for games of the past, with the tuning intended to evoke how "failure can be fun" and "that old-school feeling of 'If I fail, I deserved to fail' instead of 'the game made me fail.'"[47] Part of the idea behind differential difficulty modes embedded in Levine's comments is the individual responsibility of players for their fate in the game. As long as the game is properly designed, the logical extension of the notion that you deserve your failure is that you also earn your success when you attain it. The victory in a single-player video game is tied to your actions, your skill, your efforts, and your personal drive, absent of any cultural context.

The celebration of skill is an omnipresent thread in discourse about video games that sets it apart from other media forms. Game publications are rife with stories about how the best players do things that are unthinkable for most players. There are stories about players who conduct speed runs and complete games and objectives faster than most would think possible, about how certain players can complete key objectives without ever dying and play games in a way that developers likely never imagined, like playing through levels in *Super Mario 64* without ever jumping.[48] The excessive focus on skill means that certain elements of games are not to be questioned, as stepping out of line in the celebration of skill is likely to be met by what one game journalist describes as "an open invitation to be told how bad you are at the game and how you only need to 'git gud.'"[49] This kind of approach sets games apart from other media, as a focus on skill can be measured and assessed differently. There is certainly a literary culture around reading difficult books, like those by James Joyce or David Foster Wallace, and film fans can argue about interpretations and preferred readings, but video games quantify, measure, and celebrate skill in a manner that other media do not.

One place to clearly see the focus on skill is in discussion about the series of *Souls* games developed under Hidetaka Miyazaki. Comprising *Demon's Souls*, *Dark Souls*, *Dark Souls II*, *Dark Souls III*, and *Bloodborne*, the punishing games are best summed up as an "action series famous (or infamous) for their merciless difficulty."[50] Discussion surrounding the games includes paeans to players who are able to make the "toughest enemies look like chumps" or beat the game without ever taking advantage of the ability to level up and make their own character stronger.[51] The charitable reading of these games is provided by Laura Hudson, who sums up their appeal:

> If you're playing a Hidetaka Miyazaki game for the first time, as I was, the learning curve is often steep; for hours and hours, it feels frustrating and painful, and sometimes incredibly unfair. But here's the trick: it's not. Over time, you start to realize that the game is actually fair in the *absolute*, and you even learn to trust it. When you die, it's not usually because the game is *just mean*; it's because you screwed up. Much like a martial arts master who knocks you to the floor every time you leave yourself open, it isn't actually trying to crush your spirit; it's trying to teach you. And if you're willing to listen, it will slowly transform you into an incredible badass.[52]

The general perspective of those who enjoy the game is that "playing *Souls* is like climbing a mountain. If you're at the top it's worth bragging about, since plenty gave up along the way."[53] All the focus on skill, though, has a notable impact on how the games are discussed. For the most part, the newest entry in the series, *Bloodborne*, was met with praise, as writers focused on how the skill required by the game pushed players to their limits and made their eventual successes all the richer.

There were few critical reviews, but two focused on the harms of pursuing skill at the cost of all else. First, one reviewer contended that the success of beating the first boss "was simply not worth the aggravation" and, ultimately, "this kind of game isn't for everyone, and I'm an example of who they're not for."[54] The end result of an insular focus on skill is more harmful, however, as it actively screens potential new players out based on their lack of skill. Developing skill-screening tests means that the community of people left writing, talking, and thinking about games is far different from the pool of potential players for games. *Bloodborne* demonstrates a moment where, for one game journalist, those in game journalism and in core game culture more broadly "can't just shout to ourselves about the stuff we like. The echo chamber of praise for *Bloodborne* reminds us what an incredible lack of perspective we have within the world of games criticism, and that's not just a practical failure, it's boring to boot."[55] With an extreme emphasis on skill, games like these limit who is likely to play them. Instead of broadening the base of potential players, these games target those already part of videogame culture, especially when they are celebrated as essential, system-selling releases. It is reasonable to have games targeted at existing audiences, but the focus on skill in a single-player game is notable, especially when one considers how the computer is such a gracious loser.

A primary difference between single- and multiplayer games is locating where the wins and losses accrue. In most multiplayer games, about half the players will win and about half will lose. On the other hand, single-player is a bastion of wins for humans. In addition, instead of facing the horrific words that come with a loss in a game like *League of Legends*, when the computer loses there is only joy for the human winner. Single-player video games are typically set up to be defeated, for the player to win and claim the inevitable victory. This feeds directly into the notion of a meritocracy—just as players deserve their failure in a well-designed game, they are accountable and responsible for their eventual wins. Single-player games are often about testing limits, engaging in trial and error, and figuring out patterns that are repeated and how to conquer them. This kind of process twists meritocracy, potentially beyond recognition, because in the case of single-player video games we are all potentially winners; there quite literally is no limit to the number of people at the top and no need for downward mobility. If we are all winning, there is no space in which to get the status differential that makes those at the top feel more powerful, other than by developing and playing super-difficult games like *Bloodborne*. As such, inequality typically resides in two locations: in comparison to those outside of games and in multiplayer games.

Setting games up on a meritocratic foundation means encouraging inequity and difference. In the case of contemporary single-player games, there are three ways to foment inequality: by adding extra-difficult modes, by developing games that let the hardcore show off their skills, or by making gamers feel superior by exploiting the space in the gap between those who game and those who do not. Policing these boundaries is crucial to sustaining the hierarchy necessary to feel superior. The notion that anyone could game or anyone could win flattens social space far too much and is checked by contentions that certain games, techniques, players, designers, and people are more real or worthwhile than others. Single-player games have taught us that if we are talented enough and work hard enough we will win, which does a lovely job of making everyone feel superior, but it also sets a precedent that makes for sore losers and vocal backlash when the last few remaining pegs of differentiation between those who can beat games and those who cannot are removed.

Multiplayer games are outstanding at demonstrating inequality and difference. Because they are executed on computers, it is trivially easy to develop measuring systems that track how successful you are relative to others. Networked and placed on the Internet, suddenly the neighborhood gets a whole lot bigger, as the best person you know offline is not nearly as good as the players you can find online. We can be ranked and see just how good or bad we are. The singular conceit of playing with other people is that, at some point, you will be let down; you will lose because of the actions of another. This idea should be easy to see in *League of Legends*, as discussed previously, but it also appears in a game like *World of Warcraft*. As *WoW* released expansions, raiding, a primary way in which players interacted with large groups of people, became more difficult. Expectations for individual players were higher and the action, or lack of action, of one person could threaten the potential for victory for the other twenty-four people in a raid group.[56] As things became more difficult there was a profusion of add-ons to the game with one sole purpose: tracking who screwed up. From EnsidiaFails to YouFail to Failbot to WhoFailedWhen, suddenly it was important to monitor who was not performing up to expectations. These player-created additions to the game were set up to enforce meritocratic structures and remind players just who was doing the worst and ruining things for everyone else. While single-player gaming is based on your inevitable, earned victory, multiplayer assures that you will inevitably be let down or crushed by someone else.

These twin dynamics—that you inevitably earn success in one version of video games and are disappointed in another—frame the appeals and context in which players interact. Video games are controlled, contrived experiences, but they are also complicated symbol systems that structure what players expect and how they are likely to act. This kind of framing is perfectly suited for a meritocracy. On the one hand, players can feel good because they are successful; they can do something that other people cannot. On the other hand, the fault for failure typically resides in the actions of another. Add in the dominant masculine norms found in communities built around video games, and players are constantly placed in positions where proving their merit and their masculinity is an ongoing battle, making their status fragile and in need of defense. Assessments of merit and masculinity are clouded and losing erodes both, foreclosing efforts at deliberation and reflection. Building a community around video games based on meritocracy has one most likely outcome: toxicity and a tendency to lash out at those who question the normal order of video games.

Toxicity and Meritocracy

Video games are far from the only toxic space in the world. Video games are also far from the only meritocracy. However, I contend that video games represent a special, different place perfectly designed and controlled to actualize an idealized form of meritocracy, with all the consequences that entails. Video games are predicated on inequality, on the perception that some people are better than others and that when one is victorious it is precisely because of that player's actions, that player's timely interventions and button presses. Anything that questions that normal, meritocratic order is threatening, from opening games up to more people, to producing "games" where players do not have to show sufficient skill to complete them, to being failed by teammates you do not think are nearly as good as you are. For many years now, video games have built a culture where skill is praised and the best believe they should be rewarded because they have earned their victories. From the high-score screens in an arcade to the patches Activision would send players who beat its Atari games to the leaderboards in an online game and the gear that players acquire and then show off in a common meeting area, video games are set up to celebrate feats of skill. In the world of video games you keep what you kill, and there is an overwhelming bias in videogame design and videogame culture to reward merit and treat players as a special, gifted group of people that are, quite simply, better than those who do not have the same kind of success at play.

There are certainly reasons for toxicity in games that are not related to meritocracy. Structural barriers and inequalities of opportunity in society are represented in the people playing video games and their interactions with one another. However, a dominant norm in video games specifically and in technological culture more broadly is to reward merit and praise the skill of individual people in a way that seems blind to context and circumstance. As Katherine Sierra, a woman who has suffered frequent and sustained harassment, puts it about technology culture more broadly, "A meritocracy is exactly what I and so many others believed tech to be. 'After all,' I wrote nearly a decade ago, 'the compiler doesn't care if the person writing the code is wearing a black lace bra.' I was wrong. Embarrassingly, naïvely, wrong. Because while the compiler doesn't care, the context in which programming exists sure as hell does. To ignore that context is the essence of privilege blindness."[57] Meritocracy sets the frame and the boundaries in which players interact and in which games are developed. Given that meritocracy was originally popularized as a satirical concept pursued by a society on the brink of failure, why should it be surprising that an actualized meritocracy, like that found in video games, has a toxic culture?

The whole point of rhetorical analysis is to observe how the words used, the symbols employed, and the structures built matter. How people choose to talk about things and the frameworks they construct end up shaping what they design and how they interact. In any community the norms that are followed, the terms that are used, and the symbol systems that are established end up enabling some appeals while limiting others. In the case of video games, a system has been developed that rewards individual skill and ability. It is a system that teaches players that they are special, that they are gifted, and that their efforts should be rewarded because they have earned their plaudits. It is also a symbol system that breaks down when questioned, when people attack the potential of the individual or the quality of his or her work. It is a symbol system predicated on toxicity, one where problems are inherited because of the focus on individuals, their merit, and what they are supposed to be able to do on their own. There are problems in any type of culture, but video games certainly suffer from the impact of meritocratic norms and expectations. Addressing those problems does not have a straightforward, simple solution, but there are steps that can be taken to redefine what video games can be and to change the culture around them.

5
Learning from Others

There is no single element that causes the problems for videogame culture, but addressing the toxicity in video games requires facing up to the current situation and assessing what cultural solutions can be found to make things better. Game culture is stunted because of a limited, relatively homogenous group of players, designers, games, and experiences. An overarching lack of diversity restricts the kinds of ideas that are addressed and topics covered in games. The reach of the rhetoric, of discussion in games, is curtailed because of the small number of voices present. Diversifying the group of people making and playing games is important and should be addressed, but I believe fixing those issues will prove impossible as long as game consumers and developers valorize games predicated on meritocratic norms.

The dominance of meritocracy and the focus on skill and success in games limit the cognitive space for appeals and thought. Meritocracy functions as an apologia for why all those diverse populations are not present in games. Merit tells a story that if those people were good enough, driven enough, worthy enough, then they, too, could actively participate in videogame culture. This is a seductive, convincing story that tells those at the top of the pyramid that they deserve to be there, that they should be in positions of power to set the terms for engagement with games. A culture based on merit is reassuring and highly conservative, protecting those at the top and solidifying their control in setting the agenda. Rhetorically, using the language of merit limits the kinds of appeals that are made and judged as valid. Meritocracy is a restrictive ideology based on inequality, which is readily fueled by the lack of diversity in video games.

A limited, focused audience restricts the range of acceptable thought in games, a dynamic that is also fed by the role of computers in arbitrating what happens in video games. Offline games are subject to the human enforcement of rules, which is necessarily a social process of negotiation. From house rules to rerolls to subjective decision making to human error, offline games are riddled with imperfection. On the other hand, video games are adjudicated by computers, which are typically read as unbiased agents of rule enforcement. Although quality work in platform studies demonstrates just how different computer platforms are and how subjectivity is present in computerized systems, computers are perceived to be neutral.[1] For those already invested in meritocratic systems, computers and games can seem like a perfect pair, as a videogame system will make consistent decisions that do not change as different players get behind the controller. Although a game may be decried as unfair or cheap, it will stay the same kind of unfair for all players, which can convince those playing that their own personal, individual skill is the cause of their success. The dependence on computers in video games makes a meritocratic approach to gaming even more persuasive and further restricts the symbol system surrounding video games.

As it currently stands, the lack of diversity in and around games enables a continued focus on meritocracy, which further restricts the kinds of people interested and welcomed to play video games. Breaking the hold of meritocracy requires looking more broadly, to seeing other, related activities that can rattle the focus on skill and outline alternate ways of thinking about games. Breaking the hold of meritocracy stands to change game culture and could help facilitate a videogame culture that can address the toxicity that currently resides within it.

Deconstructing Merit

One could certainly make a strong argument that all major, contemporary Western institutions are riddled with meritocratic norms. A possible exception is the strong social safety net programs in Scandinavia, but meritocracy is currently a dominant ideology for much of the world. Lessons from a pair of major Western social structures indicate some of the ways they stand apart from video games and how thinking about them can generate approaches to building a different game culture. One of the clearest links to video games can be found in the greater institution of sports. Although periodically dismissed because of a jock–geek divide, sports offer another largely meritocratic system, but one that is far more aware of how considerations of merit are often broken. There are also the clean links between sports and video games in the paired content of sports video games and the growth of eSports within video games. A second link can be found in U.S. higher education, which ostensibly selects students based on merit and awards millions a year in merit-based scholarships, but also preserves several areas where meritocracy is disregarded in favor of developing a diverse community of people, particularly at highly selective colleges and universities.

These two institutions are largely selected because they are related to, yet independent from, videogame culture. Associations can be made, but the three cultures are largely distinct and only occasionally overlap. Sports and higher education cultures have substantial problems, some of which can be traced to meritocratic norms, but they also offer a chance to help see just how dependent on merit videogame culture is and a chance to get outside of video game culture to look at it differently. The most difficult part of disrupting a symbol system is figuring out how to get a vantage point from without to help imagine ways in which it could be structured differently. By looking at sports and U.S. higher education it is possible to see some lessons that can be taken and employed in detoxifying videogame culture. These two examples are not perfect, but they set the table for looking differently at meritocratic game design and narrative, to create a perspective that could then be used to address the toxicity at its root.

Sports and Games

Sports and video games share a substantial number of similarities. Both constitute large elements of the culture industry and are primary recreation activities for many participants, in fandom, play, or both. They are massive economic enterprises that capture billions of dollars a year. Both have cultural and institutional issues that can be tracked to meritocracy and there are certainly examples of toxicity in the player and fan cultures of both. Sports video games are a substantial part of the larger videogame ecosystem, with games like *FIFA*, *Madden NFL*, and *NBA 2K* selling millions of copies each year. Sports are far from perfect, and a critique of sports cultures and institutions can be, and is, its own searing book, but examining some crucial elements of sports culture enables a more critical look at how video games are currently designed in a way that ensures toxicity in the broader videogame community.[2]

The first key area to think about when considering sports and video games is the search for perfection and the integration of technology in that endeavor. Sports video games inhabit an odd space, as they are frequently attempts at simulation, but they are often seeking to simulate imperfect people. The history of sports video games is filled with examples of how games have sought to re-create sports in an accurate manner. *Pong* was an early attempt to re-create tennis, Intellivision advertised its football offering as a more accurate rendition of football than Atari's using the sportswriter George Plimpton and side-by-side screenshots of the games, and John Madden famously demanded that any football game with his name on it would feature eleven players on the field for each team, something that had never been done before because of technical limitations. However, sports are imperfect and have often sought out technology in an effort to make more accurate judgments within the context of individual games. The National Football League initially introduced a limited instant-replay system in 1986, which was modified and largely solidified into its current form by 1999. The system is still subject to substantial rules and restrictions, but the general idea is that each coach gets two opportunities to challenge a referee's decision during the course of a game. Certain decisions cannot be challenged and, late in each half, challenge decisions are made by a separate official, but the overarching intent of the system is to correct for human error.

The videogame version of the NFL, *Madden NFL*, is a simulation of a National Football League game. However, instead of being officiated by humans, the video game is effectively adjudicated by the game platform and game code making judgments about player input and computer-controlled artificial intelligence. In the midst of this, there is little need for an instant replay system to review referees' decisions.

The NFL system is designed to combat human error, and the computer replication of that system is actually designed to introduce error that can then be simulated within the course of the game. Add in vagaries with the representation of graphics within the game and players are subject to situations where the game is programmed to give them inaccurate information. Effectively, the offline sport is seeking to make better decisions by introducing a replay system, while the videogame analogue has to introduce doubt and error in order to make the inclusion of a replay system meaningful. This leads to questions and complaints from players, ranging from concern about how "only the computer gets successful challenges" to how the game implements the challenge resolution—"the game is smart enough to know that a challenge should be done, but its [*sic*] not smart enough to figure out how to adjust the call"—to unnecessary computer-initiated challenges that function as "pointless comic relief and nothing more."[3] The challenge feature need not be part of a video game. The call should be correct in the first place, but trying to mimic an imperfect game requires introducing elements of error into the video game, even if those errors seem ridiculous. Video games are designed from a state where we expect them to be perfect, which can make players less willing to question decisions made within them and more prone to accept the output as an accurate representation of merit. As the game designer and competitive game player David Sirlin puts it, "Debates in real life are highly subjective, but in games we can be absolutely sure who the winner is."[4] For Sirlin, one of the major factors that distinguish games is the clear platform they provide for competition; in that context, the deliberate inclusion of error is odd. However, unlike video games, sports evolved pre-digitally, so error is often seen as a problem to be solved with new digital tools, while the video games seeking simulation then attempt to copy those pre-digital dynamics into a computerized product.

The NFL is not the only league to use technology in an attempt to eliminate human judgment and officiating mistakes from the offline version of their sport. Major League Baseball was relatively late to instant replay, adding it in 2008 and slowly expanding it to review more human decisions in subsequent years. However, in 2006 MLB decided to begin installing a PITCHf/x tracking system that uses a pair of cameras to track the flight and location of every pitched ball.

That information is shared with the public via Major League Baseball Advanced Media and used to judge the performance of umpires. Including this additional level of review for umpire decisions on balls and strikes has resulted in an increased level of accuracy and an expansion of the strike zone, particularly around the knees, a fundamental change in the game that may be part of a trend toward rising strikeout rates in the league.[5] Tennis began using a system called Hawk-Eye in 2005, which replaced Cyclops, a system developed in the 1980s, that assessed whether serves were in or out. Hawk-Eye is also used as part of cricket television coverage and as a system of goal-line review by the English Football Association. Goal-line review was integrated into the 2014 FIFA World Cup, and the former head of FIFA has argued for the wider use of technology to potentially overturn refereeing decisions.[6] In order to discuss issues in officiating openly, the National Basketball Association began releasing reports that review all the major decisions in the last two minutes of close games.[7] These reports often mention errors in officiating with the ultimate goal of transparency, even when the mistakes may have resulted in a team losing a game because of an incorrect decision.[8] The point of all these choices, and the general trend throughout competitive sports, is to use technology to eliminate error in human decision making. However, there is also resistance to the trend of using technology to overrule human mistakes, as it is both expensive and changes the context of the sport. Opposition is often the strongest in soccer, as German soccer voted against installing goal-line technology because of cost and the argument by many purists that the inevitable human error is a classic part of soccer.[9] Mistakes ensure debate and discussion, one of the elements that typify reaction to what is often called "the beautiful game."

The central line of appeal by those in favor of using technology in sport to double-check human decision is that additional review can make contests more accurate. Underlying that belief is the premise that the person or team with the most skill should win and that errors in judgment necessarily reward the undeserving. Instant replay, coach's challenges, and goal-line review are designed to make sports more meritocratic and give a better chance for skill to outweigh luck. Video games have no such problem. The code may be poorly written and players could encounter bugs, glitches, or exploits, but officiating decisions can be perfect within the context of a video game. One need not have review in a video game, as the incorrect refereeing decisions have to be programmed into the game in the first place.

Replay and the integration of review in video games demonstrates two things. First, sports games are attempts to replicate and simulate their offline analogues. The pursuit of simulation leads to situations where elements are integrated into the videogame version that clearly need not be there, in an attempt to better imitate the sport with which spectators are familiar. Second, because human decisions are crucial to sports, sports cannot be perfect meritocracies. Incorrect officiating decisions will inevitably be made and, although application of technology is being used to rectify those mistakes, error is an accepted and acceptable part of sports. The rules of soccer are set up to be open to interpretation, to the point where a leading sports website can publish an article about how no one actually understands the rules of the game.[10] Replay review in baseball has led to decisions that are technically correct but contravene past practices of the game, like when a player slides into a base and has his foot leave safety for a split second that could not be spotted without a slow-motion replay, causing a sportswriter to decry the situation as "unbearable."[11] Dustin Johnson was assessed a penalty in a golf championship decided after he was finished, yet he bailed out the governing body by winning anyway (and by a large margin), ensuring that the controversy only drove discussion and debate, instead of dictating a winner and a loser.[12] The Super Bowl–winning defense of the Seattle Seahawks played with a strategy of committing fouls on every play, trusting that officials would not call all the infractions for fear of slowing down the game or seeming biased against the team.[13] Sports are full of human judgments and subjectivity, which extend to the selection of players. Research indicates that National Football League teams routinely overestimate their skill in picking players in the draft and that the actual outcomes are barely better than pure chance.[14] Sports are determined by contingency, from the weather, which can reward some athletes and punish others, to the stadium and pitch dimensions, which can encourage building a team to best fit a home park or stadium. Injuries routinely affect what happens in sport, as the winner of a season-long grind is just as likely to be the healthiest as the best.[15] Sports, driven by contemporary society and broadcast networks, are seeking to eliminate error, but the serendipity of sports has been a defining characteristic.[16] This indeterminacy of sport stands in stark contrast to sports video games, like *Madden NFL*, where players are given clear, easily interpreted ratings that are released in advance of the game and make the process of evaluating athletes transparent.[17] The human judgments that are a key part of sports do not extend to video games, which are set up to reward skill because they do not involve similar kinds of human error. A full integration of error and the potential for mistakes, which could upset a strict meritocracy, are typically written out of videogame design and culture. When chance is a part of video games, gamers frequently lobby for it to be eliminated, as in the case of *Mario Kart* and the blue shell.

A second area of contrast concerns analytics and team building. Over the past several years, substantial investments have been made in sports analytics in an effort to figure out the best possible ways to play the game. Basketball has seen a massive shift, as insights like shot mapping have led teams to recognize that a long two-point shot is the least productive play in the game.[18] Because "long twos" are less likely to draw fouls and are worth fewer points than shooting from behind the three-point line, an increasing number of teams have changed their approaches to attract a different kind of player and teach them to play in way more likely to generate additional points (i.e., fewer "long twos" and more three-point shots).[19] Acceptance of this change has become so complete in a few short years that an aversion to three-point shots has been described by prominent NBA writer Zach Lowe as an "objectively dumb strategy."[20] Similar baseball analytics were celebrated in the best-selling book and movie *Moneyball*. The companion activity in video games is known as theorycraft or game "meta." Theorycraft is an attempt to figure out the hidden rules behind a video game by solving the algorithms that govern interaction in the game world.[21] Meta has emerged as a shorthand version of "metagame," which references the optimal strategies in a given game. In both sports and video games the metagame analytics seek to solve changes and shifts over time. One approach can be matched by another, or designers can alter the rules in order to mitigate a newly dominant approach. Videogame designers can use patches and updates to change a game, just as sports leagues can develop new rules to combat hand-checking (basketball) or to redefine pass interference (American football). Altered rules spur new developments in analytics and a new meta that rewards different strategies.

However, a primary difference between analytics in sports and video games is the role of team chemistry in figuring out the optimal course. Figuring out approaches or best practices in sports is one thing, but maximizing their value in practice requires getting a bunch of human beings to perform in concert. Much like producing a television show is more difficult than writing a novel because you simply do not know how the actors will interact, building a sports team is different than playing a video game because multiple people have to work together for a common goal. To some extent, eSports and large groups of people playing together face chemistry issues, but freedom of movement is far more fluid in videogame guilds or clans than in major sports leagues. Much like you do not know when one of your star actors in a television show may ask off the program (e.g., Adewale Akinnuoye-Agbaje famously asked off of *Lost* because he was not happy shooting in Hawai'i), a player on a sports team may demand a new contract, a transfer, or a trade.[22] As one basketball writer notes, judging how players can fit and play together "is a huge factor when it comes to, you know, actually winning games."[23] The focus on managing people, on chemistry, is at the center of a dispute between two of the NBA's leading analytics teams, the Houston Rockets and the Dallas Mavericks.[24] Putting optimal talent together on a sports team is only part of the puzzle; one must also figure out how those people play with one another. In a video game it is common for the best characters to function smoothly, to the point where top players will often use highly similar approaches because there is a standard, commonly accepted best approach to be followed and all players are expected to fall in line, which places focus on individual or team skill in executing the "best" strategy.

Team building is another example of how video games present a more perfect meritocracy than sports. Sports have to account for a human factor in a way that video games do not. As with replay and other forms of technology, teams are turning toward technology in an effort to best discern their players' strengths and weaknesses.[25] However, video games, in their design and execution, demonstrate a kind of control of which the general manager of a sports team can only dream. The fundamental difference between assembling a team in a sports video game and in real life is that, in real life, the team actually has to play together. Human limitations and team chemistry are a substantial check on sports analytics, something that makes them partial and imperfect, while theorycraft and the metagame plow through video games and can actually solve the black box that resides within them.

A final important difference between sports and video games is the role of luck. Luck in video games is typically something to be ruled out. A video gamer facing a run of bad luck may attempt to brute force a solution and take the role of luck out of the computer's hands through his or her repeated effort. Sports, however, are almost defined by luck. One way to conceptualize the difference between the two is to think about the role of the short run in sports versus video games. In video games, with the exception of competitive match play, players can typically repeat a scenario as often as they desire in order to minimize the role of luck. Although there is clearly a cost in terms of time and often in terms of in-game resources, luck in video games can be reduced, or even eliminated, through repeated effort. At the very least, in many single-player games the player can simply restart the scenario and try again. In these cases, players are simply facing some sort of puzzle they need to solve through moving, jumping, shooting, or some other game mechanic. Sports, though, exist almost exclusively in the short run. One of the biggest sporting organizations in the United States, the NCAA, is nearing a billion dollars in revenue per year on the back of a month-long single-elimination men's basketball tournament.[26] In the United States, major sports champions are determined by playoffs that are, at most, best-of-seven series between the most successful regular season teams. Tennis tournaments are based on who is most successful on a given day. Ultimately, elite soccer competitions, like the UEFA Champions League and the FIFA World Cup, are determined by success or failure in a game or two. Sports are the realm of the short run, as players have limited careers and succumb to fatigue, while video games and the computers on which they run can mitigate the role of luck by simulating the same situation over and over and over. Video games are defined by the long run.

This difference in opportunity is a fundamental separation between how certain elements of sports and video games are defined. Connected to the idea of the short run, luck is an accepted factor in sports that is generally written out of video games. Baseball has the category of a perfect game, where a pitcher allows no base runners, and a no-hit game, where the pitcher allows no hits. Famed pitcher Cy Young said, "A pitcher's got to be good and he's got to be lucky to get a no hit game."[27] Extreme success in sports is generally framed and shaped by serendipity. Pitching a perfect game requires something to break in your favor. Sportswriters freely note how almost every no-hitter is "as much about luck as anything" and openly talk about how luck defines success in the NFL; along similar lines, the soccer star Javier Mascherano injured himself on a key tackle to clinch a win and responded in postgame interviews by saying, "What I did anyone could have done. To be in the [World Cup] final you need a bit of luck."[28] However, in video games, a perfect game is theoretically possible. Players talk about a perfect boss fight or a perfect encounter in which they hit all the right buttons (because there *is* a set of buttons in many game circumstances that defines perfection). Billy Mitchell has been awarded for his perfect game of *Pac-Man*.[29] As Raph Koster notes, a focus on skill is something that differentiates games from books, since "when stories and games are good, you can go back to them repeatedly and keep learning something new. But we never speak of mastering a good story."[30] The perception is that skill plays a much larger role, since player skill in a video game can determine outcomes, while in sports the outcome is subject to everything from the wind to a pebble to a stray bird. Sports are filled with stories of players who were among the greatest ever but did not make it to the big leagues because things did not break their way. Tales of outstanding players who did not make a major impact as a professional can be readily found in basketball, soccer, and American football, among others.[31] Coaches talk about the best players they have seen that simply did not pan out, and star athletes chime in with contemporaries who were better but failed at some point due to circumstance. Players, particularly in high-cost sports like baseball and hockey, openly talk about how the need for sponsors, family wealth, or a chance benefactor is a key precondition for being able to continue to play and develop their skills while growing up.[32] In sports, it is widely accepted that certain breaks are required in order to make it to the top, a dynamic that is systematically erased from considerations of success in video games.

Luck also plays a role in the success of a team overall. Building a sports team requires being ready for a trade or a transfer when it is available, and certain markets, like major cities or places with lower tax burdens (like Texas and Florida), often have an advantage over other localities. This kind of structural advantage can also extend to the level of an entire league. A recent influx of television money has allowed teams in England's Barclay's Premier League to spend far more than peers in other countries, and the director of sport for a German club observed that England's television money "posed a huge challenge for all of German football."[33] The 2016 Tour de France was won largely because the winning cyclist, Chris Froome, was supported by a team of other star riders (who were paid star salaries) to perform the role of domestiques.[34] Although the Internet makes building a guild a matter of collecting some of the best people from around the world, sports teams have to assemble their squads within restrictive structures they do not wholly control. People playing video games are subject to the whims of the corporation in charge of the game, but sports teams act within the bounds of nations, states, cities, and leagues.[35] The risk of injury is also far more likely to derail a group in sports than in video games, and staying healthy is a crucial part of winning a championship that sports teams cannot fully control.[36] Life can certainly intervene for a guild chasing a world-first, but an ill-placed basketball stanchion in a glorified practice led to a compound fracture and a missed year for an NBA All-Star when Paul George ran into a structural support in a warm-up exhibition USA Basketball played in a small, nonstandard gym.[37] Sports championships are won in competition with many other teams, and any approach to winning a title is described by one sportswriter as a "low-odds proposition filled with lucky breaks and moves that play out much differently than the people who make them anticipate."[38] Video games seek to eliminate luck through brute force and the ability to restart a fight, battle, or game, all effectively attempts to construct a perfect meritocracy. The ability to limit the potential of luck to wreck a player or team allows video games to focus on skill and merit, and to stamp out the variability and chaos that comes from simply suffering a bad day or a bad moment. Luck is all about recognizing how skill plus effort is incomplete. The role of luck in sports means that the best team does not always prevail in a game or match, which encourages reflection about how the playing field is often riddled with structural inequality.[39]

The role of contingency in sports—the combination of factors like chemistry in team building and the need for luck to be successful—means the field is often subject to something akin to serendipity.[40] There is no singular, clear way to move forward, no perfect world to which athletes and coaches can ascend. There is discussion in sports of mastery, but not nearly in the same manner that exists around video games. Sports do not get solved over time, but games can become solved problems with a definitively optimal approach. Unlike Bartle and Trubshaw's designed escape of *MUD1*, sports present a space where the laws are not fairer and the experience can be incredibly unkind. Success in sports is contingent, as careers are limited by skill that degrades over time, and good outcomes can be driven by circumstance, like ending up on the right team at the right time.[41] Elite athletes do all kinds of work to get better, but there is no real way to brute force one's way to a championship like there often is in video games. The whole notion of a labor-based game dependent on a grind emphasizes effort and teaches players that if they work hard enough and play often enough, they will be successful. Public discussion about games, even those about competitive multiplayer games like *League of Legends*, are rife with analyses of how players must play more often and try harder in order to get better. Studying sports and their design offers an example of how to get outside some of the key design features that can prop up toxic notions about masculinity in videogame and technology culture. Sports are not a place where simply trying harder or inserting more coins is enough. To be successful, athletes often need to benefit from luck, serendipity, and structural advantages.

On the face of it, sports seem like a meritocracy. Sports celebrate skill and effort at the highest level. However, the design of sports and the activities that happen within them check the tyranny of merit by adding in human judgment, variance, short-run odds, and luck. There are also occasions where sports develop rules that are explicitly anti-meritocratic. In the Olympics, smaller nations get access to universality places for one male and one female athlete, who can compete without making the Olympic qualifying standards required for others.[42] Universality places ensure that a far greater number of countries are able to send athletes to the Olympics, often with the goal of raising awareness about their country or heightening the profile of sports back home. Other rules limit or structure who is able to participate in a competition. The NCAA basketball tournaments give automatic entry to conference tournament winners—promoting broad representation, rather than selecting the most meritorious entrants—in choosing half the spots for the men's tournament. Similar rules exist in many Olympic sports that regulate the number of entrants in the competition, negatively affecting U.S. women gymnasts, Chinese table tennis players, and Brazilian women beach volleyball players, among others.[43] All of these policies prioritize driving broad interest and inclusion over efforts to engage in the best competition. Computerized video games are far easier to control, as they typically present problems that can be solved and offer the promise of a long run where variance can be minimized. There are fewer overarching governing bodies that set out to facilitate broad representation of participants. Within the difference and instability of sports, there are lessons for video games. Sports seem to be pure contests of skill, and the increased integration of technology may make that more of a reality, but sports are still imperfect and, in videogame terms, broken or ill balanced. Benefiting from errors and luck is often key to being successful at sports.

From sports, video games can learn lessons about contingency, humanity, and error. Some *Mario* games inspire strong negative reactions from the most hardcore of gamers, but they are also spaces in which video games embrace the most randomness. *Mario Party* is polarizing; for instance, the *IGN* review of *Mario Party 10* argued that "two types of people get the most enjoyment out of Mario Party: small children and inebriated adults" and that "kids gleefully absorb it, but adults only suffer through it for kids' sake."[44] As Julian Gollop, creator of the critically acclaimed *XCOM: Enemy Unknown* observes, random number generation and luck "is frowned upon" in modern game design and "lots of modern players don't like it."[45] *XCOM* is a turn-based strategy game that heavily rewards planning, one in which decisions can have lasting consequences. Luck plays a major role in the game, as the best plans can be foiled by a bad roll, which could lead to a miss that later causes the death of a key team member or wipes the whole team. The argument Gollop makes for luck is based on risk and contingency, that luck undermines the development of a clear metagame because good planning can always be trumped by an unlucky outcome. However, contemporary games are rooted in the notion that "the game is somehow being 'unfair' to a player if something is showing you a 90 percent chance of happening, and then it doesn't. You played the odds and you lost, which makes you feel cheated."[46] This perspective on contemporary players is backed up by the comments in response to Gollop's position, with players arguing that in offline games "it's very frustrating to be unlucky at the dice, but in a digital game it feels like the developer doesn't care for player experience" and "used in critical mission objectives, RNG [random number generation] gives a feeling of Luck2Win."[47] Both comments are predicated on the belief that, in modern video games, proper planning and skill should win out over all obstacles. For these kinds of players video games are different from other activities because they are proper tests of skill. Dependence on luck is considered bad form, largely because it does not represent a just adjudication of a player's merit. Even in games known to employ luck as a larger factor, developers have spoken openly about their desire to put their thumb on the scale in the favor of players. As the lead designer of *XCOM 2* puts it, "There's actually a number of things that tweak the calculations that number in the player's favor at the lower difficulty settings"; in the case of an 85 percent chance, the game actually plays out with the shot as closer to a 95 percent chance in order to "match the player's psychological feeling about that number."[48] In video games our humanity and tolerance for variance is boiled off and we expect perfection. When we do not get it we tend to cope poorly.

There can be a humanness to video games that is similar to the error built into the design of sports, thereby resisting the establishment of a pure meritocracy. Increased variance and mechanisms that upset the dominance of skill permeate the highest level of sports, and those lessons can be applied to game design to articulate a future that does not exclusively rely on merit to determine outcomes. Cheating, prominent in both video games and sports, threatens to short-circuit meritocracy, which is likely part of the reason organizing bodies behind both activities actively seek to stamp it out. From the critically reviled *Mario Party* to the adored *XCOM*, there are games that have followed a model based on randomness and contingency, which need to be reclaimed and emphasized.

Higher Education and Games

Higher education in the United States frequently attempts to follow meritocratic norms, but it still offers a number of lessons for detoxifying games. On its face, higher education may not seem like it has much in common with videogame culture. In many ways, however, the overlap between the two is tied to the fact that both have been constructed as ostensibly meritocratic spaces where people of acceptable merit are welcomed to interact with others. The first part of understanding the benefit is to look more deeply at how universities work and then turn to positive and negative lessons that can be instructive.

A combination of public and private universities, U.S. higher education is heavily subsidized by federal and state governments with the intent of educating citizens. Part of the mission of many of these institutions is to serve the greater social good. Most retain nonprofit status, which confers tax benefits to the institution in exchange for an obligation to serve the public rather than shareholders. Colleges actively recruit students, often with an eye toward gathering a diverse student population. For many institutions, assembling a diverse student body is a crucial goal because of the desire to stimulate critical thinking, and "cultural diversity inherently brings into the classroom a cultural perspective that is fundamentally diverse and thus forces students to understand issues from different points of view."[49] Diversity is not always a goal in and of itself, but it is a key component in accomplishing the deeper goal of provoking thought as a teaching tool.

A second objective in gathering a diverse student population is to select the right mix from applicants to the institution, determining who makes the cut for admission and who does not. An entire industry exists to help students maximize their chances of admission, from test-preparation courses to classes on how to write better application essays to organized tours that take potential students from campus to campus so they can learn what they need to do to have the best chance of being accepted. Colleges can consider many things from an application, typically focusing on elements like grades, test scores, and class ranking. In some states race can be a consideration, and most schools are need aware, which means that they take family income and likelihood of need for financial aid into consideration. The typical admissions criteria for a school are designed to give the appearance of a meritocratic selection process; extreme focus is placed on personal achievements, while a heavy hand is simultaneously placed on the scale for other factors. Legacy considerations are common at almost all elite institutions, conferring direct benefits to students who had family members previously attend the school. Legacy and need-aware admissions create a situation in which Josh Freedman argues it is difficult to understand how a premier school can "grant legacy preference and take most of its students from upper class households while also claiming that it cares deeply about equality, diversity, and social mobility. In other words: You cannot have your cake, eat it too, and then accept its cupcakes through legacy admissions."[50] From the outside, the admissions process is designed to seem meritocratic, but there are clear cracks where considerations having little to do with an individual applicant's merit are weighed.

According to Ross Douthat, the higher education system in the United States "was overhauled in the middle years of the twentieth century to be a force for near universal opportunity—or so the over-haulers intended," but it has transformed into a system where social elites respond to interest in restructuring the system with concerns like "Why should they [already economically elite Americans] give it up? *It's not as if our child doesn't deserve his advantages.*"[51] Although there is a heavy veneer of meritocracy, current selection processes for higher education in the United States largely replicate existing racial and class differences across generations of students.[52] Studies of white adults in California have found that they back a meritocratic selection process for college up until it is pointed out that Asian students out-perform whites on metrics like high school grades and standardized test scores.[53] College matters, as graduates make more money and are more likely to be engaged at work and happy in their lives, and yet the appearance of a meritocracy insulates admissions selection from certain critiques about how already-privileged students are advantaged because it appears fair and just.[54]

There are plenty of articles that address the myth of meritocracy in higher education, as critics frequently note how tilted the admissions or academic hiring processes actually are toward those with built-in advantages.[55] However, college admissions share a lot in common with advertising and marketing departments for videogame companies. Just as admissions officers fan out across the country each year to solicit students for their home institutions, recruiters subject videogame players to a barrage of ads that seek to draw them in, while the industry resists efforts to put women at the center of games (e.g., on game covers), often only including women, as Becky Chambers puts it, as "just victims and plot points."[56] The situation is not much better for racial depictions in games, as people of color represented in video games are likely to be exoticized and are relegated largely to roles in sports and fighting titles.[57] For black women, the situation is especially dire. A count of black female protagonists that excludes customizable and licensed characters adds up to a total of only fourteen in the entire history of video games by one game journalist's counting.[58] Where people are reached and on what terms they are contacted matters. There are some strides that have been made in higher education, however, that can demonstrate a different path and a chance to reach a broader, more diverse audience for games.

This is not to say that a university system is a perfect match for video games. There is a key difference in the relative level of commitment being made in going to a specific college or putting a new disc in the tray. College is frequently a four-plus-year, tens-of-thousands-of-dollars experience, while video games typically require a couple dozen hours and around sixty bucks, plus the cost of the console and internet access (in the case of mobile devices, free-to-play pricing can lower the barrier to entry even further). There is also a fundamental difference in the structure of the institutions supporting each industry. I expect that university adjuncts could find a number of things in common with quality assurance testers running on crunch, but most universities are nonprofits whereas most game developers and publishers are not. This leads to different kinds of incentive structures—ostensibly social good for a nonprofit, and profits for a business—but the long-term motivations of both are likely aligned in the interest of growing and sustaining their respective industries. Given these similarities and differences, there are two key lessons that can be learned by examining U.S. higher education as it pertains to video games: recruiting for diversity and the connection between inputs and outputs.

As race-based affirmative action programs have become increasingly contentious and schools have seen their enrollments dominated by students of means, many lower-income students with the potential for strong applications simply do not apply. For first-generation students, colleges have had to forge a new path for recruitment, as not knowing others who have gone to college can lead to misperceptions about how likely students are to get into a school and about how much aid they may receive in order to turn an acceptance into attendance. Universities have found that even if they are likely to qualify for highly selective schools based on their grades and test scores, most low-income students simply do not apply for admission.[59] Effectively, the background experience you have with college matters. Some of the programs that have had the best results in getting a more economically diverse population of applicants are straightforward. Targeted summer camps, sending potential students packets of information about schools, and programs that combine short-term incentives, like laptops, with long-term benefits, like full-ride scholarships, are making a dent in developing a more diverse student population of people who simply would not have applied otherwise.[60] Schools have clearly found that where people are from and what they have been invited to attend shapes what they are likely to do. These programs give a clear map about how to address a lack of diversity in games—one approach is to actively invite more people in and find ways to make them comfortable. Efforts like Girls Make Games, Girls Who Code, Dames Making Games, and the Pixelles give young women a safe space in which to develop games.[61] Those initiatives should diversify the people making games and fundamentally change the kinds of games being created. Other changes, like growth in both mobile and casual gaming, are likely to change the population of people playing games, giving the market reason to develop titles to suit a broader population of players. Seemingly basic moves to include people and make them feel welcome, while pointing them to the potential of new things, can diversify previously homogenous groups.

The second key piece that can be learned from higher education is the link between inputs and outputs when it comes to learning and experience. Directly linked to the idea of knowledge scaffolding and merit, there are extraordinarily clear relationships between graduation rates and college preparedness.[62] The most straightforward ways to improve a school's graduation rate are to improve the incoming student body's grade point average, increase the percentage of full-time students, or attract more students from families with means. Inputs lead to outputs, so changing the composition of the inputs leads to a changed set of outputs; schools themselves only do so much to change students.

It is reasonable to presuppose that games may work in a similar fashion. The skills one brings into a game help shape what happens within that game. The more background knowledge, development, and time investment that has been made prior to playing a game, the more likely one is to be successful. This factor can subvert the notion of a meritocracy before it starts. Your output, your success, is contingent on dynamics leading up to the game. Instead of being indicative of your skill, any given game is an examination of what came before, which is at least somewhat driven by whether you were encouraged to play video games in the first place. I suspect almost anyone who has played a fair chunk of video games can talk about how knowledge from one game translated directly to a new one. Being well versed in that symbol system makes you far more likely to pick it up quickly in a new game, which says less about how skilled you are than it does about the massive structural input advantages from which some players benefit.

It is notable that the world of sports and U.S. higher education are viewed externally as meritocratic, yet there is widespread acknowledgment that conceiving of them as enterprises based solely on merit is fundamentally flawed. Meritocratic structures have fallen apart in sports, where luck and timing are key, and in higher education, where schools are actively seeking diversity and recognizing the relationship between inputs and outputs, but they still remain present and prominent in the world of video games. Applying a sense of perfection to the meritocratic norms that persist in the tech world, video games hold on to perceptions that players earn their positions with true tests of skill. The stories in video games further these notions through repeated narratives about protagonists overcoming any and all reasonable, and some unreasonable, obstacles through their own efforts. Video games are built on meritocratic norms, they tell meritocratic stories, and to disrupt the toxicity in video-game culture it is necessary for both to be corralled.

There are plenty of places to look when thinking about how to get the toxicity out of videogame culture. An argument can be made that there are jerks in any community because there are jerks in the rest of the world, but there is also a real chance to make things better. Looking at other meritocracies and how they address elements that clearly connect to video games demonstrates just how reliant on meritocracy video games are. Paired against sports and education, the focus on skill, merit, and earning your position is far more apparent in video games. Learning from what other cultures do well or poorly can provide a way to think about games with a fresh perspective. Beyond the examples discussed here, I expect that links to a lack of diversity in the development of television and film, the meritocratic tendencies of contemporary technology culture and startups, and the connections between independent music and independent games all provide points from which to rethink video games and how they are designed. Increasing diversity is possible in all kinds of areas, from NASA to computer science jobs to comics.[63] There are many charted paths to follow, including the work done at *Offworld*, where Leigh Alexander and Laura Hudson actively recruited and published a diverse group of writers to analyze video games and the culture around them.[64] Sports and higher education were chosen as comparative examples because of the clear links to meritocracy, luck, and diversity, but they also set the table for engaging in a deeper look at a new path for video games.

In the midst of a toxic game culture built on meritocratic tropes, there are some promising things happening in game development that point toward a different future for games. However, maximizing that future and actually addressing the toxicity requires thinking differently about games and what they can be. Charting a new path for games largely means thinking about ways to add to what is available and to consider the repercussions of continuing along the same path. The primary idea behind rhetorical analysis is that the symbol systems we use shape what we do and how we interact with one another. Thinking deeply about the implications of those symbol systems can help us alter them. Popular, normal decisions and structures fade into the background, as they just seem like the way things are. Earning your way through a video game, showing off your skill in battle to win through your guile, and producing story after story about rising up from nothing to make it big are the background state of video games. It is just how things always have been. However, there are changes happening that can help to build a positive culture around video games.

Conclusion
An Obligation to Do Better

The whole point of a meritocracy is to reward skill, which makes the victors feel like they have earned their rewards and relegates others to their deserved lesser status. It is a system that forecloses critical thought and reflection, as the whole point is to tell the winners that they have won their place, so they begin to act accordingly. As in the Paul Piff studies that demonstrate how people act like jerks when they are winning a rigged game, videogame culture has internalized those winning lessons year after year.[1] Disturbing this system and constructing something different is a difficult task, but there are steps that point to a less toxic future.

The starting point for changing game culture is recognizing that the issue is about adding new experiences. There is nothing wrong with having games that are based on meritocratic norms if those are only some of the games, rather than almost all of the video games. I know there are games I find distasteful and I suspect the same is true for others; changing the rhetorical construction of video games need not be based on restriction and eliminating titles. Instead, the necessary step is to add more new, different types of games that offer an alternate kind of experience and, potentially, target a new kind of player. New, different games can open up space for critical reflection and destabilizing norms around merit in video games. Rather than shunning new experiences or rejecting certain genres as not "real" games, the one thing videogame culture needs to stop doing is heavily policing the notion of what constitutes a "game." A big tent approach, with a broad umbrella to include a number of different activities, gives game culture the chance to learn from new communities of people and get some joy out of doing something new and different alongside the old and beloved. New mechanics do trickle into older games, and the first step to getting rid of the toxicity in games is embracing the possibilities that exist. Meritocratic games have their place—I certainly enjoyed *Grand Theft Auto IV* and I spent plenty of time competitively raiding in *World of Warcraft*—but I am also tremendously excited about the possibility of exploring new ideas.

One broad way to start thinking about games differently is to assess what it is that games let the player do. The typical path of a game is as an empowerment fantasy. By way of a meritocratic design trope that allows the player to move forward and become more powerful over time, video games are often about making the player more capable than he or she, or any human, really is. From sports games that have players embodying All-Stars to first-person shooters that let players soak up more bullets and dish out more damage than a human ever could, games are about making the fantastic ordinary. Focusing on empowerment limits the kind of story that can be told and restricts the kind of mechanics players are likely to encounter. These elements feed a meritocratic symbol system, as these games instruct players that they are special, different, and superior to those who cannot hack it. However, there are games emerging that challenge such an expectation of empowerment.

In 2013, Richard Hofmeier's *Cart Life* dominated the Independent Games Festival Awards, winning the grand prize, an award for game narrative, and a third award given to the best abstract, unconventional game. *Cart Life* is a different kind of game; Leigh Alexander observes that the player has to "remember to pay rent, buy groceries, perhaps try to make friends in the community. If you have time. Time in *Cart Life* passes mercilessly, with no opportunity to correct for things you've missed."[2] One character in the game needs to smoke or he slows down, another character needs to pick up her daughter after school. The player is placed in a position seeking to balance all the kinds of chores and tasks a normal person has to juggle on a regular basis. Alexander argues that the game is effectively about reflection, as it "has the odd power to throw your life into sharp relief" and is effectively "a reminder of how deeply games can communicate the value of small victories."[3] Sporting a *Metacritic* rating of 79, with positive reviews from a number of mainstream game outlets, *Cart Life* provides a different kind of game experience. Instead of building a game around making a player increasingly powerful, the game has you live through the life of someone with everyday problems. The game is not about a fantasy, aspirational life; it is about reflecting on the life of people around you about whom you do not always think. The game is all about empathy and, although players are striving to make their lives better, it is not driven by the same sort of aspirational meritocratic narrative typical of most video games.

Another, related game that demonstrates a different mode of game building is Lucas Pope's *Papers, Please*. Simulating the life of a border patrol agent in Arstotzka, a communist state placed in an imagined Cold War period, *Papers, Please* requires players to make the kinds of decisions border patrol agents need to make on a regular basis. In the flow of people seeking entry into your country are smugglers, spies, and terrorists, as well as visitors simply seeking to reunite with loved ones. The game has been highly reviewed by a wide variety of sources, earning praise in publications ranging from the paragon of core gaming, *IGN*, the PC-focused *Rock, Paper, Shotgun*, and broader news sites like the *New Statesman*.[4] *Papers, Please*—with an 85 score on *Metacritic*, which would make many AAA game developers envious— forces players into a position where they are simultaneously trying to make border control decisions and take care of their family. Players are paid for each person correctly processed and can be fined for improper decisions. Side deals can be cut with shady characters, and players are often faced with such moral choices as separating families or deciding whether to let a human trafficker with proper paperwork into the country, all while trying to process enough people to buy food and medicine for your own family. The game is dark, stressful, and, as the additional levels of paperwork stack up, quite difficult. The game is also notable because of how it is built, which is fundamentally different from most video games.

Reviews of the game tell of its core features, describing how *Papers, Please* is an experience, one in which, Justin McElroy believes, players, in their work at the immigration booth, "will reduce the living, breathing humans in front of your window to a series of documents.

It's inevitable. Once you've made this essential leap, you'll be staggered at the injustice you're willing to visit on your fellow man."[5] The game instructs about the everyday grind faced by bureaucrats, and Richard Cobbett observes that "very few other games have so perfectly encapsulated just how being trapped in this kind of dehumanising role can be, in the best possible way, and both inside and out of the dreaded grey booth."[6] Not exactly "fun," but not exactly not fun; John Walker argues that the game "is unquestionably something unique" because "it is, undeniably a paperwork sim. And perhaps that's enough to put some off it entirely. But it's definitely worth getting past that (otherwise entirely sensible) prejudice in this case. It's peculiarly engrossing, darkly ominous, and a fascinating exploration of morality versus progress."[7] Players are encouraged to reassess their prior conceptions of how they would act in a pressure-filled situation, since, according to Leigh Alexander, they are forced to choose whether they wish to "perform nude body-scans on frail refugees" to prevent terrorism, which "forces you to think about the human cost of bureaucracy by creating empathy with all its living components."[8] Even through the rapid pace of the game, in which players seek to process as many people as they can, *Papers, Please* encourages reflection and critical thought. Did I really just turn that person down? What choices do I need to make to provide for my family? Is the fastest way to process people simply to turn everyone down?

Papers, Please feels and plays differently than most video games, which Leigh Alexander explains by examining the core of the game: "Most computer games are power fantasies, but in exploring the daily work of a border control agent, [game designer Lucas] Pope's concocted a *disempowerment* fantasy. What if you weren't the brave spy or roguish smuggler, but the guy who has the boring job of stopping him?"[9] Effectively, the game inverts the typical videogame experience. The player is not all-powerful but rather consistently stressed and routinely placed in situations where there are no good, easy choices. Playing more often can certainly make one more skilled at processing documentation, but the end state of the game is something more like survival than the glorious future that lies at the end of many other titles. In fact, beating the game unlocks an "endless mode" where all there is to do is process documentation. *Papers, Please*, dark and gloomy, largely breaks away from meritocratic norms in both narrative and design. It fosters space for reflection and encourages players to think about choices made both within games and within the world that exists outside them.

A third game that offers a non-meritocratic mode of play is Telltale's series *The Walking Dead: The Game*.[10] Based in the world developed by the comic books of the same name, the games are episodic and individual episodes are packaged into seasons held together by overarching stories and adventures. The game starts by placing players in the role of Lee Everett, a former University of Georgia professor who was convicted of murder and is being transported to jail when the zombie apocalypse begins. Shortly after beginning he comes across Clementine, a young girl whose parents are away and whose babysitter has been transformed into a zombie. The game, especially the first season, is well reviewed, earning praise from a variety of different outlets, with *Metacritic* scores in the high 80s and low 90s, depending on the platform being considered. However, one of the most notable aspects of the series is how it subverts typical notions of what a game is or should be.

Reviews of the series typically focus on the role of choice in its design. One reviewer contends that "the most engaging moments in the series revolve around choice" and that "choices have meaning. Characters you interact with remember what you've said and respond accordingly down the line."[11] The game is morally ambiguous, since the rules are different in a zombie apocalypse, and reviewer Hollander Cooper found that players are quickly forced to acknowledge that "there's no 'right' when right can mean shooting an innocent child before it can turn into a flesh-eating beast, and there's no 'wrong' when wrong can mean stealing the supplies you need from those just as needy as you. *The Walking Dead* is the story of the choices you can't live with, and the choices you can, coming together to create an experience as depressing and pessimistic as it is remarkable and memorable."[12] The game basically funnels players into situations where they are forced to make a decision in conversation or where they are forced to quickly respond to a quick-time event in order to defend imperiled characters. Each episode has a handful of decision points where players can choose different routes through the game, which means that, for Greg Miller, the game is effectively "like a coloring book: we each have the same black and white sketch, but it's up to us to fill it in as we see fit.

The relationships I've built, the emotions I've felt, the choices I've made—that's what makes *The Walking Dead: The Game* so endearing."[13] Choice means conferring agency to players, even if there are a limited number of scripted options from which the player is deciding. When it works, Hollander Cooper argues that the game is designed in a way that, "despite not always being in control, *The Walking Dead* makes you feel as though you are. Even though you can't always save someone from death, you can give it your best try, shaping the person you are. And it's up to you to decide if it's worth the effort to change what, in all likelihood, can not [*sic*] be changed."[14] By effectively making the game about choices, rather than combat, *The Walking Dead* works differently from many other games and becomes more accessible for a broad audience. By setting the game in a dark, postapocalyptic setting, the design and narrative of *The Walking Dead* squeeze out meritocratic narrative and design because there is no grand, escapist victory.

The game does not clearly fit in an established gaming genre; its fence straddling is best shown in the *Touch Arcade* reviews of the first two seasons. The reviews are written by different people, and the difficulty of labeling the game is clear. The first season is assessed as "an adventure game first and foremost. When there is 'action,' it occurs in QTE [quick-time event] segments that have you tapping or swiping contextually as a zombie runs towards you."[15] Fewer than two years later, the review of the second season notes, "this is less an adventure game and more of a visual novel, albeit one that does a very good job of keeping the player within the lines while simultaneously making them feel like the story is their own."[16] For me, the most interesting thing about the two seemingly oppositional statements is that I agree with both of them. The game is both an adventure game and a visual novel. *The Walking Dead: The Game* straddles boundaries and sits in a space between genres, which makes it distinct from other video games. By opting out of traditional categories, and by utilizing the narrative tropes that are typical of a zombie apocalypse, *The Walking Dead* bucks the meritocratic trends endemic to most contemporary video games.

An extension of defying established game genres is that *The Walking Dead* series does not really depend on skill in the traditional sense of video games. There are quick-time events, which can be somewhat tricky or difficult to manage, but they do not serve as the same sort of obstacle as the kinds of interactions found in most traditional titles. Instead of needing to jump on platforms, navigate three-dimensional spaces, or master complicated series of button presses, all of which are routinely found in adventure games, the actions in *The Walking Dead* are relatively rare and can be repeated as often as one needs in order to complete them. Most of the experience of playing the game is reading, moving around in small, contained areas, and simple selections made from menus. The events add depth and dynamism to play, but they are structured in a manner that is forgiving and appeal to a much broader audience than most other games. By engaging in a more accessible level of design, *The Walking Dead* and other games by Telltale subvert the typical knowledge scaffolding found in video games, as it is accessible to those well versed in video games as well as those who are not. These benefits are compounded by the fact that the game is based on a world developed in comic books and television shows. Those origin points mean that the games implicitly reward transmedia knowledge found in other texts, quite possibly inviting a larger audience to play. In blending elements of a visual novel with game play, *The Walking Dead* points to another way to avoid the meritocratic trap of video: by subverting design based on skill transfer, and thereby rejecting the structural inequality that comes with it.

The Walking Dead's focus on functioning like a visual novel provides a way of thinking about the Fullbright Company's *Gone Home*. In this "game" the player takes a first-person role as Kaitlin Greenbriar, who returns to the house where her parents and sister, Samantha, live, only to find it empty. Samantha left a note on the door to instruct Kaitlin to not look for any answers; the player can explore throughout the house to unravel what her family has been doing. Set in the mid-1990s and offering rich environmental detail, *Gone Home* is as much an experience as anything else. Unlike the visual novel of *The Walking Dead*, in *Gone Home* there are no other characters with whom to talk. Instead, everything is found through interaction with the house and the objects within it. Resonance comes in the interaction with the artifacts Kaitlin discovers and in how the game is designed to make the player "feel like you're in a space, but that you're also playing a game, and the game is playing back with you."[17] *Gone Home* is a compelling, immersive, and interesting experience that challenges the traditional structure of games.

One of the most interesting aspects of *Gone Home* is how the reception of the game encouraged reflection about what actually constitutes a video game. While one review described it as "a first-person exploratory adventure game," another went out of its way to point out that the game play is limited to "walking, reading, and the occasional mix-tape listening" and continued on to note that the game "has no action to speak of. You'll never see a character's face, and you'll never earn a score on a leaderboard. No online, no multiplayer, no DLC [downloadable content]."[18] Both reviews were quite positive, but they did not know what to do with the game, a dynamic that surprised the developers as they found *Gone Home* becoming "ingrained in the discussion of what a video game actually *is*."[19] *Gone Home* shares elements with many video games, from mode of distribution to the profile of the designers to the way in which players move through a rich world. However, you cannot win *Gone Home* or prove that you played it better than someone else did; it is not a meritocratic proving ground. These factors are precisely why *Gone Home* is an important piece in beginning to think about games differently.

Discussion of *Gone Home* typically focuses on the emotional power of the game, which is particularly meaningful because the primary characters and themes in the game are not represented in most video games. In her review, Danielle Riendeau wrote, "*Gone Home* resonated deeply for me, partially because the particulars of the story are eerily familiar. I was surprised by the story, and even more surprised by my reaction. I've mowed down thousands of bad guys and aliens and evil henchmen in my 25-plus-year gaming career. And I've enjoyed emotional experiences and fallen for a number of memorable characters in that time. But I never expected to see myself—or such a strong reflection of myself and my own life—in a video game."[20] For people who grew up in the 1990s, *Gone Home* is a version of our childhood or adolescence. It may not be our tale, but it is close enough to many of our experiences that the game prompts feeling, nostalgia, and reflection. A less lyrical, more direct assessment states that "games like *The Last of Us* and *BioShock Infinite* allow us to explore exceptionally realized worlds, but *Gone Home*'s world just feels straight-up real."[21] A third review argues that *Gone Home's* constraints make it feel "stunningly universal, even though from some angles it's unique, complicated, even difficult."[22] Simultaneously possessing a central story and compelling bits and pieces that drive the player to look deeper, *Gone Home* is largely about what it was like to live at a particular point in time.

With a different focus and different mechanics than most games, it should not be surprising that classification of *Gone Home* is difficult. The game subverts dominant expectations and is also a compelling enough experience that it is eminently worthy of attention and discussion. *Gone Home* is troublesome because it demonstrates an alternate way of doing things, proving that the games we have played up until this point were only part of what can be made. In challenging dominant norms and expectations, *Gone Home* shows how a compelling videogame experience can be made without any sort of meritocratic element. Without the leaderboards or crosshairs, one can still develop a game worthy of awards and extended analysis. Something new can be done, but when the new way of playing comes along we won't always know what to do with it.

Entire genres of games also challenge parts of the design or narrative endemic in meritocratic video games. A whole raft of so-called casual games offers alternate modes of game design, often in a way that maximizes the ability of a wide group of people to play the game and minimizes the need for finely honed skill. Often derided as "clicker" games, titles like *FarmVille, Mafia Wars,* and *Kim Kardashian: Hollywood* are not difficult to play. Most of the action in the games is relegated to a simple click, and then bars move, items spray into the air, and the cycle is repeated until your energy is exhausted, at which point you need to wait until your energy refills to play again. Often played on Facebook or mobile devices, many casual games have a fundamentally different audience than console and PC titles do, one that skews more heavily toward women and others who are left out of the traditional category of gamers.

This genre of games often employs elements of meritocratic narratives, but the mechanics often subvert key elements of meritocratic game design. Instead of designing the game around puzzles, complicated series of button presses, or the ability to maneuver with two thumb sticks, games like *Kim Kardashian: Hollywood* reward persistence, patience, and the desire to keep pushing buttons to watch bars move, all of which challenge the dominant design norms of video games. Effort is certainly involved in these games, but by stripping out skill requirements the barrier for entry is lowered and the potential audience is vast. Casual games are often regarded as lesser than more mainstream video games, but that perception is based almost exclusively on the relative level of skill involved in playing them. Calling these games "clickers" or "casual" marginalizes them, and those jeers are linked to the games' resistance of meritocratic design norms because they don't require the player to show off any "real" skills.

Core console games can also represent complicated relationships with meritocratic norms. Players in *No Man's Sky* get more powerful over the course of the game in a fairly traditional meritocratic fashion, but the design of the game is more complicated than that. Highly promoted in advance of its launch and excoriated, even sued, for not meeting prerelease expectations, *No Man's Sky* stepped outside the meritocratic framework, promoting exploration and long-term engagement. Separating the game from the hype around it is difficult, largely because the developer made so many promises that no game could possibly meet.[23] However, one of the most interesting parts of the game's release was how reviewers discussed the game. In general, game reviews are odd things to read and write. Effectively a statement of personal taste about whether an expenditure is "worth" it, game reviewers are obligated to demonstrate that they have sufficiently engaged the game and have developed a knowledgeable opinion about it. That often leads to an instrumental kind of play based on developing a perspective that can then be conveyed in an article. Reviews for *No Man's Sky* are different, largely because the game is different. The *Kotaku* review engages in two quite different approaches within a single review. The first was instrumental, as the reviewer sought to chew through the story to generate something to write about. The second was lyrical and focused on leisurely exploration. In the end, Kirk Hamilton concludes, "The first time I played *No Man's Sky*, I moved forward too fast. The second time, I stood still. Now, I'm ready to set out again, anchored by the things I'll leave behind." Hamilton's key takeaway is that, when confronted with a different kind of game, we must relearn how to play it. Forcing a non-meritocratic game into a highly rigid framework makes it harder to appreciate it on its own terms. Certainly the promotion surrounding the game led to criticism, but there is plenty of room to see how introducing a game based on exploration requires that players and journalists take time to reframe their perspectives and appreciate it on its own terms.

Another example of a video game that demonstrates resistance to meritocratic norms is *Faunasphere*, a now-defunct massively multiplayer online game (MMOG) played on browsers and Facebook. *Faunasphere*, subject to a book-length analysis by Mia Consalvo and Jason Begy, was largely popular with middle-aged women players and resisted the fantasy and science-fiction tropes that dominate most other video games. The game allowed players to have multiple pets, and the limit on how many they held was tied to whether they were paying for the game. Although there were levels to progress through, the game did not inspire the kind of competition that typifies most titles. Instead, increasing levels helped players become more successful at breeding their pets, but the best breeding opportunities required cooperation. These design choices, in combination with players who were largely unaware of typical norms in online games, meant that the game featured what Consalvo and Begy deem a "culture of niceness."[24] The early game play in *Faunasphere* "depended on players helping one another—usually by giving one another eggs for crossbreeding fauna or different items in order to decorate personal spheres [a house-like space]."[25] It is quite notable that *Faunasphere* both attracted a different player base than other games and helped structure positive interactions for players. That said, the game only survived for about two years. Although there are plenty of other short-lived MMOGs in gaming history, it is notable that a game company was unable to find a way to sufficiently market and monetize a title that did not target conventional demographics.

A final group of titles that show a different future for games, I would deem experimental. *Johann Sebastian Joust*, Die Gute Fabrik's no-graphics, motion-controller version of the folk game *Ninja*, is a great example of an alternate mode of design. Players in *Johann Sebastian Joust* are given motion controllers and tasked with keeping their motion in sync with the music while knocking opponents out of sync. As the music speeds up, players can move more quickly, but they must be ready to slow down when the tempo of the music changes. There are certainly barriers to play—one needs a whole lot of motion controllers—but when the game is being played it works as an invitation for other people to join in. There are far fewer barriers to playing a game like *Joust* than most video games, as it relies on movements and the kind of interaction that is far more typical of daily life than years of sitting behind a controller or a keyboard, even though the game design advantages those with long arms and good balance.

Other games, like thatgamecompany's *Journey* or David O'Reilly's *Mountain*, challenge fundamental notions about what games are and can be. *Journey* is a game without words, and reviews laud "its beautiful story without a line of dialogue either spoken or written out" and describe it as a game where "you never fight. You don't score points or compete with anyone. You don't make meaningful choices or venture about an open world. There is no clear set of goals or obstacles to achieve or overcome."[26] In *Journey* you can play and interact with another person in a deep, resonant manner, but you cannot talk with them. Further, the primary interaction you share is one of helping the other player move forward, instead of competing against them in an attempt to reach a mutually exclusive goal. The director of *Journey* argues that player interaction is structured by game design: "I believe that very often it's not really the player that's an asshole. It's the game designer that *made* them an asshole. If you spend every day killing one another how are you going to be a nice guy? All console games are about killing each other, or killing one another together. . . . Our games make us assholes."[27] *Journey* is designed with the explicit intent to cause players to interact positively; by changing how characters in the game interacted, *Journey* set up a system designed to encourage cooperation by awarding the most feedback to players for acts aiding others.[28] This parallels the kind of interactions Consalvo and Begy cite in *Faunasphere*: by focusing on something other than killing things, the terms of interaction change and the community can become more positive and helpful. Changing the terms for engagement and in-game incentive structures can have a massive impact on how players interact and what they choose to do.

Mountain is odd and challenging, especially as it is a game you do not really play. As an "ambient procedural mountain simulator," *Mountain* gives the player "nothing to 'play'; your mountain exists, sunlight and dark play over its green craggy face, weather happens to it. Occasionally a few words appear on the screen: The mountain has thoughts or feelings about the weather or the night."[29] In the end, *Mountain* is at least in part about talking and thinking about the experience of playing it. It has a certain kind of peace and leads some to wax eloquent about the game as a deep endurance challenge; others tend to uninstall it fairly quickly.[30] The game does have an end point, generally when the mountain is destroyed by something, but the riddle of *Mountain* lies mostly in the empty space of interaction between the player and the procedures generating the mountain. The player does not have any more control over the mountain than they do over an offline mountain; the game feels mainly like an inkblot that resists easy categorization. Even if a game like *Mountain* is quickly uninstalled, it is important and worthy of attention because it resists everything I thought a game could be.

There is also room for experimentation in game modes and design. When game companies design multiplayer modes, they have clear choices about how those modes will be played and the terms for interaction among players. From cooperative to competitive play, multiplayer can be designed in a number of ways, but the journalist Mark Serrels speaks for many when he notes that multiplayer modes in video games often make players "feel a little violent" because they often encounter situations where they face verbal harassment for making small mistakes, which is "not fun. Not fun at all. A huge barrier to entry. No-one likes to be shouted at or abused."[31] Multiplayer can be designed differently, however. Games like *Splatoon* and *Rocket League* are designed to make it okay for players to not be able to perform as well as others. Developing games that do not depend on killing, increasing the dynamics of the visual design, making the game quicker so players do not have to dwell on a loss, and giving players a clear role to play opens up opportunities and decreases the barriers to entry for new players. These kinds of chances offer up a version of multiplayer that is more like recreational sports leagues than competitive ones, which creates a multiplayer space where, Serrels argues, "everyone is playing, everyone's enjoying the experience. Even if you lose, even if you played terribly, everyone leaves happy. Everyone shakes hands at the end. Everyone is having a good time."[32] Multiplayer is a place where games still have room to innovate; the design choices made in those modes are a key factor in disrupting meritocratic norms and replacing them with collaboration and fun.

Although many of the games mentioned as positive examples could be readily classified as indie darlings, I certainly hope there are more interesting games coming on a much wider scale. For now, the independent game movement is largely where innovation in games is happening. This is likely because mainstream, AAA games now require massive budgets, which make publishers and developers exceptionally risk averse. Independent studios have more room for experimentation and exploration, so they often can take a chance and produce games that do not fit conventional norms. The important lesson that can be taken from these games is that non-meritocratic games can be designed, can be interesting, and can be successful. AAA games like *Borderlands 2* and the debut of the "Best Friends Forever" mode also demonstrate how innovation can happen across games, even if the debut of that particular mode was marred by the casual sexism of the discussion around it. Although I doubt that a few games here or there will resolve the toxicity in game culture, games like these change the terms on which players interact. There will still be jerks who play, as there are jerks everywhere, but dropping the meritocratic norms of video games puts players in a dramatically different position than they are in contemporary, mainstream games. Disrupting what currently exists is a fundamental part of addressing toxicity, which needs to reach beyond banning particular players to affect the design and narrative in the games themselves. The abandonment of meritocratic norms is likely what makes these games contentious for some, as it is readily apparent they symbolize a new future for video games.

Dear Game Designers

Changing the meritocratic norms in games and building better communities in games involves at least two major steps that can be learned from other areas where meritocracies are cracking and from the games that chart a different path for game design. The first piece of deconstructing the meritocratic norms in games is to infuse risk into or change the way competition works, particularly in single-player games. One of the key effects of the meritocratic design of games is that players are largely in control. Through their effort, skill, and persistence, they are assured a win. Competitive multiplayer takes away an assured victory, but the fault of the loss is not necessarily yours, as so many teammates are clearly performing worse than you are. Video games do not have to be this way. Early video games, like *Space Invaders* and *Donkey Kong*, did not have win conditions. Although classic arcade games often had kill screens, where the game simply stopped, the most common end state for almost all was that the game sped up to a point where the player was no longer able to keep up. Video games need the risk and contingency that, to some degree, come with sports, where players fundamentally understand that the success they see is not always their own. Serendipity and luck are primary ways to disrupt meritocratic game design, as minimizing elements of skill is part of a symbol system that stands in contrast to meritocracy. The other route is to follow the path of *Gone Home* and skip altogether the leaderboard, competition, and other elements that typify meritocratic video games. Opting out of meritocratic expectations changes both the experience of the game and the audience video games are likely to reach, all while providing a compelling product.

Developing games that have hints of meritocracy leads to bigger problems than one would think. Study after study, from Paul Piff's work with *Monopoly* to Robert H. Frank's work on skill and sharing, demonstrate how people who find themselves in a stronger position act terribly toward others.[33] Shannon K. McCoy and Brenda Major have found that any sort of meritocratic cue can cause those very human feelings to rise up, which disrupts efforts to develop a positive community around a game.[34] However, there is work that also shows the promise of a different approach. Inducing feelings of gratitude in players produces the opposite kind of response. When people are put into a state of gratitude, like when they acknowledge the role of luck in their success, Monica Y. Bartlett and David DeSteno have found they increase their efforts to help others, even if it costs them personally.[35] Even better, instead of the negative health benefits that come with meritocratic systems, Nancy Digdon and Amy Koble found that gratitude tends to make people feel better.[36] Perhaps most striking from a game design perspective, Nathan DeWall and his team of researchers found people put into a state of gratitude are more likely to feel empathy toward others and less likely to act aggressively when provoked.[37] Designing games with an eye toward prompting gratitude and reflection about good fortune is far more likely to encourage players to engage productively with one another. Instead of the relentless focus on the individual that comes with meritocracy, gratitude facilitates consideration of a group, of a larger system and the well-being of all.

A second way to disrupt the meritocracy is to think through how to seed and recruit new communities of people in an effort to detoxify games. As Richard Bartle noted long ago, when the community of a game falls out of balance, the attrition of certain player types can produce a death spiral in which no one is getting what they want out of a game.[38] Higher education demonstrates the value of recruitment, and some games have made similar efforts. *Monaco: What's Yours Is Mine* is a PC game in which players work together to execute a heist. Fundamentally a cooperative game, the efforts of any one player to subvert the mission would make the game far less fun for all of his or her teammates. The beta and early community of the game was seeded through special invitations given to active readers of *Rock, Paper, Shotgun*, with the intent of attracting positive players. Effectively, *Monaco's* developers sought to attract players seeking to play the game with other players in an effort to set positive norms before the title officially launched. In a game dependent on people working together, developing a positive community is a critical step that is far harder to fix after people have already seen negative behavior. Crafting a proper, nontoxic symbol system in advance of officially releasing the game at least gave *Monaco* and its players a chance to develop a supportive community.

Another way to think about achieving similar goals would be to take a lesson from sports and seek to include a broader representation of players, with the intent of benefiting the system in the long term, displacing a relentless focus on who is best right now. From the universality place that ensures representation from a broader range of countries to the NCAA bids given to small teams destined to get demolished in the first round of a basketball tournament, inclusivity has substantial benefits in competitive play. Finding ways to promote, celebrate, and advance players throughout the various skill levels can encourage others to see a path forward for themselves. When Riot relies on simply growing the player base of *League of Legends* to address issues of diversity, it misses opportunities to actually move things forward. Instead, it could seek out communities of people who play less or who are not as widely represented and give them a chance to participate on a prominent platform. An inclusive approach can spur the imagination and help players think about how they can become part of something larger, instead of lamenting that they simply cannot reach the heights of the best players in the game.

Our Obligation

There is no one, clear answer to fixing games. However, the videogame community stands apart in its willingness to attack its own. As I write, GamerGate is still ongoing—and I am sure that more will occur between when I write this and when you read this—but among the many takeaways from GamerGate is the undercurrent that those in the videogame community understand what is going on, but those outside it do not.[39] There are certainly elements of game journalism worthy of questioning—from the pro-consumption standpoint of most reviews to the money paid to YouTubers in exchange for favorable coverage of games and the promotion of questionably legal, assuredly rigged gambling sites through online videos—but, as a movement, GamerGate functions more like a mob of harassment than a bona fide organization for addressing structural problems in video games.[40] The general technology community calls it "the most depressing thing to have happened in games in quite some time," and larger, general-purpose publications refer to it as a "misogynist and racist movement" that should be considered a hate group: "There is no neutral stance to take on that—we are either with them or against them."[41] Videogame culture is insular, restricted, and toxic. There are real impacts to these kinds of campaigns beyond the people harassed and bullied out of covering video games—namely, many won't take on writing about video games as a topic in the first place. One journalist recounted talking to a colleague who was grateful for not covering video games even though "here is a guy who spends all day on the phone with officials from the Pentagon trying to ferret out which multi-billion dollar weapon systems are actually expensive boondoggles and, thanks to Gamergate, he's terrified to even spill a drop of virtual ink covering video games."[42] Toxic culture and repressive campaigns have the effect of pushing people out, silencing voices, and cutting off discussion. Reconstructing videogame culture requires recognizing that many talented, good people are being bullied and have stopped thinking about, writing about, and playing games before they even started. Although some people at the heart of GamerGate have been linked to misogynist, white supremacist, and other hate campaigns, the videogame community provided a fertile ground within which to attract adherents to their message and sustain the effort long past its sell-by date.

Games have been telling gamers for a long time that if they are good enough and work hard enough they will have earned the wins they collect at the end of the level. There is no single cause to all these problems, but these concerns are closely linked to the kinds of issues Michael Young originally hypothesized would occur under a meritocracy. The hate, the lack of understanding, the feelings of superiority, all these elements are tightly linked to symbol systems related to merit and earning one's advancements. As Whitney Phillips observed about trolls and discourse online, it is often the systems and structures that need to be addressed, as changing problematic norms is a key factor in addressing troublesome communities.

The job of rhetorical analysis is to disrupt moments like this one in video games. Rhetorical criticism is well designed to assess a symbol system and how it works to enable certain kinds of appeals and discourage others. The new perspective that can be given by rhetoric is similar to the direct engagement that can be furthered by certain kinds of education. In advocating for the active learning that often typifies a Jesuit education, Rev. Peter-Hans Kolvenbach explained that "when the heart is touched by direct experience, the mind may be challenged to change."[43] The beautiful thing about video games is that they can provide a direct experience for their players. The horrible thing is that they have primarily offered only a limited, meritocratic experience. However, there is plenty of room for change. Addressing toxicity in games requires taking on the meritocratic design and narratives woven within them. Certain games and elements of other parts of culture give a roadmap for how video games can change, which can disrupt what exists now with something new. I hope that is a journey we, as a part of videogame culture, take on in order to make video games a more accepting, less toxic place. It is dangerous for any of us to go alone, so we must gather what resources we can to make video games and game culture better. We have an obligation and an opportunity to fix a desperately broken system. It's time for change. We can do it. We need to do it. Let's get started.

Acknowledgments

Although my name is the one on the cover of this book, there are many people without whom this project simply could not have happened. Thank you to everyone who helped make this possible.

The initial seeds of this project began in the Arrupe Seminar at Seattle University. Thank you to Father Peter Ely, SJ, and Jennifer Tilghman-Havens for being exceptional moderators and to all of my Arrupe group mates. I would not have thought about this project in the way I did without the Arrupe Seminar. Funding for the beginning of this project came as a part of a Seattle University College of Arts and Sciences Dean's Research Fellowship. Thank you to Anina Walas and Katheryn Smith for rocking your projects. Thanks to the colleagues in my department for supporting my work.

Professional feedback at many conferences and presentations was incredibly valuable. My first presentation on this topic was given as part of an invitation by Mia Consalvo at her M-Lab at Concordia University. Thank you to Mia for offering the opportunity to present the work in a nascent stage and to all who attended. In particular, Bart Simon made huge contributions to the early stages of my thinking, and many of my responses to his comments show up in the final version of the work. Thank you to Adrienne Shaw for answering all of my questions about the University of Minnesota Press. Thank you to all who made contributions or comments that helped push and adapt my thinking or provided an example for how to think about these concepts. Substantial credit for the quality of the arguments in the book is due to the contributions of its reviewers: Mia Consalvo, Torill Mortensen, Carly Kocurek, and the anonymous "Reviewer 2." Thank you to Cathy Hannabach and Emma Johnson at Ideas on First for the awesome index.

The University of Minnesota Press has been amazing throughout this process. I am deeply indebted to Jason Weidemann, who gave great advice for my first book; I am so glad we got to work together on this one. His comments on the manuscript were insightful and provocative, and he definitely made the book better. Danielle Kasprzak and Erin Warholm gave great guidance and feedback, and I hope to work with them more in the future. Nicholas Taylor and Mike Stoffel deserve credit for quality copyediting. Thanks to Daniel Ochsner for moving the book through the production process. Thank you to everyone at the Press who made this possible and consistently made it a better book.

Thank you to all the people who kept me going and asked good questions. Thank you to Fatima Azami and everyone at Mother's Place for watching Piper. Thank you to Caitlin Ring Carlson for running and keeping me sane, and to Wayno for driving us to races and introducing me to SWGOH. Thanks to Rick Malleus for helping me keep perspective. Thank you to Beth Slattery for providing the first feedback on the written version of this project. Thank you to Melissa Marion Rosenberry and my best friend, Suzanne, for keeping me laughing. Thank you to Martha Aby for quality walks and talks. Thanks to Eleanor, Addy, Amy, and Beth Meyer for helping me keep perspective on life. Thanks to the fine folks at Georgetown Brewery, particularly Lauren and Max, for keeping me hydrated. Thank you to the people involved in *Lost* and *Battlestar Galactica*, who gave me something to watch as I wrote.

Most of all, thank you to my family. Lisa, your constant requests for a dedication amused me. Maybe one of these days. Mom and Dad, thanks for asking questions, giving feedback, and supporting me. I appreciate it. Thanks to the Minnesota crew of Trudie Harris, Greg Harris, Richard Wieser, and Ashley Wieser for making each trip there fun. Thanks to Casey Byrne and Chris Lott. Thank you to Adam Conway. Most of all, thank you to Erin, Piper, and Ingrid. I could not do what I do without you three. Thank you so much for all you add to life.

Notes

Introduction

1. Taylor Wofford, "APA Says Video Games Make You Violent, but Critics Cry Bias," *Newsweek*, 20 August 2015, http://www.newsweek.com/apa-video-games-violence-364394.

2. Tom Chatfield, "Videogames Now Outperform Hollywood Movies," *The Guardian*, 27 September 2009, http://www.theguardian.com/technology/gamesblog/2009/sep/27/videogames-hollywood; Aphra Kerr, *The Business and Culture of Digital Games: Gamework and Gameplay* (London: Sage, 2006).

3. In this text I generally use videogame culture and the culture around video games as interchangeable terms. I contend that there is a culture around video games that is distinct from other cultures. Although the people participating in the culture around video games are also part of other cultures, the interactions around video games offer a specific set of common texts and experiences. It is important to remember that videogame culture is certainly affected by other cultural norms, including meritocracy, norms and practices of the internet, and various other social and cultural factors. This culture is largely populated by people who would describe themselves as gamers and is often referred to as a hardcore audience for video games.

4. Keith Stuart, "Gamer Communities: The Positive Side," *The Guardian*, 31 July 2014, http://www.theguardian.com/technology/gamesblog/2013/jul/31/gamer-communities-positive-side-twitter.

5. Leigh Alexander, "GDC Online: Bartle on *MUD*'s 'Soul,' Design 'Must Want to Say Something,'" *Gamasutra*, 8 October 2010, http://www.gamasutra.com/view/news/121595/GDC_Online_Bartle_On_MUDs_Soul_Design_Must_Want_To_Say_Something.php.

6. Simon Parkin, "The Man Who Made a Game to Change the World," *Eurogamer*, 30 October 2014, http://www.eurogamer.net/articles/2014-10-30 -the-utopia-that-never-died.

7. Ibid.

8. Chief Pat, "The State of Clash Royale," *YouTube*, 15 July 2016, https:// www.youtube.com/watch?v=C_vHdhSgGmw.

9. PandabBoj, "What Part of This Game Is Fun Exactly?" *Clash Royale Forum*, 27 July 2016, http://forum.supercell.net/showthread.php/1213578 -What-part-of-this-game-is-fun-exactly; QuaternionsRock, "Legendaries Are Slowly Breaking the Game (Not Just Another Rant Post)," reddit, 27 July 2016, https://www.reddit.com/r/ClashRoyale/comments/4uvxbc/legendaries_are_ slowly_breaking_the_game_not_just/.

10. International Game Developers Association, "Game Developer De- mographics: An Exploration of Workforce Diversity," October 2005, http://c .ymcdn.com/sites/www.igda.org/resource/collection/9215B88F-2AA3-4471 -B44D-B5D58FF25DC7/IGDA_DeveloperDemographics_Oct05.pdf.

11. International Game Developers Association, "Developer Satisfaction Sur- vey 2015: Summary Report," 2 September 2015, https://c.ymcdn.com/sites/www .igda.org/resource/collection/CB31CE86-F8EE-4AE3-B46A-148490336605/ IGDA%20DSS%202015-SummaryReport_Final_Sept15.pdf.

12. Robin Potanin, "Forces in Play: The Business and Culture of Videogame Production," in *Fun and Games '10: Proceedings of the 3rd International Confer- ence on Fun and Games*, ed. Vero Vanden Abeele et al. (New York: ACM, 2010), 138.

13. Matthew Handrahan, "Ubisoft: Creativity and Commerce in AAA Devel- opment," *Games Industry*, 28 June 2016, http://www.gamesindustry.biz/articles /2016-06-28-ubisoft-creativity-and-commerce-in-aaa-development.

14. Paul Tamburro, "Top 10 Most Memorable GTA Characters," *Crave*, 2 November 2012, http://www.craveonline.com/site/198965-top-10-most-mem orable-gta-characters.

15. Arthur Chu, "It's Dangerous to Go Alone: Why Are Gamers So Angry?" *The Daily Beast*, 28 August 2014, http://www.thedailybeast.com/articles/2014 /08/28/it-s-dangerous-to-go-alone-why-are-gamers-so-angry.html.

16. Paul Kennedy, "The Dangerous Game: Gamergate and the 'Alt-Right,'" *CBC Radio*, 30 November 2016, http://www.cbc.ca/radio/ideas/the-dangerous -game-gamergate-and-the-alt-right-1.3874259.

17. Whitney Phillips, *This Is Why We Can't Have Nice Things: Mapping the Relationship between Online Trolling and Mainstream Culture* (Cambridge, Mass.: MIT Press, 2015), 11.

18. The website *100 People: A World Portrait* tracks breakdowns in what our lives would be like if we were a village of one hundred people; see http://www

.100people.org/statistics_100stats.php. This is also one of Father Steven Sundborg's favorite anecdotes to use in his speeches.

19. Kovie Biakolo, "The Lie of Meritocracy and the Illusion of the American Dream," *Thought Catalog*, 8 January 2014, http://thoughtcatalog.com/kovie-biakolo/2014/01/the-lie-of-meritocracy-and-the-illusion-of-the-american-dream/; Christopher L. Hayes, *Twilight of the Elites: America after Meritocracy* (New York: Crown, 2012); Leanne S. Son Hing, D. Ramona Bobocel, and Mark P. Zanna, "Meritocracy and Opposition to Affirmative Action: Making Concessions in the Face of Discrimination," *Journal of Personality and Social Psychology* 83, no. 3 (2002): 493–509; Leanne S. Son Hing, D. Ramona Bobocel, Mark P. Zanna, Donna M. Garcia, Stephanie S. Gee, and Katie Orazietti, "The Merit of Meritocracy," *Journal of Personality and Social Psychology* 101, no. 3 (2011): 433–50.

20. Matthew H. Barton and Paul D. Turman, "VH1's 'Behind the Music' and American Culture: The Role of Myth in a Meritocracy," *Texas Speech Communication Journal* 34 (Summer 2009): 8–23; Jennifer Goodman, "The Meritocracy Myth: National Exams and the Depoliticization of Thai Education," *Sojourn: Journal of Social Issues in Southeast Asia* 28, no. 1 (2013): 101–31; Naa Oyo A. Kwate and Ilan H. Meyer, "The Myth of Meritocracy and African American Health," *American Journal of Public Health* 100, no. 10 (2010): 1831–34; Stephen J. McNamee and Robert K. Miller, *The Meritocracy Myth* (Lanham, Md.: Rowman & Littlefield, 2004).

21. Dylan Matthews, "Donald Trump Isn't Rich Because He's a Great Investor: He's Rich Because His Dad Was Rich," *Vox*, 2 September 2015, http://www.vox.com/2015/9/2/9248963/donald-trump-index-fund.

22. Ezra Klein, "Ta-Nehisi Coates: 'I'm a Big Believer in Chaos,'" *Vox*, 19 December 2016, http://www.vox.com/conversations/2016/12/19/13952578/ta-nehisi-coates-ezra-klein.

23. Glenn Kessler, "Trump's False Claim He Built His Empire with a 'Small Loan' from His Father," *Washington Post*, 20 December 2016, https://www.washingtonpost.com/news/fact-checker/wp/2016/03/03/trumps-false-claim-he-built-his-empire-with-a-small-loan-from-his-father/.

24. Alex Abad-Santos, "Donald Trump and Kim Kardashian Are Kindred Spirits," *Vox*, 19 December 2016, http://www.vox.com/culture/2016/12/19/13956596/donald-trump-kim-kardashian-kindred-spirits.

25. Henry Farrell, "How the Chris Hayes Book Twilight of the Elites Explains Trump's Appeal," *Vox*, 13 October 2016, http://www.vox.com/the-big-idea/2016/10/13/13259860/twilight-elites-trump-meritocracy.

26. Daniel Bell, *The Coming of Post-Industrial Society: A Venture in Social Forecasting* (New York: Basic Books, 1973), 453; Michael Young, *The Rise of the Meritocracy* (1958; repr., New Brunswick, N.J.: Transaction, 2008).

27. Peter Saunders, "Might Britain Be a Meritocracy?" *Sociology* 29, no. 1 (1995): 27.

28. Peter Saunders, "Social Mobility in Britain: An Empirical Evaluation of Two Competing Explanations," *Sociology* 31, no. 2 (1997): 283.

29. Sigal Alon and Marta Tienda, "Diversity, Opportunity, and the Shifting Meritocracy in Higher Education," *American Sociological Review* 72, no. 4 (2007): 489.

30. Jo Littler, "Celebrity and 'Meritocracy,'" *Soundings* 26 (Spring 2004): 122.

31. Jo Littler, "Meritocracy as Plutocracy: The Marketing of 'Equality' under Neoliberalism," *New Formations* 80–81 (2013): 52.

32. Ruth Levitas, "Shuffling Back to Equality?" *Soundings* 26 (Spring 2004): 69.

33. Littler, "Meritocracy as Plutocracy," 54.

34. Son Hing, Bobocel, and Zanna, "Meritocracy and Opposition to Affirmative Action," 433.

35. Phillips, *This Is Why We Can't Have Nice Things*; Adrienne Shaw, "The Internet Is Full of Jerks, Because the World Is Full of Jerks: What Feminist Theory Teaches Us about the Internet," *Communication and Critical/Cultural Studies* 11, no. 3 (2014): 273–77.

36. Amanda Hess, "Why Women Aren't Welcome on the Internet," *Pacific Standard*, 6 January 2014, http://www.psmag.com/navigation/health-and-behavior/women-arent-welcome-internet-72170/.

37. Laura Hudson, "That *Game of Thrones* Scene Wasn't a 'Turn-On,' It Was Rape," *Wired*, 21 April 2014, http://www.wired.com/2014/04/game-of-thrones-rape/; Maureen Ryan, "'Tyrant's' Rape Cliches Are Just the Last Straw," *Huffington Post*, 24 June 2014, http://www.huffingtonpost.com/2014/06/24/tyrant-fx_n_5525441.html.

38. Zeynep Tufekci, "No, Nate, Brogrammers May Not Be Macho, but That's Not All There Is to It," *The Message*, 19 March 2014, https://medium.com/technology-and-society/2f1fe84c5c9b.

39. Lea Coligado, "A Female Computer Science Major at Stanford: 'Floored' by the Sexism," *Fortune*, 17 February 2015, http://fortune.com/2015/02/17/a-female-computer-science-major-at-stanford-floored-by-the-sexism/; Michelle Goldberg, "Feminist Writers Are So Besieged by Online Abuse That Some Have Begun to Retire," *Washington Post*, 20 February 2015, https://www.washingtonpost.com/opinions/online-feminists-increasingly-ask-are-the-psychic-costs-too-much-to-bear/2015/02/19/3dc4ca6c-b7dd-11e4-a200-c008a01a6692_story.html; Hess, "Why Women Aren't Welcome on the Internet"; Ellen Pao, "Former Reddit CEO Ellen Pao: The Trolls Are Winning the Battle for the Internet," *Washington Post*, 16 July 2015, https://www.washingtonpost.com/opinions/we-cannot-let-the-internet-trolls

-win/2015/07/16/91b1a2d2-2b17-11e5-bd33-395c05608059_story.html; Julia Carrie Wong, "Women Considered Better Coders—but Only If They Hide Their Gender," *The Guardian*, 12 February 2016, http://www.theguardian .com/technology/2016/feb/12/women-considered-better-coders-hide-gender -github.

40. Leigh Alexander, "EA's LGBT Event Aims to Be a First Step toward Cultural Change," *Gamasutra*, 7 March 2013, http://www.gamasutra.com/view/ news/187769/EAs_LBGT_event_aims_to_be_a_first_step_toward_cultural_ change.php; Mia Consalvo, "Confronting Toxic Gamer Culture: A Challenge for Feminist Game Studies Scholars," *Ada*, November 2012, http://adanewmedia .org/2012/11/issue1-consalvo/; Adrienne Shaw, "Changing the Conversation, Not Just the Games," *Antenna*, 12 March 2013, http://blog.commarts.wisc .edu/2013/03/12/changing-the-conversation-not-just-the-games/; John Walker, "Misogyny, Sexism, and Why RPS Isn't Shutting Up," *Rock, Paper, Shotgun*, 6 April 2013, http://www.rockpapershotgun.com/2013/04/06/misogyny-sexism -and-why-rps-isnt-shutting-up/.

41. Jenny Haniver, "About," *Not in the Kitchen Anymore*, 21 February 2016, http://www.notinthekitchenanymore.com/about/; gtz jaspir, likeOMGitsFE- DAY, and inklesspen, "Fat, Ugly, or Slutty," n.d., *Fat, Ugly, or Slutty*, http:// fatuglyorslutty.com/.

42. Amanda Marcotte, "Online Misogyny: Can't Ignore It, Can't Not Ig- nore It," *Slate*, 13 June 2012, http://www.slate.com/blogs/xx_factor/2012/06/13/ online_misogyny_reflects_women_s_realities_though_in_a_cruder_way_than_ is_customary_offline_.html.

43. Consalvo, "Confronting Toxic Gamer Culture"; Mathew Jones, "Com- ments Aren't Disabled: Here's What People Are Saying about Tropes vs. Women," *Gameranx*, 8 March 2013, http://www.gameranx.com/features/ id/13300/article/comments-aren-t-disabled-here-s-what-people-are-saying -about-tropes-vs-women/.

44. Leigh Alexander, "Opinion: In the Sexism Discussion, Let's Look at Game Culture," *Gamasutra*, 16 July 2012, http://www.gamasutra.com/view/ news/174145/.

45. Chu, "It's Dangerous to Go Alone."

46. Film Crit Hulk, "Film Crit Hulk Smash: on despair, gamergate and quitting the hulk," *Badass Digest*, 27 October 2014, http://badassdigest .com/2014/10/27/film-crit-hulk-smash-on-despair-gamergate-and-quitting -the-hulk/.

47. Maeve Duggan, "Online Harassment," *Pew Research Center: Internet, Sci- ence & Tech*, 22 October 2014, http://www.pewinternet.org/2014/10/22/online -harassment/.

48. Edge Staff, "Why Is the Game Industry Still Fixated on Breasts?" *Edge*

Online, 15 March 2013, http://www.edge-online.com/features/why-is-the-game -industry-still-fixated-on-breasts/.

49. Rory Young, "Team Ninja Studio Head Says DOA 5's Female Depiction Is Cultural," *Neoseeker*, 23 August 2012, http://www.neoseeker.com/news/20486 -team-ninja-studio-head-says-doa-5s-female-depiction-is-cultural/.

50. Becky Chambers, "Why Games with Female Protagonists Don't Sell, and What It Says about the Industry," *The Mary Sue*, 23 November 2012, http:// www.themarysue.com/why-games-with-female-protagonists-dont-sell-and -what-it-says-about-the-industry/.

51. Rich McCormick, "Adding Female Characters to New 'Assassin's Creed' Would 'Double the Work,' Says Ubisoft," *The Verge*, 11 June 2014, http://www .theverge.com/2014/6/11/5799386/no-female-characters-in-assassins-creed -unity-too-much-work; Rachel Weber, "Naughty Dog: We've Been Asked to Push Ellie to the Back of the Box Art," *Games Industry*, 12 December 2012, http://www.gamesindustry.biz/articles/2012-12-12-naughty-dog-theres-a -misconception-that-if-you-put-a-girl-on-the-cover-the-game-sells-less; Mike Williams, "Rockstar's Houser Explains Lack of Female Protagonist in GTA V," *Games Industry*, 10 September 2013, http://www.gamesindustry.biz/articles /2013-09-10-rockstars-houser-explains-lack-of-female-protagonist-in-gta-v.

52. Nathan Ditum, "FIFA's Struggle to Include Women Reveals a Lot about Gaming's Problems with Diversity," *Kotaku*, 15 July 2015, http://www.kotaku.co .uk/2015/07/15/fifas-struggle-to-include-women-reveals-a-lot-about-gamings -problems-with-diversity.

53. Evan Narcisse, "Video Games' Blackness Problem," *Kotaku*, 19 February 2015, http://kotaku.com/video-games-blackness-problem-1686694082.

54. Tauriq Moosa, "Colorblind: On The Witcher 3, Rust, and Gaming's Race Problem," *Polygon*, 3 June 2015, http://www.polygon.com/2015/6/3/8719389/ colorblind-on-witcher-3-rust-and-gamings-race-problem.

55. Ibid.

56. Sidney Fussell, "Video Games without People of Color Are Not 'Neutral,'" *Offworld*, 26 June 2015, http://boingboing.net/2015/06/26/race-video -games-witcher-3.html.

57. Don Crothers, "GamerGate Drives Critic Tauriq Moosa Off Twitter," *Inquisitr*, 27 June 2015, http://www.inquisitr.com/2207377/gamergate-drives -critic-tauriq-moosa-off-twitter/; Jessica Lachenal, "#IStandWithTauriq: Tauriq Moosa Leaves Twitter After Sustained Harassment Campaign Led by Gamer-Gate," *The Mary Sue*, 27 June 2015, http://www.themarysue.com/i-stand-with -tauriq/.

58. Potanin, "Forces in Play," 136.

59. Ibid., 140, 141.

60. Carly A. Kocurek, *Coin-Operated Americans: Rebooting Boyhood at the Video Game Arcade* (Minneapolis: University of Minnesota Press, 2015), 188.

61. Kishonna L. Gray, *Race, Gender, and Deviance in Xbox Live: Theoretical Perspectives from the Virtual Margins* (New York: Routledge, 2014), 16.

62. Ibid.

63. Nathan Grayson, "Twitch Chat Racism Changed *Hearthstone* Pro Terrence Miller's Career," *Kotaku*, 7 October 2016, http://kotaku.com/hearthstone-pro-terrence-miller-hopes-to-clean-up-twitc-1787551043.

64. Mia Consalvo and Christopher A. Paul, "Welcome to the Discourse of the Real: Constituting the Boundaries of Games and Players," *FDG* (2013): 55–62.

65. Adrienne Shaw, *Gaming at the Edge: Sexuality and Gender at the Margins of Gamer Culture* (Minneapolis: University of Minnesota Press, 2014).

66. Stephanie Llamas, "Why all Gamers Matter—My View as a Female Games Analyst," *Superdata*, 28 October 2014, http://www.superdataresearch.com/blog/why-all-gamers-matter/.

67. To view the opening cinematics and early game play, see kingdavidgaming, "The Beginning of Skyrim (Part 1)" and "The Beginning of Skyrim (Part 2)," *YouTube*, 12 November 2011, https://www.youtube.com/watch?v=5Cdoyqs NdaE and https://www.youtube.com/watch?v=MiqjhkpNqg8.

68. Statistic Brain, "Skyrim: The Elder Scrolls V Statistics," *Statistic Brain*, 12 April 2015, http://www.statisticbrain.com/skyrim-the-elder-scrolls-v-statistics/.

69. For more on rhetoric, see Ian Bogost, "Writing Books People Want to Read: Or, How to Stake Vampire Publishing," *Ian Bogost*, 30 May 2011, http://bogost.com/writing/blog/writing_books_people_want_to_r/; Ian Bogost, "The Rhetoric of Video Games," in *The Ecology of Games: Connecting Youth, Games, and Learning*, ed. Katie Salen, 117–39 (Cambridge, Mass.: MIT Press, 2008); Kenneth Burke, *A Rhetoric of Motives* (Berkeley, CA: University of California Press, 1969); Karlyn Kohrs Campbell and Susan Schultz Huxman, *The Rhetorical Act: Thinking, Speaking, and Writing Critically* (Belmont, Calif.: Thomson/Wadsworth, 2009); Ronald Greene, "The Aesthetic Turn and the Rhetorical Perspective on Argumentation," *Argumentation & Advocacy* 35, no. 1 (1998): 19; Todd Harper, "Rules, Rhetoric, and Genre: Procedural Rhetoric in Persona 3," *Games and Culture* 6, no. 5 (2011): 395–413; Christopher A. Paul, *Wordplay and the Discourse of Video Games: Analyzing Words, Design, and Play* (New York: Routledge, 2012); Edward Schiappa, "Second Thoughts on the Critiques of Big Rhetoric," *Philosophy and Rhetoric* 34, no. 3 (2001): 260–74; Robert L. Scott, "On Viewing Rhetoric as Epistemic," *Central States Speech Journal* 18, no. 1 (1967): 9–17; Gerald A. Voorhees, "The Character of Difference: Procedurality, Rhet-

oric, and Roleplaying Games," *Game Studies* 9, no. 2 (2009): http://gamestudies
.org/0902/articles/voorhees; David Zarefsky, "Knowledge Claims in Rhetorical
Criticism," *Journal of Communication* 58, no. 4 (2008): 629–40.

70. For a thorough explanation of "The Journey" and how it plays in practice, see Chris Tapsell, "FIFA 17 The Journey Walkthrough—How to Play a
Full Season and Get All Rewards," *Eurogamer*, 25 November 2016, http://www
.eurogamer.net/articles/2016-11-25-fifa-17-the-journey-walkthrough-how
-to-play-a-full-season-and-get-all-rewards. Also, the mode was not included
in PS3 and Xbox 360 versions of the game, as EA claimed there were technical limitations with the older consoles, likely having to do with their use of the
Frostbite game engine.

1. Leveling Up in Life

1. Henry Farrell, "How the Chris Hayes Book Twilight of the Elites
Explains Trump's Appeal," *Vox*, 13 October 2016, http://www.vox.com/the-
big-idea/2016/10/13/13259860/twilight-elites-trump-meritocracy.

2. The Guodian manuscripts are tremendously informative about ancient
China, to the point where it has been said that they transformed "our understanding of the formative era of China's religious and political philosophy." See
Kenneth Holloway, *Guodian: The Newly Discovered Seeds of Chinese Religious
and Political Philosophy* (New York: Oxford University Press, 2009), 1.

3. Ibid., 13, 14, 110, 130.

4. Benjamin A. Elman, *Civil Examinations and Meritocracy in Late Imperial
China* (Cambridge, Mass.: Harvard University Press, 2013), 1.

5. The most thorough integrations of meritocracy that I have read about
in China happened during the T'ang (618–906), Ming (1368–1644), and Qing
(1644–1912) dynasties. There are also some mentions of a move toward meritocracy in the Sui dynasty (581–618). For more, see Denis Twitchett, *The Birth
of Chinese Meritocracy: Bureaucrats and Examinations in T'ang China* (London:
China Society, 1976).

6. Elman, *Civil Examinations and Meritocracy in Late Imperial China*, 316.

7. Robin Potanin, "Forces in Play: The Business and Culture of Videogame
Production," in *Fun and Games '10: Proceedings of the 3rd International Conference on Fun and Games*, ed. Vero Vanden Abeele et al. (New York: ACM, 2010),
135–43. Another excellent argument from a similar perspective is Janine Fron,
Tracy Fullerton, Jacquelyn Ford Morie, and Celia Pearce, "The Hegemony of
Play," *DiGRA '07: Proceedings of the 2007 DiGRA International Conference: Situated Play* 4 (September 2007): 1–10.

8. The first published use of the term I have seen actually comes in the
writing of Alan Fox, who wrote an essay called "Class and Equality" for *Socialist
Quarterly* two years before Young's book. Fox's use of the term is overwhelm-

ingly negative, as the meritocracy is seen as an extension of a social system that furthered the "distance between the extremes of the social strata." Fox also casts meritocracy in moral terms, with those at the top taking advantage of the "unblessed" and not recognizing that they are "blessed." See Alan Fox, "Class and Equality," *Socialist Commentary*, May 1956, 11–13.

9. Michael Young, *The Rise of the Meritocracy* (1958; repr., New Brunswick, N.J.: Transaction, 2008), xvii.

10. Patricia Hernandez, "*Overwatch*: The *Kotaku* Review," *Kotaku*, 1 June 2016, http://kotaku.com/overwatch-the-kotaku-review-1779831636.

11. Ibid.

12. Nathan Grayson, "*Overwatch* Doesn't Do Enough for Its Support Heroes," *Kotaku*, 1 June 2016, http://kotaku.com/overwatch-doesnt-do-enough-for-its-support-heroes-1779909864; Philippa Warr, "Overwatch: Why We Need a 2-Person Play of the Game," *Rock, Paper, Shotgun*, 31 May 2016, https://www.rockpapershotgun.com/2016/05/31/overwatch-play-of-the-game/.

13. Grayson, "*Overwatch* Doesn't Do Enough for Its Support Heroes."

14. Nathan Grayson, "The *Overwatch* Characters Who Get Play of the Game Most (and Least) Often," *Kotaku*, 7 September 2016, http://kotaku.com/the-overwatch-characters-who-get-play-of-the-game-most-1786354626.

15. Nathan Grayson, "*Overwatch*'s Director on Competitive Mode, Controversies, and the Future," *Kotaku*, 18 July 2016, http://kotaku.com/overwatchs-director-on-competitive-controversies-and-1783869335.

16. Ibid.

17. Blizzard Entertainment, "Welcome to Competitive Play," *Overwatch*, 28 June 2016, https://playoverwatch.com/en-us/blog/20167051.

18. Nathan Grayson, "How *Overwatch*'s Competitive Mode Works," *Kotaku*, 29 June 2016, http://kotaku.com/how-overwatchs-competitive-mode-works-1782839858.

19. Patricia Hernandez, "*Overwatch* Fans Have Turned Soldier 76 into a Dad," *Kotaku*, 29 July 2016, http://kotaku.com/overwatch-fans-have-turned-soldier-76-into-a-dad-1784531869.

20. Nathan Grayson, "*Overwatch*'s Competitive Mode Is at Odds with the Rest of the Game," *Kotaku*, 1 July 2016, http://kotaku.com/overwatchs-competitive-mode-is-at-odds-with-the-rest-of-1782990226.

21. Ibid.

22. InternetBitch6969, "Competitive Community Is Mostly Toxic," reddit, 1 July 2016, https://www.reddit.com/r/Overwatch/comments/4qsntg/competitive_community_is_mostly_toxic/.

23. Nathan Grayson, "How Blizzard Is Trying to Fix *Overwatch*'s Toxicity Problem," *Kotaku*, 15 July 2016, http://kotaku.com/how-blizzard-is-trying-to-fix-overwatchs-toxicity-probl-1783749976.

24. Ibid.

25. Whitney Phillips, *This Is Why We Can't Have Nice Things: Mapping the Relationship between Online Trolling and Mainstream Culture* (Cambridge, Mass.: MIT Press, 2015).

26. Geoff Colvin, "A CEO's Passionate Defense of 'Stack Ranking' Employees," *Fortune*, 19 November 2013, http://fortune.com/2013/11/19/a-ceos-passion ate-defense-of-stack-ranking-employees/; Jodi Kantor and David Streitfeld, "Inside Amazon: Wrestling Big Ideas in a Bruising Workplace," *New York Times*, 15 August 2015, https://www.nytimes.com/2015/08/16/technology/inside-amazon -wrestling-big-ideas-in-a-bruising-workplace.html.

27. Young, *Rise of the Meritocracy*, 96.

28. Michael Young, "Down with Meritocracy," *The Guardian*, 28 June 2001, http://www.guardian.co.uk/politics/2001/jun/29/comment.

29. Nathan Grayson, "The Guy with the Lowest Possible Rank in *Overwatch*," *Kotaku*, 23 August 2016, http://kotaku.com/the-guy-with-the-lowest -possible-rank-in-overwatch-1785662123.

30. Ibid.

31. Jesper Juul, *The Art of Failure: An Essay on the Pain of Playing Video Games* (Cambridge, Mass.: MIT Press, 2013), 81.

32. Ibid., 1.

33. David Harvey summarizes many of these changes, arguing that the acceleration of consumption in modern society was driven by two key factors that permeated society: the expansion of mass markets in video and children's games, and a transition toward the consumption of services and away from the consumption of goods. For more, see David Harvey, *The Condition of Postmodernity* (Oxford, U.K.: Basil Blackwell, 1989).

34. Young, "Down with Meritocracy."

35. Christopher L. Hayes, *Twilight of the Elites: America after Meritocracy* (New York: Crown, 2012), 45.

36. Robert Guthrie, "Inside the Grim World of *Minecraft*'s Prison Servers," *Kotaku*, 24 June 2016, http://kotaku.com/inside-the-grim-world-of-minecrafts -prison-servers-1782517890.

37. Ibid.

38. Young, *Rise of the Meritocracy*, xi.

39. Ibid., xi–xii.

40. Daniel Bell, "On Meritocracy and Equality," *Public Interest* 29 (Fall 1972): 30.

41. R. J. Herrnstein, *I.Q. in the Meritocracy* (Boston: Little, Brown, 1971), 221–22.

42. Daniel Bell, *The Coming of Post-Industrial Society: A Venture in Social Forecasting* (New York: Basic Books, 1973), 426–27.

43. Bell consistently uses the universal "man" to refer to all people. Claiming that there are not substantial structural barriers to exhibiting skill and effort is particularly rich when relying on sexist language to make the case.

44. Herrnstein, *I.Q. in the Meritocracy*, 221.

45. Peter Saunders, "Social Mobility in Britain: An Empirical Evaluation of Two Competing Explanations," *Sociology* 31, no. 2 (1997): 282.

46. Bell, "On Meritocracy and Equality," 31–32.

47. Ibid., 40.

48. Ibid., 67.

49. Saunders, "Social Mobility in Britain," 562.

50. Bell, *Coming of Post-Industrial Society*, 454.

51. Stephen J. McNamee and Robert K. Miller, "The Meritocracy Myth," *Sociation Today* 2, no. 1 (2004): 3.

52. Ibid., 4.

53. Naa Oyo A. Kwate and Ilan H. Meyer, "The Myth of Meritocracy and African American Health," *American Journal of Public Health* 100, no. 10 (2010): 1831–34.

54. Jo Littler, "Celebrity and 'Meritocracy,'" *Soundings* 26 (Spring 2004): 60.

55. Ibid.

56. Meritocracy and meritocratic norms can also be seen in plenty of other contexts and in many other countries. For more, see Livia Barbosa, "Meritocracy and Brazilian Society," *Revista de Administração de Empresas* 54, no. 1 (2014): 80–85; Jennifer Goodman, "The Meritocracy Myth: National Exams and the Depoliticization of Thai Education," *Sojourn: Journal of Social Issues in Southeast Asia* 28, no. 1 (2013): 101–31; Surinder S. Jodhka and Katherine Newman, "In the Name of Globalisation: Meritocracy, Productivity and the Hidden Language of Caste," *Economic and Political Weekly* 42, no. 41 (2007): 4125–32; Takehiko Kariya, *Education Reform, and Social Class in Japan: The Emerging Incentive Divide*, trans. Michael Burtscher (New York: Routledge, 2013); Kenneth Paul Tan, "Meritocracy and Elitism in a Global City: Ideological Shifts in Singapore," *International Political Science Review* 29, no. 1 (2008): 7–27; Godfrey B. Tangwa, *Road Companion to Democracy and Meritocracy: Further Essays from an African Perspective* (Bamenda, Cameroon: Langaa RPCIG, 2010).

57. Hayes, *Twilight of the Elites*, 22.

58. Shannon K. McCoy and Brenda Major, "Priming Meritocracy and the Psychological Justification of Inequality," *Journal of Experimental Social Psychology* 43, no. 3 (2007): 341.

59. John Beck, *Meritocracy, Citizenship and Education: New Labour's Legacy* (London: Continuum, 2008), 25.

60. Kwate and Meyer, "Myth of Meritocracy and African American Health."

61. Richard Breen and John H. Goldthorpe, "Class Inequality and Meritocracy: A Critique of Saunders and an Alternative Analysis," *British Journal of Sociology* 50, no. 1 (1999): 22.

62. Brian Ashcraft, "Korean Woman Kicks Ass at *Overwatch*, Gets Accused of Cheating [Update]," *Kotaku*, 21 June 2016, http://kotaku.com/korean-woman-kicks-ass-at-overwatch-gets-accused-of-ch-1782343447.

63. Aja Romano, "How a Teen Girl's Mad Overwatch Skills Struck a Major Blow to Sexism in Gaming," *Vox*, 23 June 2016, http://www.vox.com/2016/6/23/12002454/how-a-teen-girl-s-mad-overwatch-skills-struck-a-major-blow-to-sexism-in-gaming.

64. Ashcraft, "Korean Woman Kicks Ass at *Overwatch*, Gets Accused of Cheating."

65. Romano, "How a Teen Girl's Mad Overwatch Skills Struck a Major Blow to Sexism in Gaming."

66. Samuel Lingle, "Blizzard Vows Zero Tolerance for Overwatch Cheaters but Adds: 'Some Players Are Just Really Good,'" *Daily Dot*, 13 May 2016, http://www.dailydot.com/esports/blizzard-overwatch-anti-cheat/.

67. The treatment of people of color in video games is complicated, particularly given the prominence and success of many high-profile Asian, particularly Korean, players. Racism is a massive issue in game culture regardless.

68. Hayes, *Twilight of the Elites*, 225.

69. Jeff Spross, "You're Probably Richer Than You Think You Are: How Inequality Screws with Our Perspective," *The Week*, 27 January 2015, http://theweek.com/articles/535887/youre-probably-richer-than-think-are-howinequality screws-ourperspective.

70. Craig Haney and Aida Hurtado, "The Jurisprudence of Race and Meritocracy: Standardized Testing and 'Race-Neutral' Racism in the Workplace," *Law and Human Behavior* 18, no. 3 (1994): 240.

71. James Brightman, "I'm Doing This Because I'm a Gamer," *Games Industry*, 2 June 2016, http://www.gamesindustry.biz/articles/2016-06-02-im-doing-this-because-im-a-gamer; Potanin, "Forces in Play."

72. Carly A. Kocurek, *Coin-Operated Americans: Rebooting Boyhood at the Video Game Arcade* (Minneapolis: University of Minnesota Press, 2015), xxiii.

73. Halli Bjornsson, "Smart Lessons 17 Million Organic Installs Taught Us about Mobile," *Games Industry*, 19 July 2016, http://www.gamesindustry.biz/articles/2016-07-19-smart-lessons-17-million-organic-installs-taught-us-about-mobile.

74. Ageism is relatively under-discussed as it pertains to video games, but one take on it can be found in Jeff Vogel, "Age, Pleasing Apple, and Trying to Climb Out of the Hole," *Bottom Feeder*, 10 June 2015, http://jeff-vogel.blogspot.com/2015/06/age-pleasing-apple-and-trying-to-climb.html.

75. Neil Irwin, "Ben Bernanke on Life, Love, and Intestinal Parasites," *Washington Post*, 2 June 2013, http://www.washingtonpost.com/blogs/wonkblog/wp/2013/06/02/ben-bernanke-on-life-cynicism-beauty-and-love.

76. Robert H. Frank, *Success and Luck: Good Fortune and the Myth of Meritocracy* (Princeton, N.J.: Princeton University Press, 2016), Kindle ed., loc. 318.

77. Ibid., loc. 82.

78. Zack Beauchamp, "One Graphic That Shows Your Mom Was Right: The World Isn't Fair," *Vox*, 28 May 2015, http://www.vox.com/2015/5/28/8663065/inequality-global-income; Matt O'Brien, "Poor Kids Who Do Everything Right Don't Do Better Than Rich Kids Who Do Everything Wrong," *Washington Post*, 18 October 2014, http://www.washingtonpost.com/blogs/wonkblog/wp/2014/10/18/poor-kids-who-do-everything-right-dont-do-better-than-rich-kids-who-do-everything-wrong/.

79. William Deresiewicz, "Don't Send Your Kid to the Ivy League: The Nation's Top Colleges Are Turning Our Kids into Zombies," *New Republic*, 21 July 2014, http://www.newrepublic.com/article/118747/ivy-league-schools-are-over rated-send-your-kids-elsewhere.

80. Danielle Douglas-Gabriel, "College Is Not the Great Equalizer for Black and Hispanic Graduates," *Washington Post*, 17 August 2015, http://www.washingtonpost.com/news/wonkblog/wp/2015/08/17/college-is-not-the-great-equalizer-for-black-and-hispanic-graduates/; Christopher Ingraham, "Still Think America Is the 'Land of Opportunity'? Look at This Chart," *Washington Post*, 22 February 2016, https://www.washingtonpost.com/news/wonk/wp/2016/02/22/still-think-america-is-the-land-of-opportunity-look-at-this-chart/.

81. Jo Littler, "Meritocracy as Plutocracy: The Marketing of 'Equality' under Neoliberalism," *New Formations* 80–81 (2013): 55.

82. Stephen J. McNamee and Robert K. Miller, *The Meritocracy Myth* (Lanham, Md.: Rowman & Littlefield, 2004), 208.

83. Thank you to Mia Consalvo for lending this phrasing.

84. Anna Anthropy, *Rise of the Videogame Zinesters: How Freaks, Normals, Amateurs, Artists, Dreamers, Drop-Outs, Queers, Housewives, and People Like You Are Taking Back an Art Form* (New York: Seven Stories Press, 2012), Kindle ed., loc. 100.

85. Raph Koster, *Theory of Fun for Game Design* (Sebastopol, Calif.: O'Reilly, 2013), Kindle ed., loc. 1314.

86. Adrienne Shaw, *Gaming at the Edge: Sexuality and Gender at the Margins of Gamer Culture* (Minneapolis: University of Minnesota Press, 2014), 41.

87. Matthew Handrahan, "Ubisoft: Creativity and Commerce in AAA Development," *Games Industry*, 28 June 2016, http://www.gamesindustry.biz/articles/2016-06-28-ubisoft-creativity-and-commerce-in-aaa-development.

88. Potanin, "Forces in Play."

89. Hayes, *Twilight of the Elites*, 40.

90. Kocurek, *Coin-Operated Americans*.

91. Anthropy, *Rise of the Videogame Zinesters*, loc. 105.

92. Koster, *Theory of Fun for Game Design*, loc. 1343.

93. Kocurek, *Coin-Operated Americans*; Potanin, "Forces in Play."

94. Anthropy, *Rise of the Videogame Zinesters*, loc. 236.

95. Peter Kellner, "Yes, We Still Need Meritocracy," *New Statesman*, 9 July 2001, http://www.newstatesman.com/node/153755; Ruth Levitas, "Shuffling Back to Equality?" *Soundings* 26 (Spring 2004): 69.

96. Jennifer de Winter, *Shigeru Miyamoto: Super Mario Bros., Donkey Kong, The Legend of Zelda* (New York: Bloomsbury, 2015).

97. Emilio J. Castilla and Stephen Benard, "The Paradox of Meritocracy in Organizations," *Administrative Science Quarterly* 55, no. 4 (2010): 572.

98. Robin DiAngelo, "White Fragility," *International Journal of Critical Pedagogy* 3, no. 3 (2011): 54–70; Ryan D. Enos, "Casual Effect of Intergroup Contact on Exclusionary Attitudes," *Proceedings of the National Academy of Sciences of the United States of America* 111, no. 10 (2014): 3699–704; German Lopez, "Research Says There Are Ways to Reduce Racial Bias: Calling People Racist Isn't One of Them," *Vox*, 15 November 2016, http://www.vox.com/identities/2016/11/15/13595508/racism-trump-research-study; Dylan Matthews, "Donald Trump Has Every Reason to Keep White People Thinking about Race," *Vox*, 30 November 2016, http://www.vox.com/policy-and-politics/2016/11/30/13765248/donald-trump-race-priming-political-science.

99. Shannon K. McCoy and Brenda Major, "Priming Meritocracy and the Psychological Justification of Inequality," *Journal of Experimental Social Psychology* 43, no. 3 (2007): 342.

100. Ibid., 351.

101. Frank, *Success and Luck*, 1472.

102. Craig Haney and Aida Hurtado, "The Jurisprudence of Race and Meritocracy: Standardized Testing and 'Race-Neutral' Racism in the Workplace," *Law and Human Behavior* 18, no. 3 (1994): 224.

103. James Fraser and Edward Kick, "The Interpretive Repertoires of Whites on Race-Targeted Policies: Claims Making of Reverse Discrimination," *Sociological Perspectives* 43, no. 1 (2000): 26–27.

104. McCoy and Major, "Priming Meritocracy and the Psychological Justification of Inequality," 342.

105. McNamee and Miller, *Meritocracy Myth*, 40.

106. For much more on eSports, see "e-Sports and Pro Gaming Literature," *T. L. Taylor*, n.d., http://tltaylor.com/teaching/e-sports-and-pro-gaming-litera

ture/. For more on competitive gaming and Korea, see Dal Yong Jin, *Korea's Online Gaming Empire* (Cambridge, Mass.: MIT Press, 2010).

107. Todd Harper, *The Culture of Digital Fighting Games: Performance and Practice* (New York: Routledge, 2014).

108. Littler, "Meritocracy as Plutocracy," 66.

109. Christopher A. Paul, "Eve Online Is Hard and It Matters," in *Internet Spaceships Are Serious Business: An Eve Online Reader*, ed. Marcus Carter, Kelly Bergstrom, and Darryl Woodford, 17–30 (Minneapolis: University of Minnesota Press, 2016).

110. Nick Monroe, "'Git Gud' Culture Gives Us the Best of Gaming," *Gameranx*, 18 May 2016, http://gameranx.com/features/id/54186/article/git-gud -culture-gives-us-the-best-of-gaming/.

111. Carol C. Mukhopadhyay, "StarPower: Experiencing a Stratified Society," *What's Race Got to Do with It?*, 2004, http://www.whatsrace.org/pages/ starpower.htm; Simulation Training Systems, "StarPower—Use & Abuse of Power, Leadership & Diversity," n.d., http://www.simulationtrainingsystems .com/schools-and-charities/products/starpower/.

112. Donella Meadows, "Why Would Anyone Want to Play Starpower," *Donella Meadows Institute*, 4 December 2011, http://www.donellameadows.org/ archives/why-would-anyone-want-to-play-starpower/.

113. Lisa Miller, "The Money-Empathy Gap," *New York Magazine*, 1 July 2012, http://nymag.com/news/features/money-brain-2012-7/.

114. Jessica Gross, "6 Studies on How Money Affects the Mind," *TED Blog*, 20 December 2013, http://blog.ted.com/2013/12/20/6-studies-of-money-and -the-mind/.

115. Current norms of merit and success in games were set by early players, and the most successful helped craft systems that were self-beneficial; those practices then filtered out to the wider community of players. For more on ideology, see Antonio Gramsci, *Prison Notebooks: Volume One*, trans. Joseph A. Buttigieg and Antonio Callari (New York: Columbia University Press, 1992).

2. A Toxic Culture

1. John Banks and Sal Humphreys, "The Labour of User Co-creators: Emergent Social Network Markets?" *Convergence* 14, no. 4 (2008): 401–18; John Banks and Jason Potts, "Co-creating Games: A Co-evolutionary Analysis," *New Media & Society* 12, no. 2 (2010): 253–70; Ian Bogost, *Persuasive Games: The Expressive Power of Videogames* (Cambridge, Mass.: MIT Press, 2007); Mia Consalvo and Jason Begy, *Players and Their Pets: Gaming Communities from Beta to Sunset* (Minneapolis: University of Minnesota Press, 2015); T. L. Taylor, "The

Assemblage of Play," *Games and Culture* 4, no. 4 (2009): 331–39; T. L. Taylor, *Play between Worlds: Exploring Online Game Culture* (Cambridge, Mass.: MIT Press, 2006); Gerald A. Voorhees, "I Play Therefore I Am: Sid Meier's Civiliza-tion, Turn-Based Strategy Games and the Cogito," *Games and Culture* 4, no. 3 (2009): 254–75.

2. Kenneth Burke, *Language as Symbolic Action: Essays on Life, Literature, and Method* (Berkeley: University of California Press, 1966); Kenneth Burke, *A Rhetoric of Motives* (Berkeley: University of California Press, 1969).

3. Ellie Zolfagharifard, "Could Our Ancestors See Blue? Ancient People Didn't Perceive the Colour Because They Didn't Have a Word for It, Say Scien-tists," *Daily Mail Online*, 2 March 2015, http://www.dailymail.co.uk/sciencetech/article-2976405/Could-ancestors-blue-Ancient-civilisations-didn-t-perceive-colour-didn-t-word-say-scientists.html.

4. David Zarefsky, "Knowledge Claims in Rhetorical Criticism," *Journal of Communication* 58, no. 4 (2008): 629–40.

5. Bogost, *Persuasive Games*; Jeroen Bourgonjon, Kris Rutten, Ronald Soe-taert, and Martin Valcke, "From *Counter-Strike* to *Counter-Statement*: Using Burke's Pentad as a Tool for Analysing Video Games," *Digital Creativity* 22, no. 2 (2011): 91–102; Todd Harper, "Rules, Rhetoric, and Genre: Procedural Rhet-oric in Persona 3," *Games and Culture* 6, no. 5 (2011): 395–413; Ken S. McAl-lister, *Game Work: Language, Power, and Computer Game Culture* (Tuscaloosa: University of Alabama Press, 2004); Christopher A. Paul, *Wordplay and the Dis-course of Video Games: Analyzing Words, Design, and Play* (New York: Routledge, 2012); Gerald A. Voorhees, "The Character of Difference: Procedurality, Rhet-oric, and Roleplaying Games," *Game Studies* 9, no. 2 (2009): http://gamestudies.org/0902/articles/voorhees.

6. Mia Consalvo and Christopher A. Paul, "Welcome to the Discourse of the Real: Constituting the Boundaries of Games and Players," *FDG* (2013): 55–62.

7. Taylor, "Assemblage of Play."

8. Banks and Humphreys, "Labour of User Co-creators"; Banks and Potts, "Co-creating Games."

9. Adrienne Shaw, "What Is Video Game Culture? Cultural Studies and Game Studies," *Games and Culture* 5, no. 4 (2010): 403–24.

10. Charlie Hall and Danielle Riendeau, "Mass Surveillance, Watch Dogs and the Militarized Police: When Strapping Cameras on People Is a Good Idea," *Polygon*, 14 August 2014, http://www.polygon.com/2014/8/14/6000267/ferguson-police-cameras-watch-dogs; Htown, "Polygon—'What Watch Dogs Can Teach Us About the Situation in Ferguson,'" *NeoGAF*, 14 August 2014, http://www.neogaf.com/forum/showthread.php?t=874691; Stephen Totilo, "Antonin Scalia's Landmark Defense of Violent Video Games," *Kotaku*, 13 Feb-

ruary 2016, http://kotaku.com/antonin-scalias-landmark-defense-of-violent
-video-games-1758990360.

11. Carly A. Kocurek, *Coin-Operated Americans: Rebooting Boyhood at the
Video Game Arcade* (Minneapolis: University of Minnesota Press, 2015).

12. Adrienne Shaw, "Do You Identify as a Gamer? Gender, Race, Sexuality,
and Gamer Identity," *New Media & Society* 14, no. 1 (2012): 28–44; Adrienne
Shaw, "On Not Becoming Gamers: Moving beyond the Constructed Audience,"
Ada: A Journal of Gender, New Media, and Technology 2 (2013): http://adanew
media.org/2013/06/issue2-shaw/.

13. Mia Consalvo, Timothy Dodd Alley, Nathan Dutton, Matthew Falk,
Howard Fisher, Todd Harper, and Adam Yulish, "Where's My Montage? The
Performance of Hard Work and Its Reward in Film, Television, and MMOGs,"
Games and Culture 5, no. 4 (2010): 381–402; Nick Yee, "The Labor of Fun: How
Video Games Blur the Boundaries of Work and Play," *Games and Culture* 1, no.
1 (2006): 68–71.

14. Adrienne Shaw, "The Internet Is Full of Jerks, Because the World Is Full
of Jerks: What Feminist Theory Teaches Us about the Internet," *Communication
and Critical/Cultural Studies* 11, no. 3 (2014): 273–77.

15. Brad McCarty, "70 Million Users, 1+ Billion Hours Every Month:
League of Legends Is the World's Most Played Video Game," *The Next Web*,
12 October 2012, http://thenextweb.com/shareables/2012/10/12/70-million
-users-1-billion-hours-every-month-league-of-legends-is-the-worlds-most
-played-game/; Paul Tassi, "Monstrous Viewership Numbers Show 'League of
Legends' Is Still eSports King," *Forbes*, 11 December 2015, http://www.forbes
.com/sites/insertcoin/2015/12/11/monstrous-viewership-numbers-show-league
-of-legends-is-still-esports-king; Paul Tassi, "Riot's 'League of Legends' Reveals
Astonishing 27 Million Daily Players, 67 Million Monthly," *Forbes*, 27 January 2014,
http://www.forbes.com/sites/insertcoin/2014/01/27/riots-league-of-legends
-reveals-astonishing-27-million-daily-players-67-million-monthly/.

16. Jeffrey Lin, "Why Do You Hate 'Toxic' Players? They Are Fun and If
Needed They Can Be Muted Anyway," *ask.fm*, 2015, http://ask.fm/RiotLyte/
answer/130575100866; Christian Nutt, "*League of Legends*: Changing Bad Player
Behavior with Neuroscience," *Gamasutra*, 5 December 2012, http://www.gama
sutra.com/view/news/178650/League_of_Legends_Changing_bad_player_
behavior_with_neuroscience_.php.

17. Game Politics Staff, "Riot Cracking Down on Unruly 'League of Legends' Players," *Game Politics*, 22 July 2014, http://gamepolitics.com/2014/07/22/
riot-cracking-down-unruly-league-legends-players.

18. Megan Farokhmanesh, "Riot Continues to Crack Down on 'Toxic'
League of Legends Pro Players," *Polygon*, 2 June 2014, http://www.polygon
.com/2014/6/2/5772642/riot-league-of-legends-ban-pro-players; Ethan Gach,

"*League of Legends* Pro Suspended during Worlds for Toxic Chat, Will Be Fined $2,000," *Kotaku*, 9 October 2016, http://kotaku.com/league-of-legends-pro -suspended-during-worlds-for-toxic-1787589483; Michael McWhertor, "The League of Legends Team of Scientists Trying to Cure 'Toxic Behavior' On-line," *Polygon*, 13 October 2012, http://www.polygon.com/2012/10/17/3515178/ the-league-of-legends-team-of-scientists-trying-to-cure-toxic; Jenna Pitcher, "Riot Tests New League of Legends Insta-Ban Feature," *IGN*, 27 August 2014, http://www.ign.com/articles/2014/08/27/riot-tests-new-league-of-legends-insta -ban-feature.

19. Timothy Burke, "Hell Is Other Gamers (and Some Games)," *Easily Distracted*, 2 August 2012, http://blogs.swarthmore.edu/burke/blog/2012/08/02/ hell-is-other-gamers-and-some-games/.

20. Andrew Todd, "Video Games, Misogyny, and Terrorism: A Guide to Assholes," *Badass Digest*, 26 August 2014, http://badassdigest.com/2014/08/26/ video-games-misogyny-and-terrorism-a-guide-to-assholes.

21. Colin Campbell, "Sarkeesian Driven out of Home by Online Abuse and Death Threats," *Polygon*, 27 August 2014, http://www.polygon .com/2014/8/27/6075679/sarkeesian-driven-out-of-home-by-online-abuse -and-death-threats.

22. Zoë Quinn, "Once Again, I Will Not Negotiate with Terrorists," *Quinnspiracy*, August 19, 2014, http://ohdeargodbees.tumblr.com/post/9518865 7119/once-again-i-will-not-negotiate-with-terrorists.

23. Zoë Quinn, "Final Thoughts on This Whole Kerfuffle," *Zoë Quinn*, 29 August 2014, http://ohdeargodbees.tumblr.com/post/96115946094/final -thoughts-on-this-whole-kerfuffle.

24. Carolyn Cox, "[updated] Female Game Journalists Quit over Harassment, #GamerGate Harms Women," *The Mary Sue*, 4 September 2014, http:// www.themarysue.com/gamergate-harms-women/.

25. Anna Merlan, "A Man Is Making Bizarre, Terrifying YouTube Videos about Brianna Wu," *Jezebel*, 2 February 2015, http://jezebel.com/a-man-is -making-bizarre-terrifying-youtube-videos-abou-1683221832; Stephen Totilo, "Another Woman in Gaming Flees Home Following Death Threats," *Kotaku*, 11 October 2014, http://kotaku.com/another-woman-in-gaming -flees-home-following-death-thre-1645280338; Brianna Wu, "Why GSX Is Withdrawing from PAX East," *Space Channel 6*, 2015, http://spacechannel6 .com/post/111384260988/why-gsx-is-withdrawing-from-pax-east.

26. Brianna Wu, "No Skin Thick Enough: The Daily Harassment of Women in the Game Industry," *Polygon*, 22 July 2014, http://www.polygon .com/2014/7/22/5926193/women-gaming-harassment.

27. Crystal K. M., "Having Thick Skin: Harassment in the Industry," *Phoe-*

nixDown, 23 July 2014, http://iphoenixdown.com/2014/07/23/having-thick
-skin-harassment-in-the-industry/.

28. It is notable how having two people who likely have vastly different
amounts of experience with a game or game genre leads to the more experienced person being more successful. This certainly seemed to be testing something other than merit or skill at *Killer Instinct*.

29. Rebecca Greenfield, "The Rape 'Joke' at Microsoft's E3 Reveal Is a Bigger Deal Than Another Bad 'Joke,'" *The Atlantic*, 10 June 2013, https://www
.theatlantic.com/technology/archive/2013/06/microsoft-e3-rape-joke/314326/.

30. Jillian Scharr, "What the Xbox Press Event Rape Joke Says about
the Gaming Industry," *NBC News*, 11 June 2013, http://www.nbcnews.com/
id/52175677/ns/technology_and_science-tech_and_gadgets/t/what-xbox-press
-event-rape-joke-says-about-gaming-industry.

31. Carol Pinchefsky, "Really? IGDA Party at GDC Brings on the Female
Dancers," *Forbes*, 27 March 2013, http://www.forbes.com/sites/carolpinchefsky
/2013/03/27/really-igda-party-at-gdc-brings-on-the-female-dancers/.

32. Megan Farokhmanesh, "Women in the Gaming Industry Share Their
Reason to Be in the Business," *Polygon*, 28 March 2013, http://www.polygon
.com/2013/3/28/4155650/women-in-the-gaming-industry-share-their-number
-one-reason-to-be-in.

33. Griffin McElroy, "IGDA Draws Backlash, Member Resignations over
Female Dancers at GDC Party (Update: IGDA Responds)," *Polygon*, 28 March
2013, http://www.polygon.com/2013/3/28/4157266/igda-gdc-party-brenda
-romero-resignation.

34. Lesley, "What Are Dickwolves, and What Do They Have to Do with
Rape Culture? A Cautionary Tale of How Not to Respond to Feminist Criticism," *xoJane*, 4 September 2013, http://www.xojane.com/issues/dickwolves
-penny-arcade-pax-rape-culture-mike-krahulik; Maddy Myers, "Gaming, Rape
Culture, and How I Stopped Reading Penny Arcade," *Boston Phoenix*, 7 March
2011, http://thephoenix.com/boston/life/116456-gaming-rape-culture-and
-how-i-stopped-reading-pe/; Anastasia Salter and Bridget Blodgett, "Hypermas-
culinity & Dickwolves: The Contentious Role of Women in the New Gaming
Public," *Journal of Broadcasting & Electronic Media* 56, no. 3 (2012): 401–16.

35. Rachel Edidin, "Why I'm Never Going Back to Penny Arcade Expo,"
Wired, 5 September 2013, http://www.wired.com/2013/09/penny-arcade-expo
-dickwolves/.

36. Elizabeth Sampat, "Quit Fucking Going to PAX Already, What Is Wrong
with You," *Elizabeth Sampat*, 3 September 2013, http://elizabethsampat.com/
quit-fucking-going-to-pax-already-what-is-wrong-with-you/.

37. Nicholas T. Taylor, "Play Globally, Act Locally: The Standardization of

Pro Halo 3 Gaming," *International Journal of Gender, Science and Technology* 3, no. 1 (2011); T. L. Taylor, *Raising the Stakes: The Professionalization of Computer Gaming* (Cambridge, Mass.: MIT Press, 2012); Emma Witkowski, "On the Digital Playing Field: How We 'Do Sport' with Networked Computer Games," *Games and Culture* 7, no. 5 (2012): 349–74.

38. Todd Harper, *The Culture of Digital Fighting Games: Performance and Practice* (New York: Routledge, 2014), 125.

39. Nathan Grayson, "Twitch Chat Racism Changed *Hearthstone* Pro Terrence Miller's Career," *Kotaku*, 7 October 2016, http://kotaku.com/hearthstone -pro-terrence-miller-hopes-to-clean-up-twitc-1787551043.

40. IGN Staff, "Cross Assault: The Full Story," *IGN*, 21 March 2012, http://www.ign.com/articles/2012/03/21/cross-assault-the-full-story.

41. Dylan Garner, "Capcom Announces Cast for 'Cross Assault' Reality Series," *Video Game Writers*, 16 February 2012, http://videogamewriters.com/cap-com-announces-cast-for-cross-assault-reality-series-39004.

42. IGN Staff, "Cross Assault."

43. Patrick Klepek, "When Passions Flare, Lines Are Crossed [updated]," *Giant Bomb*, 2012, http://www.giantbomb.com/articles/when-passions-flare-lines-are-crossed-updated/1100-4006/.

44. Ibid.

45. Jim Sterling, "Sexual Harassment and Fightin' Drama, Together at Last!" *Destructoid*, 28 February 2012, http://www.destructoid.com/sexual -harassment-and-esports-drama-together-at-last-222877.phtml.

46. Amy O'Leary, "In Virtual Play, Sex Harassment Is All Too Real," *New York Times*, 1 August 2012, http://www.nytimes.com/2012/08/02/us/sexual -harassment-in-online-gaming-stirs-anger.html.

47. Harper, *Culture of Digital Fighting Games*; Maddy Myers, "One Woman's Battle against the Anxious Masculinity of the Fighting-Games Scene," *Boston Phoenix*, 16 October 2012, http://thephoenix.com/boston/rec room/145892-one-womans-battle-against-the-anxious-masculinity/.

48. Wesley Yin-Poole, "Borderlands 2: Gearbox Reveals the Mechromancer's 'Girlfriend Mode' Update: Randy Pitchford Unhappy with Connotations," *Eurogamer*, 13 August 2012, http://www.eurogamer.net/articles/2012-08-13-border lands-2-gearbox-reveals-the-mechromancers-girlfriend-mode.

49. Ibid.

50. Ian Miles Cheong, "Girlfriend Mode: Casual Sexism in the Game Industry," *Gameranx*, 13 August 2012, http://www.gameranx.com/features/id/8535/ article/girlfriend-mode-casual-sexism-in-the-game-industry/.

51. Brandon Sheffield, "Opinion: *Borderlands 2*'s 'Girlfriend Mode' and Casual Sexism," *Gamasutra*, 14 August 2012, http://www.gamasutra.com/view/

news/175878/Opinion_Borderlands_2s_Girlfriend_Mode_and_casual_sexism
.php.

52. Colin Moriarty, "Opinion: Borderlands 2 and the Girlfriend Mode Farce," *IGN*, 13 August 2012, http://www.ign.com/articles/2012/08/14/opinion -borderlands-2-and-the-girlfriend-mode-farce.

53. Leigh Alexander, "The Mixed Blessing of 'Girlfriend Mode,'" *Gamasutra*, 20 September 2012, http://www.gamasutra.com/view/news/177006/The_ mixed_blessing_of_Girlfriend_Mode.php.

54. "The Pledge," *Gamers against Bigotry*, 2014, http://gamersagainstbigotry .org/.

55. Jason Schreier, "Anti-bigotry Gaming Site Defaced with Racial Slurs," *Kotaku*, 24 July 2012, http://kotaku.com/5928723/anti+bigotry-gaming-site -defaced-with-racial-slurs; Jason Simon, "Gamers against Bigotry Targeted by Hackers, 1500 Pledges Erased," *Kill Screen Daily*, 24 July 2012, http:// killscreendaily.com/articles/news/gamers-against-bigotry-targeted-hackers -pledges-erased/.

56. One of the best analyses of race in video games is Kishonna L. Gray, *Race, Gender, and Deviance in Xbox Live: Theoretical Perspectives from the Virtual Margins* (New York: Routledge, 2014).

57. David Leonard, "Not a Hater, Just Keepin' It Real : The Importance of Race- and Gender-Based Game Studies," *Games and Culture* 1, no. 1 (2006): 83–88.

58. David Leonard, "Young, Black (& Brown) and Don't Give a Fuck: Virtual Gangstas in the Era of State Violence," *Cultural Studies ↔ Critical Methodologies* 9, no. 2 (2009): 248–72; Paul, *Wordplay and the Discourse of Video Games*.

59. Kishonna L. Gray, "Deviant Bodies, Stigmatized Identities, and Racist Acts: Examining the Experiences of African-American Gamers in Xbox Live," *New Review of Hypermedia and Multimedia* 18, no. 4 (2012): 261–76.

60. Derek A. Burrill, *Die Tryin': Videogames, Masculinity, Culture* (New York: Peter Lang, 2008), 138.

61. R. W. Connell, *Masculinities: Knowledge, Power, and Social Change* (Berkeley: University of California Press, 1995), 54–56.

62. Many of the articles referenced in this section have at least some element of the origins of GamerGate in them, though I am partial to Jack Gardner's. An ongoing timeline of GamerGate is being maintained as of this writing at GamerGhazi, "A Comprehensive Timeline of Gamergate (with Sources)," reddit, 3 September 2015, https://www.reddit.com/r/GamerGhazi/wiki/time line. Additional histories can be found in the following: Zachary Jason, "Game of Fear," *Boston Magazine*, May 2015, http://www.bostonmagazine.com/news/ article/2015/04/28/gamergate/; Helen Lewis, "Gamergate: A Brief History of

a Computer-Age War," *The Guardian*, 11 January 2015, http://www.theguard ian.com/technology/2015/jan/11/gamergate-a-brief-history-of-a-computer -age-war.

63. Jack Gardner, "GamerGate's Origins and What It Is Now," *Game Informer*, 20 October 2014, http://www.gameinformer.com/blogs/members/b/ jackalope38_blog/archive/2014/10/20/gamergate-39-s-origins-and-what-it-is -now.aspx.

64. Ibid.

65. Quinn, "Once Again, I Will Not Negotiate with Terrorists." There is an interlude here, wherein Quinn is accused of ruining an event put on by the Fine Young Capitalists. 4Chan raised money to fund the Fine Young Capitalists and spite Quinn, which also led to the creation of Vivian James, who was taken up as a symbol for the movement, was to feature in video games, was designed as the average female gamer, and whose color scheme is a reference to a rape GIF.

66. Andy Baio, "72 Hours of #Gamergate," *The Message*, 27 October 2014, https://medium.com/message/72-hours-of-gamergate-e00513f7cf5d; Cox, "[updated] Female Game Journalists Quit over Harassment"; Aja Romano, "Zoe Quinn Claims 4chan Was Behind GamerGate the Whole Time," *Daily Dot*, 6 September 2014, http://www.dailydot.com/geek/zoe-quinn-outs -4chan-behind-gamergate/; Brianna Wu, "Rape and Death Threats Are Terrorizing Female Gamers: Why Haven't Men in Tech Spoken Out?" *Washington Post*, 20 October 2014, http://www.washingtonpost.com/posteverything/ wp/2014/10/20/rape-and-death-threats-are-terrorizing-female-gamers-why -havent-men-in-tech-spoken-out/.

67. Zoë Quinn, "5 Things I Learned as the Internet's Most Hated Person," *Cracked*, 16 September 2014, http://www.cracked.com/blog/5-things-i-learned -as-internets-most-hated-person/.

68. Frank Lantz, "#Gamergate," *Gamasutra*, 24 October 2014, http://www .gamasutra.com/blogs/FrankLantz/20141024/228523/GamerGate.php.

69. Film Crit Hulk, "Film Crit Hulk Smash: on despair, gamergate and quitting the hulk," *Badass Digest*, 27 October 2014, http://badassdigest .com/2014/10/27/film-crit-hulk-smash-on-despair-gamergate-and-quitting -the-hulk/.

70. This was also turned into a meme in critique of GamerGate. Cf. Victoria McNally, "Gamergate Roundup: IGN & Occupy Wall Street Comment on GG, Internet Makes Hella Memes," *The Mary Sue*, 24 October 2014, http:// www.themarysue.com/gamergate-round-up/.

71. There are various arguments to make about how game journalism is broken, but I am partial to ones like Dave Cook, "How Modern Games Coverage Has Reduced Critics to Human Punching Bags," *Vice*, 13 April 2015, http://

www.vice.com/en_uk/read/how-modern-games-coverage-has-reduced-critics
-to-human-punching-bags-224.

72. Leigh Alexander, "'Gamers' Don't Have to Be Your Audience: 'Gamers'
Are Over," *Gamasutra*, 28 August 2014, http://www.gamasutra.com/view/news
/224400/Gamers_dont_have_to_be_your_audience_Gamers_are_over.php;
Dan Golding, "The End of Gamers," *Dan Golding*, 28 August 2014, http://
dangolding.tumblr.com/post/95985875943/the-end-of-gamers.

73. Andy Chalk, "BioWare Breaks Down *Mass Effect 3* Game Modes," *The
Escapist*, 11 January 2012, http://www.escapistmagazine.com/news/view/115186
-BioWare-Breaks-Down-Mass-Effect-3-Game-Modes.

74. Jonathan Holmes, "Why Does the Term 'Gamer' Feel Important?" *Destructoid*, 31 August 2014, http://www.destructoid.com/why-does-the-term-gamer
-feel-important-280451.phtml.

75. Casey Johnston, "The Death of the 'Gamers' and the Women Who
'Killed' Them," *Ars Technica*, 28 August 2014, http://arstechnica.com/gaming
/2014/08/the-death-of-the-gamers-and-the-women-who-killed-them/.

76. The saga of the "Sad Puppies" and the 2015 Hugo Awards for science
fiction points to how readers can have substantial cultural conflicts. For more,
see Amy Wallace, "Who Won Science Fiction's Hugo Awards, and Why It
Matters," *Wired*, 23 August 2015, http://www.wired.com/2015/08/won-science
-fictions-hugo-awards-matters/.

77. Rich McCormick, "Intel Buckles to Anti-feminist Campaign by Pulling Ads from Gaming Site," *The Verge*, 2 October 2014, http://www.theverge
.com/2014/10/2/6886747/intel-buckles-to-anti-feminist-campaign-by-pulling
-ads-from-gaming.

78. Owen S. Good, "Intel Issues Apology Regarding Its Advertising and
'Gamergate,'" *Polygon*, 4 October 2014, http://www.polygon.com/2014/10/4
/6906909/intel-gamergate-advertising-gamasutra; Josh Lowensohn, "Intel
Opposes Gamergate as Part of $300 Million Effort to Fix Diversity in Tech,"
The Verge, 6 January 2015, http://www.theverge.com/2015/1/6/7505929/intel
-investing-300-million-to-fix-diversity-ces-2015.

79. Eric Johnson, "Adobe Distances Itself from Gawker after Writer's Gamergate Tweet," *Recode*, 22 October 2014, http://recode.net/2014/10/22/adobe
-distances-self-from-gawker-after-writers-gamergate-tweet/.

80. Adobe Corporate Communications, "When Anti-bullying Efforts Backfire," *Adobe News*, 28 October 2014, http://blogs.adobe.com/conversations
/2014/10/when-anti-bullying-efforts-backfire.html.

81. Max Read, "How We Got Rolled by the Dishonest Fascists of Gamergate," *Gawker*, 22 October 2014, http://gawker.com/how-we-got-rolled-by-the
-dishonest-fascists-of-gamergat-1649496579.

82. In an effort at disclosure, I was elected a board member of DiGRA at this conference, am serving as vice president as of this writing, and was both an invited member of the fishbowl and an active note taker for the session.

83. Shira Chess and Adrienne Shaw, "A Conspiracy of Fishes, or, How We Learned to Stop Worrying about #Gamergate and Embrace Hegemonic Masculinity," *Journal of Broadcasting & Electronic Media* 59, no. 1 (2015): 208–20; Shira Chess and Adrienne Shaw, "We Are All Fishes Now: DiGRA, Feminism, and Gamergate," *Transactions of the Digital Games Research Association* 2, no. 2 (2016): 21–30; Torill Elvira Mortensen, "Anger, Fear, and Games: The Long Event of #Gamergate," *Games and Culture*, 13 April 2016, 1–20.

84. Mortensen, "Anger, Fear, and Games."

85. Jose Zagal, "On Chairing a Games Research Conference," *Transactions of the Digital Games Research Association* 2, no. 2 (2016): 16.

86. Chess and Shaw, "Conspiracy of Fishes," 214.

87. Chess and Shaw, "We Are All Fishes Now."

88. Mortensen, "Anger, Fear, and Games."

89. Adrienne Shaw, "Do You Identify as a Gamer? Gender, Race, Sexuality, and Gamer Identity," *New Media & Society* 14, no. 1 (2012): 28–44.

90. Keith Stuart, "Brianna Wu and the Human Cost of Gamergate: 'Every Woman I Know in the Industry Is Scared,'" *The Guardian*, 17 October 2014, http://www.theguardian.com/technology/2014/oct/17/brianna-wu-gamergate-human-cost.

91. Emily Greer, "A Natural A/B Test of Harassment," *Kongregate Developer News*, 23 October 2014, http://developers.kongregate.com/blog/a-natural-a-b-test-of-harassment.

92. Chris Kluwe, "Why #Gamergaters Piss Me the F*** Off," *The Cauldron*, 21 October 2014, https://medium.com/the-cauldron/why-gamergaters-piss-me-the-f-off-a7e4c7f6d8a6; Sarah Gray, "'Gamergate Is Now Irredeemably Toxic': The Top 10 Takeaways from Chris Kluwe's Reddit AMA," *Salon*, 23 October 2014, http://www.salon.com/2014/10/23/gamergate_is_now_irredeemably_toxic_the_top_10_takeaways_from_chris_kluwes_reddit_ama/.

93. Felicia Day, "The Only Thing I Have to Say about Gamer Gate," *Felicia's Melange*, 23 October 2014, http://thisfeliciaday.tumblr.com/post/100700417809/the-only-thing-i-have-to-say-about-gamer-gate.

94. Brandon Griggs, "Actress Harassed Online over #Gamergate," *CNN*, 23 October 2014, http://www.cnn.com/2014/10/23/living/felicia-day-gamergate/index.html; Kirk Hamilton, "Felicia Day and Gamergate: This Is What Happens Now," *Kotaku*, 24 October 2014, http://kotaku.com/felicia-day-and-gamergate-this-is-what-happens-now-1650544129.

95. Sam Laird, "Chris Kluwe: GamerGate a Symptom of Society's Misog-

yny Problem," *Mashable*, 26 October 2014, http://mashable.com/2014/10/25/gamergate-chris-kluwe/.

96. Chris Suellentrop, "Can Video Games Survive?" *New York Times*, 25 October 2014, http://www.nytimes.com/2014/10/26/opinion/sunday/the-disheartening-gamergate-campaign.html; Anita Sarkeesian, "It's Game Over for 'Gamers,'" *New York Times*, 28 October 2014, http://www.nytimes.com/2014/10/29/opinion/anita-sarkeesian-on-video-games-great-future.html.

97. Dave Lee, "Zoe Quinn: Gamergate Must Be Condemned," *BBC News*, 29 October 2014, http://www.bbc.com/news/technology-29821050; Todd VanDerWerff, "#Gamergate Has Won a Few Battles: It Will Lose the War," *Vox*, 23 October 2014, http://www.vox.com/2014/10/23/7044593/gamergate; Leigh Alexander, "Sexism, Lies, and Video Games: The Culture War Nobody Is Winning," *Time*, 5 September 2014, http://time.com/3274247/video-game-culture-war/; Taylor Wofford, "Is Gamergate about Media Ethics or Harassing Women? Harassment, the Data Shows," *Newsweek*, 25 October 2014, http://www.newsweek.com/gamergate-about-media-ethics-or-harassing-women-harassment-data-show-279736; Wu, "Rape and Death Threats Are Terrorizing Female Gamers."

98. Alex Abad-Santos, "#Gamergate Loves Stephen Colbert: Stephen Colbert Does Not Love Them Back," *Vox*, 30 October 2014, http://www.vox.com/xpress/2014/10/30/7131071/stephen-colbert-anita-sarkeesian-gamergate; Brian Crecente, "Brianna Wu: 'I'm Not Going to Get Bullied out of This Industry,'" *Polygon*, 14 October 2014, http://www.polygon.com/2014/10/14/6974547/brianna-wu-im-not-going-to-get-bullied-out-of-this-industry; Lee, "Zoe Quinn."

99. Chris Plante, "Gamergate Is Dead," *The Verge*, 30 October 2014, http://www.theverge.com/2014/10/30/7131931/gamergate-is-dead.

100. Adi Robertson, "The Law & Order Gamergate Episode Manages to Be Even More Depressing Than Gamergate," *The Verge*, 12 February 2015, http://www.theverge.com/2015/2/12/8026175/law-and-order-svu-gamergate-episode. Discussion about the episode was widespread both before and after it aired. Other perspectives on it can be found in Leigh Alexander, "Law & Order: SVU 'Intimidation Game' Is Not What Games Are About," *Hopes & Fears*, 13 February 2015, http://www.hopesandfears.com/hopes/culture/video-games/168413-gamergate-svu-episode-reviewed-by-leigh-alexander; Caitlin Dewey, "This Is the Final Word on Gamergate—and It's from 'Law & Order: SVU,'" *Washington Post*, 11 February 2015, https://www.washingtonpost.com/news/the-intersect/wp/2015/02/11/this-is-the-final-word-on-gamergate-and-its-from-law-order-svu/; Philip Kollar, "Law & Order: SVU to Air Episode Based on GamerGate," *Polygon*, 29 January 2015, http://www.polygon.com/2015/1/29/7949153/law-order-svu-gamergate-episode-nbc-tv; Jason

Schreier, "So That Was *Law & Order*'s Gamergate Episode," *Kotaku*, 11 February 2015, http://kotaku.com/so-that-was-law-orders-gamergate-episode-1685333828.

101. Eric Johnson, "Shadows of Gamergate, but Few Answers, Materialize at Gaming Industry Shindig," *Recode*, 9 February 2015, http://recode.net/2015/02/09/shadows-of-gamergate-but-few-answers-materialize-at-gaming-industry-shindig/.

102. Natalie Zina Walschots, "Finish Him!" *This*, 10 March 2015, http://this.org/magazine/2015/03/10/finish-him/.

103. Ben Kuchera, "The Year of GamerGate: The Worst of Gaming Culture Gets a Movement," *Polygon*, 30 December 2014, http://www.polygon.com/2014/12/30/7460777/gamergate-2014-just-the-worst.

104. mr stroke, "GAF FOTY 2014-Fail of the Year-Results- Winner of the 2014 Shit Sandwich Goes to . . . ," *NeoGAF*, 23 December 2014, http://www.neogaf.com/forum/showthread.php?t=957568; Paul Verhoeven, "The Biggest Nerd Stories of 2014," *TheVine*, 28 December 2014, http://www.thevine.com.au/life/tech/the-biggest-nerd-stories-of-2014-20141228-292442/; Nadia Kayyali and Danny O'Brien, "Facing the Challenge of Online Harassment," *Electronic Frontier Foundation*, 8 January 2015, https://www.eff.org/deeplinks/2015/01/facing-challenge-online-harassment.

105. Brian Crecente, "Depression Quest Creator Speaks at Congressional Briefing on Cyberstalking," *Polygon*, 15 April 2015, http://www.polygon.com/2015/4/15/8420237/depression-quest-creator-speaks-at-congressional-briefing-on; Jeff Grubb, "Massachusetts Congresswoman Urges FBI to Take Gamergate Seriously," *VentureBeat*, 10 March 2015, http://venturebeat.com/2015/03/10/massachusetts-congresswoman-urges-fbi-to-take-gamergate-seriously/; Mary Elizabeth Williams, "Twitter Trolls, Your Days Are Numbered: The Department of Justice Is Finally Taking Online Harassment Like #Gamergate Seriously," *Salon*, 29 May 2015, http://www.salon.com/2015/05/29/twitter_trolls_your_days_are_numbered_the_department_of_justice_is_finally_taking_online_harassment_like_gamergate_seriously/; Brianna Wu, "It's Time for the FBI to Prosecute Gamergate Trolls," *Daily Dot*, 12 March 2015, http://www.dailydot.com/opinion/brianna-wu-fbi-death-threats-gamergate/; Brianna Wu, "[updated] Gamergate Death Threat Is a Slam Dunk for Prosecutors: Will They Act?" *The Mary Sue*, 22 May 2015, http://www.themarysue.com/will-prosecutors-act-on-gamergate-death-threat/.

106. Benjamin Barber, *Twitter*, 15 October 2014, https://twitter.com/endomorphosis/status/522520577249001473.

107. Hayes, *Twilight of the Elites*.

108. Lantz, "#GamerGate."

109. Matt Lees, "What Gamergate Should Have Taught Us about the 'Alt-

Right,'" *The Guardian*, 1 December 2016, https://www.theguardian.com/tech nology/2016/dec/01/gamergate-alt-right-hate-trump. See also Paul Kennedy, "The Dangerous Game: Gamergate and the 'Alt-Right,'" *CBC Radio*, 30 November 2016, http://www.cbc.ca/radio/ideas/the-dangerous-game-gamergate -and-the-alt-right-1.3874259.

3. Coding Meritocracy

1. Jesper Juul, *The Art of Failure: An Essay on the Pain of Playing Video Games* (Cambridge, Mass.: MIT Press, 2013).

2. Robin Potanin, "Forces in Play: The Business and Culture of Videogame Production," in *Fun and Games '10: Proceedings of the 3rd International Conference on Fun and Games*, ed. Vero Vanden Abeele et al. (New York: ACM, 2010), 135–43.

3. Christopher L. Hayes, *Twilight of the Elites: America after Meritocracy* (New York: Crown, 2012); Ruth Levitas, "Shuffling Back to Equality?" *Soundings* 26 (Spring 2004): 59–72; Jo Littler, "Meritocracy as Plutocracy: The Marketing of 'Equality' under Neoliberalism," *New Formations* 80–81 (2013): 52–72; Kenneth Paul Tan, "Meritocracy and Elitism in a Global City: Ideological Shifts in Singapore," *International Political Science Review* 29, no. 1 (2008): 7–27; Michael Young, "Down with Meritocracy," *The Guardian*, 28 June 2001, http:// www.guardian.co.uk/politics/2001/jun/29/comment; Michael Young, *The Rise of the Meritocracy* (1958; repr., New Brunswick, N.J.: Transaction, 2008).

4. Jennifer Goodman, "The Meritocracy Myth: National Exams and the Depoliticization of Thai Education," *Sojourn: Journal of Social Issues in Southeast Asia* 28, no. 1 (2013): 101–31; Naa Oyo A. Kwate and Ilan H. Meyer, "The Myth of Meritocracy and African American Health," *American Journal of Public Health* 100, no. 10 (2010): 1831–34; Stephen J. McNamee and Robert K. Miller, *The Meritocracy Myth* (Lanham, Md.: Rowman & Littlefield, 2004).

5. Juul, *Art of Failure*, 74–75.

6. Ben Barrett, "Getting Better at Hearthstone with Computers," *Rock, Paper, Shotgun*, 4 September 2014, http://www.rockpapershotgun.com/2014 /09/04/getting-better-at-hearthstone-with-computers/.

7. At the first ever *Clash Royale* tournament the mortar player was mercilessly booed and the card was made weaker shortly after the tournament. The card creates a building that enables players to attack from their side of the map, which is a more defensible position and does not facilitate "fun" play. In tournament fighting games, certain characters and stages are often banned as players find them too powerful and unbalanced, thereby subverting the contest of skill they are seeking. Sports games are based on unbalanced teams, but those teams are all given ratings. It is typically considered bad form to use a radically more

powerful team than your opponent does, unless an agreement was made to do so in advance. That agreement typically is made to pursue a more equal contest where the more skilled player (I'm looking at you, Miguel Sicart) takes a lesser team and still beats me.

8. Mia Consalvo, *Cheaters: Gaining Advantage in Videogames* (Cambridge, Mass.: MIT Press, 2007).

9. Chris Kohler, "Why Can't Nintendo Stop Ruining *Mario Kart?*" *Wired*, 15 May 2014, http://www.wired.com/2014/05/mario-kart-8-wii-u/.

10. Celestius, "Most Annoying Mario Kart Wii Items," *TheTopTens*, 19 July 2016, http://www.thetoptens.com/annoying-mario-kart-wii-items/.

11. Stephen Totilo, "The Maker of *Mario Kart* Justifies the Blue Shell," *Kotaku*, 9 March 2011, http://kotaku.com/5780082/the-maker-of-mario-kart -justifies-the-blue-shell.

12. BlazeAssassin, "I Wish They Would Add a 'Skill' Mode to MP Games," *GameFAQs*, 28 March 2012, http://www.gamefaqs.com/boards/632974-mario -party-9/62381927; Turbo_TRex, "There's Too Much Reliance on Luck in This Game," *GameFAQs*, 19 January 2014, http://www.gamefaqs.com/boards /711406-mario-party-island-tour/68375685.

13. "Banned Stage," *SmashWiki*, n.d., http://www.ssbwiki.com/Banned_ stage.

14. Mia Consalvo, "Hardcore Casual: Game Culture Return(s) to Raven-hearst," *FDG '09: Proceedings of the 4th International Conference on Foundations of Digital Games* (New York: ACM, 2009), 50–54.

15. Derek Strickland, "Halo Online Pay to Win Microtransactions Revealed," *VR World*, 26 March 2015, http://www.vrworld.com/2015/03/26/halo -online-pay-to-win-microtransactions-revealed/.

16. Leigh Alexander, "Watergun Assassin: The Grand Game Story of Street Wars," *Gamasutra*, 6 August 2014, http://www.gamasutra.com/view/news /222713/Watergun_assassin_The_grand_game_story_of_Street_Wars.php.

17. Stephen Totilo, "The Uncracked Secrets of *Pokémon Go* Egg-Hatching," *Kotaku*, 28 July 2016, http://kotaku.com/the-uncracked-secrets-of-pokemon-go -egg-hatching-1784339902.

18. Alexander, "Watergun Assassin."

19. Ethan Ham, "Rarity and Power: Balance in Collectible Object Games," *Game Studies* 10, no. 1 (2010): http://gamestudies.org/1001/articles/ham.

20. Eli Hodapp, "'Hearthstone' Curse of Naxxramas Review: Easily the Best Way New Collectable Card Game Cards Have Ever Been Released," *Touch Arcade*, 21 August 2014, http://toucharcade.com/2014/08/21/hearthstone -curse-of-naxxramas-review/.

21. Ibid.

22. Eugene Lee, "Tomb Raider to Survivor, Reimagining Lara Croft," *En-

tropy, 30 June 2014, http://entropymag.org/tomb-raider-to-survivor-reimagin ing-lara-croft/.

23. Evan Narcisse, "*Tomb Raider*: The *Kotaku* Review," *Kotaku*, 25 February 2013, http://kotaku.com/5986619/tomb-raider-the-kotaku-review.

24. This is especially interesting in consideration of how Lara Croft was rebooted away from her lineage of inheritance and wealth in the newest installment of the series.

25. Edward Castronova, *Synthetic Worlds: The Business and Culture of Online Games* (Chicago: University of Chicago Press, 2005), 114.

26. Simon Parkin, "If You Love Games, You Should Refuse to Be Called a Gamer," *New Statesman*, 9 December 2013, http://www.newstatesman.com/if -you-love-games-you-are-not-a-gamer.

27. Ibid.

28. Elizabeth Harper, "Should You Lose Experience When You Die?" *Engadget*, 7 April 2007, https://www.engadget.com/2007/04/07/should-you-lose -experience-when-you-die/.

4. Judging Skill

1. Jesper Juul, *The Art of Failure: An Essay on the Pain of Playing Video Games* (Cambridge, Mass.: MIT Press, 2013).

2. Benjamin Sell and Michael Hartman, "Gear Score in World of Warcraft: What Is It and How Do I Know What Mine Is?" *Altered Gamer*, 18 April 2012, http://world-of-warcraft.alteredgamer.com/wow-basics/71203-gear-score -in-world-of-warcraft-what-is-it-and-how-do-i-know-what-mine-is/; "Gear Score," *WoWWiki*, n.d., http://wowwiki.wikia.com/wiki/Gear_score.

3. Gus Mustrapa, "Gamer Earns Every *World of Warcraft* Achievement," *Wired*, 3 December 2009, http://www.wired.com/2009/12/world-of-warcraft -achievement/; Starym, "A History of World Firsts: Vanilla," *Manaflask*, 1 March 2014, http://manaflask.com/en/articles/a-history-of-world-firsts -vanilla#; Gergo Vas, "The First Player to Unlock All 2,057 of *World of Warcraft's* Achievements," *Kotaku*, 22 April 2014, http://kotaku.com/russian-player -unlocks-all-2-057-achievements-in-world-1566029494.

4. For general background on raiding, please see Mark Chen, *Leet Noobs: The Life and Death of an Expert Player Group in World of Warcraft* (New York: Peter Lang, 2011).

5. A general background on DKP can be found in Krista-Lee Malone, "Dragon Kill Points: The Economics of Power Gamers," *Games and Culture* 4, no. 3 (2009): 296–316.

6. Mark Silverman and Bart Simon, "Discipline and Dragon Kill Points in the Online Power Game," *Games and Culture* 4, no. 4 (2009): 364.

7. Ibid., 371.

8. Michael McWhertor, "The League of Legends Team of Scientists Trying to Cure 'Toxic Behavior' Online," *Polygon*, 13 October 2012, http://www.poly gon.com/2012/10/17/3515178/the-league-of-legends-team-of-scientists-trying -to-cure-toxic; Paul Tassi, "Riot's 'League of Legends' Reveals Astonishing 27 Million Daily Players, 67 Million Monthly," *Forbes*, 27 January 2014, http:// www.forbes.com/sites/insertcoin/2014/01/27/riots-league-of-legends-reveals -astonishing-27-million-daily-players-67-million-monthly/.

9. McWhertor, "League of Legends Team of Scientists Trying to Cure 'Toxic Behavior' Online."

10. Colin Campbell, "How Riot Games Encourages Sportsmanship in League of Legends," *Polygon*, 20 March 2014, http://www.polygon.com /2014/3/20/5529784/how-riot-games-encourages-sportsmanship-in-league -of-legends.

11. Luke Plunkett, "Pro *League of Legends* Player Banned for Harassment, Abuse & 'Negative Attitude,'" *Kotaku*, 4 December 2012, http://kotaku .com/5965713/pro-league-of-legends-player-banned-for-harassment-abuse -negative-attitude. For academic studies of the governance systems in *League of Legends*, see Jeremy Blackburn and Haewoon Kwak, "stfu noob! Predicting Crowdsourced Decisions on Toxic Behavior in Online Games," in *WWW '14: Proceedings of the 23rd International Conference on World Wide Web* (New York: ACM, 2014), 877–88; Yubo Kou and Bonnie Nardi, "Governance in League of Legends: A Hybrid System," *FDG* (2014): https://pdfs.semanticscholar.org/; Haewoon Kwak, Jeremy Blackburn, and Seungyeop Han, "Exploring Cyberbullying and Other Toxic Behavior in Team Competition Online Games," in *CHI '15: Proceedings of the 33rd Annual ACM Conference on Human Factors in Computing Systems* (New York: ACM, 2015), 3739–48.

12. Elo is a system originally designed for chess that has found its way into a number of technical products in some form, from video games to the forerunner to Facebook. The system is based on trying to match players of equal skill against each other. Players start out with a baseline rating, which goes up and down as they lose matches. Beating a higher-rated player leads to a larger boost than beating a player with a similar rating to your own. Conversely, losing to a lower-ranked player can lead to a substantial lowering of your own rating. In my experience, Elo makes games feel weightier as there are somewhat durable consequences to each match.

13. YurdleTheTurtle, "Beginner's Guide to Ranked Games," *League of Legends Community*, 5 May 2013, http://forums.na.leagueoflegends.com/board/ showthread.php?t=1194168.

14. Ibid.

15. Nathan Grayson, "The Guy with the Lowest Possible Rank in *Over-*

watch," *Kotaku*, 23 August 2016, http://kotaku.com/the-guy-with-the-lowest
-possible-rank-in-overwatch-1785662123.

16. Dillion Skiffington, "*League of Legends*' Neverending War on Toxic
Behavior," *Kotaku*, 19 September 2014, http://kotaku.com/league-of-legends
-neverending-war-on-toxic-behavior-1636894289.

17. Riot Socrates, "Ranked Restrictions," *League of Legends Boards*, 24
September 2014 http://boards.na.leagueoflegends.com/en/c/miscellaneous
/1LJP1ovA-ranked-restrictions.

18. Nathan Grayson, "*League of Legends* Restricting Toxic Players from
Ranked Games," *Kotaku*, 23 September 2014, http://kotaku.com/league-of
-legends-restricting-toxic-players-from-ranked-1638305092.

19. Skiffington, "League of Legends' Neverending War on Toxic Behavior."

20. Ibid.

21. Yannick LeJacq, "Losing in MOBAs Should Be More Fun," *Kotaku*, 29 April 2015, http://kotaku.com/losing-in-mobas-should-be-more
-fun-1701067967.

22. Philippa Warr, "Wot I Learned: League of Legends Q&A," *Rock, Paper,
Shotgun*, 26 October 2014, http://www.rockpapershotgun.com/2014/10/26/lol
-2015-changes/.

23. Yannick LeJacq, "Why Riot Tweaks *League of Legends* to Make It Better
for Its Best Players," *Kotaku*, 19 May 2015, http://kotaku.com/why-riot-tweaks
-league-of-legends-to-make-it-better-for-1705527275.

24. Jeffrey Lin, "Tweet," *Twitter*, 28 May 2015, https://twitter.com/riotlyte/
status/604005785245335552.

25. Brenna Hillier, "Only 2% of League of Legends Matches Include Abuse,
Says Riot," *VG247*, 9 July 2015, http://www.vg247.com/2015/07/09/only-2-of
-league-of-legends-matches-include-abuse-says-riot/.

26. Vikki Blake, "'Online Harassment Is Not an Impossible Problem,' Says
Riot," *Destructoid*, 9 July 2015, http://www.destructoid.com/-online-harassment
-is-not-an-impossible-problem-says-riot-295658.phtml.

27. Five-star heroes have a 0.01 percent chance of being drawn out of the
free pack that players get once a day and a 0.25 percent chance of being drawn
out of a paid pack. A paid character costs about five dollars as of this writing.

28. Paul Tassi, "The World's Best 'Clash Royale' Player Has Spent $12k
on the Game, and for Good Reason," *Forbes*, 1 April 2016, http://www.forbes
.com/sites/insertcoin/2016/04/01/the-worlds-best-clash-royale-player-has
-spent-12k-on-the-game-and-for-good-reason.

29. Eli Hodapp, "Seven Ways 'Clash Royale' Should Be More Like Pepper-
oni Pizza," *Touch Arcade*, 20 May 2016, http://toucharcade.com/2016/05/20/
seven-ways-clash-royale-should-be-more-like-pepperoni-pizza/.

30. Dean Takahashi, "With Patience, I Defeated Supercell's Monetization

Strategy in Clash Royale," *VentureBeat*, 28 April 2016, http://venturebeat.com /2016/04/28/with-patience-i-defeated-supercells-monetization-strategy-in -clash-royale/.

31. dragonroar3, "Tournaments Make Me Not Want to Play Ranked," reddit, 10 July 2016, https://www.reddit.com/r/ClashRoyale/comments/4s45yv /tournaments_make_me_not_want_to_play_ranked/.

32. Eli Hodapp, "Supercell Doubles Down on Never Muting Emotes in 'Clash Royale,'" *Touch Arcade*, 14 June 2016, http://toucharcade.com/2016/06/14 /supercell-doubles-down-on-never-muting-emotes-in-clash-royale/.

33. Clash Royale Team, "Emotes," *Clash Royale*, 14 June 2016, https:// clashroyale.com/blog/news/emotes.

34. Hodapp, "Supercell Doubles Down on Never Muting Emotes in 'Clash Royale.'"

35. Clash Royale Team, "Rethinking Emotes," *Clash Royale*, 6 September 2016, https://clashroyale.com/blog/news/rethinking-emotes.

36. David Amsden, "'Madden' and Me: How Football's Biggest Video Game Took Over My Life," *Rolling Stone*, 28 August 2015, http://www.rollingstone.com /sports/features/madden-and-me-how-footballs-biggest-video-game-took -over-my-life-20150828.

37. Owen S. Good, "Meet the Million-Point Man of Xbox Live," *Polygon*, 22 March 2014, http://www.polygon.com/2014/3/22/5533384/meet-the-million -point-man-of-xbox-live; Greg Kumparak, "It Took 8 Years, but Someone Just Broke One Million Gamerscore on Xbox Live," *TechCrunch*, 12 March 2014, http://techcrunch.com/2014/03/12/it-took-8-years-but-someone-just -broke-one-million-gamerscore-on-xbox-live/; Luke Plunkett, "Meet the First Gamer to Get *One Million* Achievement Points," *Kotaku*, 13 March 2014, http://kotaku.com/watch-live-as-a-hero-gets-a-gamerscore-of-over-one-mill -1542821937/1542852654.

38. Good, "Meet the Million-Point Man of Xbox Live."

39. Joel Goodwin, "The Trouble with Serious Games," *Electron Dance*, 14 September 2014, http://www.electrondance.com/the-trouble-with-serious -games/.

40. Jen Gerson, "Dragon Age Writer Jennifer Hepler Talks about Leaving Bioware, but Not for Being Harrassed," *National Post*, 19 August 2013, http:// news.nationalpost.com/2013/08/19/jennifer-hepler/.

41. Susana Polo, "Inclusion: What Jennifer Hepler's Story Is All About," *The Mary Sue*, 20 February 2012, http://www.themarysue.com/inclusion-what -jennifer-heplers-story-is-all-about/.

42. Ibid.

43. Andy Chalk, "BioWare Breaks Down *Mass Effect 3* Game Modes," *The*

Escapist, 11 January 2012, http://www.escapistmagazine.com/news/view/115186 -BioWare-Breaks-Down-Mass-Effect-3-Game-Modes.

44. Tina Amini, "BioWare Writer Describes Her Gaming Tastes; Angry Gamers Call Her a 'Cancer,'" *Kotaku*, 20 February 2012, http://kotaku.com /5886674/bioware-writer-describes-her-gaming-tastes-angry-gamers-call-her -a-cancer; Stephanie Gutowski, "Attack of the Internet: Saving Bioware's Jennifer Hepler," *RipTen Videogame Blog*, 24 February 2012, http://www.ripten .com/2012/02/24/attack-of-the-internet-saving-biowares-jennifer-hepler/.

45. Chris Priestly, "Our Statement Supporting a Valued Employee," *BioWare Forum*, 21 February 2012, http://forum.bioware.com/topic/259859-our-state ment-supporting-a-valued-employee/.

46. Mike Fahey, "Average Gamers Are Going to Hate *Bioshock Infinite*'s 1999 Mode," *Kotaku*, 23 January 2012, http://kotaku.com/5878338/average-gamers -are-going-to-hate-bioshock-infinites-1999-mode.

47. Ibid.

48. Patricia Hernandez, "*GTA* Players Beat All of the Heists without Ever Dying," *Kotaku*, 16 March 2015, http://kotaku.com/gta-v-players-beat-all-of -heists-without-ever-dying-1691705013; Patricia Hernandez, "The Man Who Does the Impossible in *Super Mario 64*," *Kotaku*, 17 March 2015, http://kotaku .com/the-man-who-does-the-impossible-in-super-mario-64-1656869221; Jason Schreier, "Someone Beat *Pillars of Eternity* in under 40 Minutes," *Kotaku*, 14 April 2015, http://kotaku.com/someone-beat-pillars-of-eternity-in-under -40-minutes-1697709938.

49. Nic Rowen, "Review: Evolve," *Destructoid*, 13 February 2015, http://www .destructoid.com/review-evolve-287650.phtml.

50. Laura Hudson, "In Bloodborne's Brutal World, I Found Myself," *Offworld*, 10 April 2015, http://boingboing.net/2015/04/10/bloodborne.html.

51. Patricia Hernandez, "Incredible *Bloodborne* Player Beats Game without Ever Leveling Up," *Kotaku*, 3 April 2015, http://kotaku.com/incredible-blood borne-player-beats-game-without-ever-le-1695418129; Patrick Klepek, "Skilled *Dark Souls II* Player Makes Toughest Enemies Look Like Chumps," *Kotaku*, 10 February 2015, http://kotaku.com/skilled-dark-souls-ii-player-makes-toughest -enemies-loo-1684963271.

52. Hudson, "In Bloodborne's Brutal World, I Found Myself."

53. Patrick Klepek, "Apparently I'm Not Playing *Demon's Souls* the 'Right Way,'" *Kotaku*, 19 February 2015, http://kotaku.com/apparently-im-not-playing -demons-souls-the-right-way-1686815820.

54. Dan Stapleton, "How and Why Bloodborne Lost Me," *IGN*, 26 March 2015, http://www.ign.com/articles/2015/03/26/how-and-why-bloodborne-lost -me.

55. Dave Thier, "Echo Chamber: 'Bloodborne's' Critical Praise Is Gaming Journalism's Failure," *Forbes*, 27 March 2015, http://www.forbes.com/sites/davidthier/2015/03/27/echo-chamber-bloodbornes-critical-praise-is-gaming-journalisms-failure/print/.

56. Or nine, or thirty-nine, depending on when and what you were raiding.

57. Katherine Sierra, "Silicon Valley Could Learn a Lot from Skater Culture: Just Not How to Be a Meritocracy," *Wired*, 23 February 2015, http://www.wired.com/2015/02/silicon-valley-thinks-can-learn-skater-culture-terrible-idea/.

5. Learning from Others

1. Steven E. Jones and George K. Thiruvathukal, *Codename Revolution: The Nintendo Wii Platform* (Cambridge, Mass.: MIT Press, 2012); Nick Montfort and Ian Bogost, *Racing the Beam: The Atari Video Computer System* (Cambridge, Mass.: MIT Press, 2009).

2. An excellent example of a book about sports culture is Dave Zirin, *Game Over: How Politics Has Turned the Sports World Upside Down* (New York: New Press, 2013).

3. feedmeacid, "Challenging the Play Is Broken," *GameFAQs*, 9 October 2012, http://www.gamefaqs.com/boards/656454-madden-nfl-13/64260364, robd42; "Challenging the Refs Call?" *GameFAQs*, 5 October 2011, http://www.gamefaqs.com/boards/625123-madden-nfl-12/60536576; Ebenezer Samuel, "System Update: Madden 15 Fumbled a Couple of Details," *Daily News*, 29 August 2014, http://nydailynews.com/entertainment/tv/system-update-madden-15-fumbled-couple-details-article-1.1921335.

4. David Sirlin, *Playing to Win: Becoming the Champion* (n.p.: David Sirlin, 2005), Kindle ed., loc. 96.

5. David Leonhardt, "The Strike-Zone Revolution," *New York Times*, 23 October 2014, http://www.nytimes.com/2014/10/24/upshot/the-strike-zone-revolution.html; Jeff Sullivan, "Umpires Are Improving," *FanGraphs Baseball*, 28 February 2013, http://www.fangraphs.com/blogs/umpires-are-improving/.

6. Rich Trenholm, "Coaches Could Challenge Refs with TV Replays, Says Soccer Boss Sepp Blatter," *CNET*, 8 September 2014, http://www.cnet.com/news/coaches-could-challenge-refs-with-tv-replays-says-soccer-boss-sepp-blatter/.

7. "NBA to Share 'Last Two Minutes' Officiating Reports Beginning March 2," *National Basketball Association*, 27 February 2015, http://www.nba.com/2015/news/02/27/officating-reports-official-release/.

8. Kevin Draper, "NBA Says Refs Missed Five Calls on Final Thunder-Spurs Possession," *Deadspin*, 3 May 2016, http://deadspin.com/nba-says-refs-missed-five-calls-on-final-spurs-thunder-1774523941.

9. Kit Holden, "Why Did the Bundesliga Turn Down Goal Line Technology?" *The Independent*, 24 March 2014, http://www.independent.co.uk/sport /football/european/why-did-the-bundesliga-turn-down-goal-line-technology -9213017.html.

10. Bobby Warshaw, "No One Understands Soccer's Rules, and That's a Problem," *Deadspin*, 14 June 2016, http://screamer.deadspin.com/no-one -understands-soccers-rules-and-thats-a-problem-1781973591.

11. Tom Ley, "Replay Is Turning Baseball into Football and I Hate It," *Deadspin*, 12 October 2015, http://deadspin.com/replay-is-turning-baseball-into -football-and-i-hate-it-1736111661.

12. Jaime Diaz, "After Further Review, the USGA Got Real Lucky Dustin Johnson Won the U.S. Open by More Than One Stroke," *Golf Digest*, 20 June 2016, http://www.golfdigest.com/story/after-further-review-the-usga-got-real -lucky-dustin-johnson-won-the-us-open-by-more-than-one-stroke.

13. Barry Petchesky, "The Secret of the Seahawks' Defense? Fouling, Maybe," *Deadspin*, 10 January 2014, http://deadspin.com/the-secret-of-the -seahawks-defense-fouling-maybe-1498806994.

14. Daniel Rich, "For Wharton Professor Cade Massey, the NFL Draft Is a Crapshoot," *Daily Pennsylvanian*, 14 October 2013, http://www.thedp.com/ article/2013/10/nfl-draft-analysis-cade-massey.

15. Dave McMenamin, "LeBron James: Warriors Are 'Most Healthy Team I've Ever Seen in NBA History,'" *ESPN*, 23 November 2015, http://espn.go .com/nba/story/_/id/14204846/lebron-james-says-golden-state-warriors-most -healthy-team-ever-seen.

16. Claire McNear, "The End of Mike Carey, and the Twilight of Human Error," *The Ringer*, 13 June 2016, https://theringer.com/nfl-mike-carey-rules -analyst-human-error-edd2226e9a29.

17. EA Sports, "Madden NFL 16 Player Ratings," 2015, https://www.easports .com/madden-nfl/player-ratings.

18. Mark McClusky, "This Guy's Quest to Track Every Shot in the NBA Changed Basketball Forever," *Wired*, 28 October 2014, http://www.wired.com /2014/10/faster-higher-stronger.

19. Dylan Burkhardt, "How Iowa State Eliminated the Mid-Range Jumper," *Shot Analytics*, 18 March 2014, http://www.shotanalytics.com/2014/03/18/iowa -state-eliminated-mid-range-jumper/.

20. Zach Lowe, "The Tiers of the NBA: Ranking the Teams from Top to Bottom," *Grantland*, 28 October 2014, http://grantland.com/the-triangle/nba -rankings-san-antonio-spurs-los-angeles-clippers-oklahoma-city-thunder -cleveland-cavaliers/.

21. Christopher A. Paul, "Optimizing Play: How Theorycraft Changes Gameplay and Design," *Game Studies* 11, no. 2 (2011): http://gamestudies.org

/1102/articles/paul; Christopher A. Paul, *Wordplay and the Discourse of Video Games: Analyzing Words, Design, and Play* (New York: Routledge, 2012); Karin Wenz, "Theorycrafting: Knowledge Production and Surveillance," *Information, Communication & Society* 16, no. 2 (2013): 178–93.

22. Jennifer Armstrong, "Life after Death for the Man behind *Lost's* Mr. Eko," *Entertainment Weekly*, 3 November 2006, http://www.ew.com/ew/article /0,,1553848,00.html.

23. Brett Koremenos, "Assets and Fit," *Grantland*, 5 March 2015, http:// grantland.com/the-triangle/nba-shootaround-physical-graffiti/.

24. Adrian Wojnarowski, "Rockets GM Daryl Morey Fires Back at Mavericks Owner Mark Cuban," *Yahoo Sports*, 29 September 2014, http://sports .yahoo.com/news/rockets-gm-daryl-morey-fires-back-at-mavericks-owner -mark-cuban-082844311.html.

25. Pablo S. Torre and Tom Haberstroh, "New Biometric Tests Invade the NBA," *ESPN*, 6 October 2014, http://espn.go.com/nba/story/_/id/11629773/ new-nba-biological-testing-less-michael-lewis-more-george-orwell.

26. Gary Jacobson, "Inside the Final Four Finances: The March toward $1 Billion in Revenue," *Dallas Morning News*, 4 April 2014, http://www.dallasnews .com/sports/college-sports/ncaa-tournament/the-scene/20140403-inside-final -four-finances-cuban-ncaa-tournament-won-t-get-fat-like-nfl.ece.

27. Cy Young, "Cy Young Perfect Game Box Score," *Baseball Almanac*, n.d., http://www.baseball-almanac.com/boxscore/05051904.shtml.

28. Jeff Passan, "Tim Lincecum's No-Hitter Shows His Very Best Is Still Better Than Most," *Yahoo Sports*, 25 June 2014, https://sports.yahoo.com/news/ tim-lincecum-still-good-enough-for-no-hitter-even-if-he-s-a-different-than -before-011427676.html; Maxi Rodriguez, "Javier Mascherano Says He Tore His Anus During Semifinal against Netherlands," *Yahoo Sports*, 10 July 2014, https://sports.yahoo.com/blogs/soccer-dirty-tackle/javier-mascherano-says-he -tore-his-anus-during-semifinal-against-netherlands-154255457-soccer.html; Chris Sprow, "The NFL's 'Luckiest' Teams," *ESPN*, 30 December 2011, http:// insider.espn.go.com/nfl/story/_/id/7400317/the-luckiest-teams-nfl-sometimes -turn-the-greatest-nfl.

29. Mike Fahey, "Pac-Man World Record Broken," *Kotaku*, 11 September 2009, http://kotaku.com/5357260/pac-man-world-record-broken.

30. Raph Koster, *Theory of Fun for Game Design* (Sebastopol, Calif.: O'Reilly, 2013), Kindle ed., loc. 890.

31. Angel Diaz and Rafael Canton, "The 20 Greatest Basketball Players to Never Play in the NBA," *Complex*, 9 November 2012, http://www.complex .com/sports/2012/11/the-20-greatest-players-who-never-played-in-the-nba/; "World Football: The Top 10 Most Promising Players That Never Made It,"

Bleacher Report, 3 June 2011, http://bleacherreport.com/articles/708618-guti-and
-the-top-10-promising-players-that-never-made-it-and-busted; Adam Lazarus,
"10 Best NFL Players That Never Were," *Bleacher Report*, 12 April 2012, http://
bleacherreport.com/articles/1143472-the-10-best-nfl-players-that-never-were.

32. Andrew McCutchen, "Left Out," *The Players' Tribune*, 13 February 2015,
http://www.theplayerstribune.com/left-out/.

33. PA Sport, "Manchester City's Kevin De Bruyne Offer 'Astonishing'—
Wolfsburg Chief," *ESPN FC*, 28 August 2015, http://www.espnfc.us/story
/2584407/manchester-city-kevin-de-bruyne-offer-astonishing-chief.

34. Patrick Redford, "How Chris Froome Dominated the Tour De France,"
Deadspin, 26 July 2016, http://fittish.deadspin.com/how-chris-froome-dominated
-the-tour-de-france-1784285012.

35. One example of the importance of corporations being in charge of eSports
and how that affects play can be seen in the debate surrounding relegation and
League of Legends. For more, see Vince Nairn, "LCS Owners Send Letter to Riot
Games about Concerns Regarding Relegation, Financial Stability and Char-
ter Membership," *Slingshot*, 12 November 2016, https://slingshotsports.com
/2016/11/12/riot-games-lett-lcs-owners-league-of-legends-concerns-relegation
-financial-stability/.

36. Andrew Sharp, "The Warriors Were Too Good at Everything to Ever
Really Lose Anything," *Grantland*, 17 June 2015, http://grantland.com/the-tri
angle/the-warriors-were-too-good-at-everything-to-ever-really-lose-anything/.

37. Dan Diamond, "Paul George Injury: Why the Stanchions Were So
Close, and How to Fix It," *Forbes*, 2 August 2014, http://www.forbes.com/sites
/dandiamond/2014/08/02/paul-george-injury-how-one-expert-would-make
-sure-it-never-happens-again/.

38. Zach Lowe, "A Playoff Problem: If the Celtics Are Trying to Rebuild,
Then Why the Postseason Push?" *Grantland*, 31 March 2015, http://grantland
.com/the-triangle/a-playoff-problem-if-the-celtics-are-trying-to-rebuild-then
-why-the-postseason-push/.

39. Sports certainly has its own structural inequalities, not the least of which
is the cost to play certain sports. For a perspective on how this affects hockey, see
Geordie Tait, "The Puck Stops Here," *Star City Games*, 20 October 2010, http://
www.starcitygames.com/magic/misc/20314_The_Puck_Stops_Here.html.

40. I deeply appreciate this suggestion from the anonymous "Reviewer 2,"
who read an earlier version of this chapter.

41. The best example of this may be the AAAA baseball player, who is good
enough to dominate AAA baseball but not good enough to play consistently in
Major League Baseball.

42. Rodger Sherman, "The Story of the Slowest Athletes at the Rio Olym-

pics, and Why They Compete," *SBNation*, 19 August 2016, http://www.sbnation
.com/2016/8/19/12467438/rio-olympics-2016-athletes-small-nations-richson
-simeon.

43. Rodger Sherman, "This Is Why Gabby Douglas Isn't in the Olympics Gymnastics All-Around Finals," *SBNation*, 11 August 2016, http://www.sbnation
.com/2016/8/7/12400004/team-usa-gymnastics-olympics-all-around-simone
-biles-aly-raisman-gabby-douglas-2-per-country-rule.

44. Samuel Claiborn, "Mario Party 10 Review: Party Yawn," *IGN*, 17 March 2015, http://www.ign.com/articles/2015/03/17/mario-party-10-review.

45. Phill Cameron, "A Quick Argument for 'Luck' in Strategy Game Design, from *XCOM 2*'s Creator," *Gamasutra*, 6 August 2015, http://www.gamasutra.com
/view/news/249978/A_quick_argument_for_luck_in_strategy_game_design
_from_XCOMs_creator.php.

46. Ibid.

47. Tiago Raposo, comment on ibid.; Anton Temba, comment on ibid.

48. Roy Graham, "Jake Solomon Explains the Careful Use of Randomness in *XCOM 2*," *Gamasutra*, 1 March 2016, http://www.gamasutra.com/view/news
/266891/Jake_Solomon_explains_the_careful_use_of_randomness_in_XCOM
_2.php.

49. Matthew Lynch, "Diverse Conversations Recruiting a Diverse Student Population," *Huffington Post*, 4 February 2014, http://www.huffingtonpost.com
/matthew-lynch-edd/diverse-conversations-rec_b_4724817.html.

50. Josh Freedman, "The Farce of Meritocracy: Why Legacy Admissions Might Actually Be a Good Thing," *Forbes*, 14 November 2013, http://www
.forbes.com/sites/joshfreedman/2013/11/14/the-farce-of-meritocracy-in-elite
-higher-education-why-legacy-admissions-might-be-a-good-thing/.

51. Ross Douthat, "Does Meritocracy Work?" *The Atlantic*, 1 November 2005, http://www.theatlantic.com/magazine/archive/2005/11/does-meritocracy
-work/304305/.

52. Tamar Lewin, "Colleges Seek New Paths to Diversity after Court Ruling," *New York Times*, 22 April 2014 http://www.nytimes.com/2014/04/23/us/
turning-to-new-means-of-promoting-diversity.html.

53. Scott Jaschik, "Meritocracy or Bias?" *Inside Higher Ed*, 13 August 2013, https://www.insidehighered.com/news/2013/08/13/white-definitions-merit-and
-admissions-change-when-they-think-about-asian-americans.

54. Libby Nelson, "The Formula for a Good Life after College," *Vox*, 6 May 2014, http://www.vox.com/2014/5/6/5683788/the-science-of-a-good-life-after
-college.

55. Jia Tolentino, "All the Greedy Young Abigail Fishers and Me," *Jezebel*, 28 June 2016, http://jezebel.com/all-the-greedy-young-abigail-fishers-and
-me-1782508801; Marcus Woo, "Infoporn: College Faculties Have a Serious

Diversity Problem," *Wired*, 19 February 2015, http://www.wired.com/2015/02/infoporn-college-faculties-serious-diversity-problem/.

56. Becky Chambers, "Why Games with Female Protagonists Don't Sell, and What It Says about the Industry," *The Mary Sue*, 23 November 2012, http://www.themarysue.com/why-games-with-female-protagonists-dont-sell-and-what-it-says-about-the-industry; Matthew Handrahan, "No Female Assassin's Creed Characters a 'Reality of Development,'" *Games Industry*, 12 June 2014, http://www.gamesindustry.biz/articles/2014-06-11-no-female-assassins-creed-characters-a-reality-of-development; Cameron Kunzelman, "In Watch Dogs, Women Are Just Victims and Plot Points," *Paste*, 28 May 2014, http://www.pastemagazine.com/articles/2014/05/in-watch-dogs-women-are-victims-and-plot-points.html; Carolyn Petit, "Fear of a Woman Warrior," *GameSpot*, 22 February 2013, https://www.gamespot.com/articles/fear-of-a-woman-warrior/1100-6404142/; Rachel Weber, "Naughty Dog: We've Been Asked to Push Ellie to the Back of the Box Art," *Games Industry*, 12 December 2012, http://www.gamesindustry.biz/articles/2012-12-12-naughty-dog-theres-a-misconception-that-if-you-put-a-girl-on-the-cover-the-game-sells-less; Mike Wehner, "Devs Had to Demand Female Focus Testers for *The Last of Us*," *The Escapist*, 8 April 2013, http://www.escapistmagazine.com/news/view/123139-Devs-Had-to-Demand-Female-Focus-Testers-for-The-Last-of-Us.

57. David Leonard, "Not a Hater, Just Keepin' It Real: The Importance of Race- and Gender-Based Game Studies," *Games and Culture* 1, no. 1 (2006): 83–88.

58. Jef Rouner, "Would You Believe There Have Been Only 14 Playable Black Women in Gaming?" *Houston Press*, 5 June 2015, http://www.houstonpress.com/arts/would-you-believe-there-have-been-only-14-playable-black-women-in-gaming-7484017.

59. Richard Pérez-Peña, "Generation Later, Poor Are Still Rare at Elite Colleges," *New York Times*, 25 August 2014, http://www.nytimes.com/2014/08/26/education/despite-promises-little-progress-in-drawing-poor-to-elite-colleges.html.

60. David Leonhardt, "'A National Admissions Office' for Low-Income Strivers," *New York Times*, 16 September 2014, http://www.nytimes.com/2014/09/16/upshot/a-national-admissions-office-for-low-income-strivers.html; David Leonhardt, "A Simple Way to Send Poor Kids to Top Colleges," *New York Times*, 29 March 2013, http://www.nytimes.com/2013/03/31/opinion/sunday/a-simple-way-to-send-poor-kids-to-top-colleges.html; Peg Tyre, "Improving Economic Diversity at the Better Colleges," *New York Times*, 5 February 2014, http://opinionator.blogs.nytimes.com/2014/02/05/improving-economic-diversity-at-the-better-colleges/.

61. Leigh Alexander, "These Girls Are Ready to Shape the Future of Game

Development," *Gamasutra*, 29 July 2014, http://www.gamasutra.com/view/news/221883/These_girls_are_ready_to_shape_the_future_of_game_development.php; Tanya X. Short, "Gaming the System: How Pixelles Make (More and More) Games," *Gamasutra*, 20 March 2015, http://www.gamasutra.com/blogs/TanyaXShort/20150320/238808/Gaming_the_System_How_Pixelles_Make_More_and_More_Games.php.

62. Paul Fain, "Inputs Trump Outputs," *Inside Higher Ed*, 1 August 2013, https://www.insidehighered.com/news/2013/08/01/incoming-student-characteristics-determine-graduation-rates-studies-find.

63. "Please Come Work with Me," *Brie Code*, 2015, http://briecode.tumblr.com/post/123327104135/please-come-work-with-me; Jenny Kutner, "Feminist Thor Selling *Way* More Comic Books Than Dude Thor," *Salon*, 29 March 2015, http://www.salon.com/2015/03/19/feminist_thor_selling_way_more_comic_books_than_dude_thor/; Melissa Jun Rowley, "How NASA Broke the Gender Barrier in STEM," *Fast Company*, 23 June 2015, http://www.fastcompany.com/3047618/strong-female-lead/how-nasa-broke-the-gender-barrier-in-stem.

64. Leigh Alexander, "The Good News," *Leigh Alexander*, 10 March 2015, http://leighalexander.net/the-good-news/.

Conclusion

1. TEDxMarin, "Paul Piff: Does Money Make You Mean?" *TED*, October 2013, https://www.ted.com/talks/paul_piff_does_money_make_you_mean.

2. Leigh Alexander, "Gamer's Paradise: The Bleak, Toilsome World of Cart Life," *Creators Project*, 13 March 2013, http://thecreatorsproject.vice.com/blog/gamers-paradise-the-bleak-toilsome-world-of-icart-lifei.

3. Ibid.

4. Alexander, "Gamer's Paradise"; Richard Cobbett, "Papers, Please Review," *IGN*, 12 August 2013, http://www.ign.com/articles/2013/08/12/papers-please-review; John Walker, "Wot I Think: Papers, Please," *Rock, Paper, Shotgun*, 12 August 2013, http://www.rockpapershotgun.com/2013/08/12/wot-i-think-papers-please/.

5. Justin McElroy, "Papers, Please Review: Mundane Tyranny," *Polygon*, 9 August 2013, http://www.polygon.com/2013/8/9/4606420/papers-please-review-mundane-tyranny.

6. Cobbett, "Papers, Please Review."

7. Walker, "Wot I Think."

8. Leigh Alexander, "GTA V Is Not Subversive—but These Games Are," *The Guardian*, 27 September 2013, http://www.theguardian.com/technology/2013/sep/27/gta-v-transgressive-video-games.

9. Leigh Alexander, "Papers, Please: Why Make a Computer Game about

Border Control?" *New Statesman*, 16 September 2013, http://www.newstatesman .com/sci-tech/2013/09/papers-please%20why-make-computer-game-about -border-control.

10. Thank you to Nicholas T. Taylor for suggesting I analyze *The Walking Dead.*

11. Brad Nicholson, "'Walking Dead: The Game' Review—a Dark Zombie Tale," *Touch Arcade*, 27 November 2012, http://toucharcade.com/2012/11/27 /the-walking-dead-the-game-review-a-dark-zombie-tale/.

12. Hollander Cooper, "The Walking Dead Game Review," *GamesRadar*, 26 November 2012, http://www.gamesradar.com/the-walking-dead-review/.

13. Greg Miller, "The Walking Dead: The Game Review," *IGN*, 12 December 2012, http://www.ign.com/articles/2012/12/12/the-walking-dead-the -game-review.

14. Cooper, "Walking Dead Game Review."

15. Nicholson, "Walking Dead."

16. Shaun Musgrave, "'The Walking Dead: Season Two' Review: Experience the Apocalypse from a Different Perspective," *Touch Arcade*, 29 August 2014, http://toucharcade.com/2014/08/29/the-walking-dead-season-two-review/.

17. Brandon Sheffield, "What Makes *Gone Home* a Game?" *Gamasutra*, 20 March 2014, http://gamasutra.com/view/news/213612/What_makes_Gone _Home_a_game.php.

18. Dale North, "Review: Gone Home," *Destructoid*, 1 October 2013, http:// www.destructoid.com/review-gone-home-262626.phtml.

19. Kris Graft, "For *Gone Home*'s Designer, 'What Is a Game?' Is a Question Worth Exploring," *Gamasutra*, 14 March 2014, http://www.gamasutra.com/view/ news/212853/For_Gone_Homes_designer_what_is_a_game_is_a_question_ worth_exploring.php.

20. Danielle Riendeau, "Gone Home Review: Living Room," *Polygon*, 15 August 2013, http://www.polygon.com/2013/8/15/4620172/gone-home-review -if-these-walls-could-talk.

21. Marty Sliva, "Gone Home Review," *IGN*, 15 August 2013, http://www .ign.com/articles/2013/08/15/gone-home-review.

22. Leigh Alexander, "How *Gone Home*'s Design Constraints Lead to a Powerful Story," *Gamasutra*, 15 August 2013, http://gamasutra.com/view/ news/198340/How_Gone_Homes_design_constraints_lead_to_a_powerful_ story.php.

23. Jason Schreier, "The *No Man's Sky* Hype Dilemma," *Kotaku*, 18 August 2016, http://kotaku.com/the-no-mans-sky-hype-dilemma-1785416931.

24. Mia Consalvo and Jason Begy, *Players and Their Pets: Gaming Communities from Beta to Sunset* (Minneapolis: University of Minnesota Press, 2015), 44.

25. Ibid., 67.

26. Erik Kain, "'Journey' Review: Making Video Games Beautiful," *Forbes*, 4 December 2012, http://www.forbes.com/sites/erikkain/2012/12/04/journey-review-making-video-games-beautiful/.

27. Simon Parkin, "Jenova Chen: Journeyman," *Eurogamer*, 21 July 2015, http://www.eurogamer.net/articles/2012-04-02-jenova-chen-journeyman.

28. Ibid.

29. Leigh Alexander, "There Is Nothing to 'Do' in O'Reilly's Mountain—and That's a Good Thing," *Gamasutra*, 8 July 2014, http://gamasutra.com/view/news/220443/There_is_nothing_to_do_in_OReillys_Mountain__and_thats_a_good_thing.php.

30. Ben Kuchera, "Mountain Could Be a \$1 Joke, and I Think I'm the Butt," *Polygon*, 3 July 2014, http://www.polygon.com/2014/7/3/5868087/mountain-indie-game-joke-satire-self-loathing; Cameron Kunzelman, "*Mountain* Review (PC/Mac/iOS)," *Paste*, 3 July 2014, http://www.pastemagazine.com/articles/2014/07/mountain-review-pcmacios.html.

31. Mark Serrels, "Multiplayer Games Where It's Okay to Suck," *Kotaku*, 28 July 2015, http://kotaku.com/multiplayer-games-where-its-okay-to-suck-1720756255.

32. Ibid.

33. TEDxMarin, "Paul Piff: Does Money Make You Mean?"; Robert H. Frank, *Success and Luck: Good Fortune and the Myth of Meritocracy* (Princeton, N.J.: Princeton University Press, 2016), Kindle ed.

34. Shannon K. McCoy and Brenda Major, "Priming Meritocracy and the Psychological Justification of Inequality," *Journal of Experimental Social Psychology* 43 (2007): 341–51.

35. Monica Y. Bartlett and David DeSteno, "Gratitude and Prosocial Behavior: Helping When It Costs You," *Psychological Science* 17, no. 4 (2006): 319–25.

36. Nancy Digdon and Amy Koble, "Effects of Constructive Worry, Imagery Distraction, and Gratitude Interventions on Sleep Quality: A Pilot Trial," *Applied Psychology: Health and Well-Being* 3, no. 2 (2011): 193–206.

37. C. Nathan DeWall, Nathaniel M. Lambert, Richard S. Pond Jr., Todd B. Kashdan, and Frank D. Fincham, "A Grateful Heart Is a Nonviolent Heart: Cross-Sectional, Experience Sampling, Longitudinal, and Experimental Evidence," *Social Psychological and Personality Science* 3, no. 2 (2012): 232–40.

38. Richard Bartle, "Hearts, Clubs, Diamonds, Spades: Players Who Suit Muds," *Muse*, 28 August 1996, http://www.mud.co.uk/richard/hcds.htm.

39. Jay Hathaway, "What Is Gamergate, and Why? An Explainer for Non-Geeks," *Gawker*, 10 October 2014, http://gawker.com/what-is-gamergate-and-why-an-explainer-for-non-geeks-1642909080; Matt Lees, "What Gamergate Should Have Taught Us about the 'Alt-Right,'" *The Guardian*, 1 December

2016, https://www.theguardian.com/technology/2016/dec/01/gamergate-alt
-right-hate-trump.

40. Mike Fahey, "YouTube Corruption Sinks Even Deeper into the Gutter,"
Games Industry, 8 July 2016, http://www.gamesindustry.biz/articles/2016-07-08
-youtube-corruption-sinks-even-deeper-into-the-gutter; Rob Fahey, "Dirty
Videos," *Games Industry*, 10 October 2014, http://www.gamesindustry.biz
/articles/2014-10-10-dirty-videos.

41. Jennifer Allaway, "#Gamergate Trolls Aren't Ethics Crusaders; They're
a Hate Group," *Jezebel*, 13 October 2014, http://jezebel.com/gamergate
-trolls-arent-ethics-crusaders-theyre-a-hate-1644984010; Tadhg Kelly, "The
#Gamergate Question," *TechCrunch*, 7 September 2014, http://techcrunch
.com/2014/09/07/the-gamergate-question/; Leo Reyna, "#Gamergate Revealed
as Misogynist and Racist Movement from 4chan," *The Examiner*, 6 September
2014, http://www.examiner.com/article/gamergate-revealed-as-misogynist-and
-racist-movement-from-4chan; Jon Stone, "Gamergate's Vicious Right-Wing
Swell Means There Can Be No Neutral Stance," *The Guardian*, 13 October
2014, http://www.theguardian.com/technology/2014/oct/13/gamergate-right
-wing-no-neutral-stance.

42. Aaron Sankin, "Why the Trolls Are Winning #Gamergate," *The Daily Dot*,
17 October 2014, http://www.dailydot.com/opinion/trolls-winning-gamergate
-anita-sarkeesian/.

43. Peter-Hans Kolvenbach, "The Service of Faith and the Promotion of
Justice in American Jesuit Higher Education," Santa Clara University, 6 October 2000, https://www.scu.edu/ic/programs/ignatian-tradition-offerings/stories/
the-service-of-faith-and-the-promotion-of-justice-in-american-jesuit-higher
-education.html.

Gameography

Games discussed in this book are listed here in alphabetical order by title. More information about most of the console and PC games mentioned can be found at MobyGames.com. Other games can be found on Wikipedia, apps are most likely to be found on the iOS App Store, and board games are likely to be found on BoardGameGeek.com.

Ascension: Deckbuilding Game. Card game. Designed by John Fiorillo and Justin Gary. Stone Blade Entertainment, 2010. Also available on iOS. https://boardgamegeek.com/boardgame/69789/ascension-deckbuilding-game.

Bioshock (series). The first game was developed by 2K Australia and 2K Boston. 2K Games, 2007. http://www.mobygames.com/game-group/bioshock-series.

Bioshock Infinite. PS3. Developed by Irrational Games. 2K Games, 2013. http://www.mobygames.com/game/bioshock-infinite_.

Bloodborne. PS4. Developed by FromSoftware. Sony Computer Entertainment, 2015. http://www.mobygames.com/game/playstation-4/bloodborne.

Borderlands (series). The first game was developed by Gearbox Software. 2K Games, 2009. http://www.mobygames.com/game-group/borderlands-series.

Borderlands 2. Xbox 360. Developed by Gearbox Software. 2K Games, 2012. Android, Linux, PS3, Windows. http://www.mobygames.com/game/borderlands-2.

Bully. PS2. Developed by Rockstar Vancouver. Rockstar Games, 2006. PS3, PS4. http://www.mobygames.com/game/bully.

Candy Crush Saga. iOS. Developed by Midasplayer AB. King.com, 2012. Android, browser, Windows Apps. http://www.mobygames.com/game/candy-crush-saga.

Cart Life. Windows. Developed by Richard Hofmeier. Open source, 2011. https://en.wikipedia.org/wiki/Cart_Life.

Civilization (series). The first game was developed by MPS Labs. MicroProse Software, 1991. http://www.mobygames.com/game-group/civilization-series.

Clash of Clans. iOS. Developed by Supercell. Supercell, 2012. Android. http://www.mobygames.com/game/clash-of-clans.

Clash Royale. iOS. Developed by Supercell. Supercell, 2016. Android. https://en.wikipedia.org/wiki/Clash_Royale.

Cook, Serve, Delicious. iOS. Developed by Vertigo Gaming. Vertigo Gaming, 2013. Windows. https://itunes.apple.com/us/app/cook-serve-delicious!/id582153229.

Cow Clicker. Browser. Developed by Ian Bogost. Ian Bogost, 2010. https://en.wikipedia.org/wiki/Cow_Clicker.

Dark Souls. PS3. Developed by FromSoftware. FromSoftware, 2011. Xbox 360. http://www.mobygames.com/game/dark-souls.

Dark Souls II. PS3. Developed by FromSoftware. Namco Bandai, 2014. Windows, Xbox 360. http://www.mobygames.com/game/dark-souls-ii.

Dark Souls III. PS4. Developed by FromSoftware. FromSoftware, 2016. Windows, Xbox One. http://www.mobygames.com/game/dark-souls-iii.

Dear Esther. Windows. Developed by The Chinese Room. The Chinese Room, 2012. Linux, Macintosh. http://www.mobygames.com/game/dear-esther.

Demon's Souls. PS3. Developed by FromSoftware and Sony Computer Entertainment Japan. Atlus USA, 2009. http://www.mobygames.com/game/ps3/demons-souls.

Destiny. PS4. Developed by Bungie. Activision Publishing, 2014. PS3, Xbox 360, Xbox One. http://www.mobygames.com/game/destiny_.

Diablo. Windows. Developed by Blizzard Entertainment and Blizzard North. Blizzard Entertainment, 1996. Macintosh, PlayStation. http://www.mobygames.com/game/diablo.

Dominion. Card game. Designed by Donald X. Vaccarino. Rio Grande Games, 2008. Also available on iOS. https://boardgamegeek.com/boardgame/36218/dominion.

Donkey Kong. Arcade. Developed by Ikegami Tsushinki and Nintendo. Nintendo, 1981. Available on many, many platforms. http://www.mobygames.com/game/donkey-kong.

Dragon Age II. PS3. Developed by BioWare. Electronic Arts, 2011. Macintosh, Windows, Xbox 360. http://www.mobygames.com/game/dragon-age-ii.

The Elder Scrolls V: Skyrim. PS3. Developed by Bethesda Game Studio.

Bethesda Softworks, 2011. Windows, Xbox 360. http://www.mobygames
.com/game/elder-scrolls-v-skyrim.

EVE Online. Windows. Developed by CCP Games. Crucial Entertainment,
2003. Linux, Macintosh. http://www.mobygames.com/game/eve-online.

EverQuest. Windows. Developed by Verant Interactive. 989 Studios, 1999. Macintosh. http://www.mobygames.com/game/everquest.

FarmVille. Browser. Developed by Zynga Game Network. Zynga Game Network, 2009. iOS. http://www.mobygames.com/game/farmville.

Fashion Story. iOS. Developed by TeamLava. TeamLava, 2011. Android. http://
www.mobygames.com/game/fashion-story.

Faunasphere. Browser. Developed by BigFish Games. BigFish Games, 2009.
http://www.mmorpg.com/faunasphere.

FIFA 14. PS4. Developed by Electronic Arts Canada. Electronic Arts, 2013. Xbox
One. http://www.mobygames.com/game/fifa-14.

FIFA 16. PS4. Developed by Electronic Arts Canada. Electronic Arts, 2015. Windows, Xbox One. http://www.mobygames.com/game/fifa-16.

FIFA 17. PS4. Developed by Electronic Arts Canada and Bucharest. EA Sports,
2016. PS3, Windows, Xbox 360, Xbox One. https://en.wikipedia.org/wiki/
FIFA_17.

Final Fantasy (series). The first game was developed by Square. Square, 1987.
http://www.mobygames.com/game-group/final-fantasy-series.

Final Fantasy XI Online. PS2. Developed by Square Enix. Square Enix, 2003.
Windows. http://www.mobygames.com/game/final-fantasy-xi-online_.

Gone Home. Windows. Developed by The Fullbright Company. The Fullbright
Company, 2013. Linux, Macintosh, PS4, Xbox One. http://www.mobygames
.com/game/gone-home.

Grand Theft Auto (series). The first game was developed by DMA Design Limited. BMG Interactive Entertainment, 1997. http://www.mobygames.com/
game-group/grand-theft-auto-series.

Grand Theft Auto III. PS2. Developed by DMA Design Limited. Rockstar
Games, 2001. Android, iOS, Macintosh, PS3, PS4, Windows. http://www
.mobygames.com/game/grand-theft-auto-iii.

Grand Theft Auto IV. PS3. Developed by Rockstar North. Rockstar Games,
2008. Windows, Xbox 360. http://www.mobygames.com/game/grand
-theft-auto-iv.

Grand Theft Auto V. PS4. Developed by Rockstar North. Rockstar Games, 2013.
PS3, Windows, Xbox 360, Xbox One. http://www.mobygames.com/game/
grand-theft-auto-v.

Grand Theft Auto: Chinatown Wars. Nintendo DS. Developed by Rockstar
Leeds and Rockstar North. Rockstar Games, 2009. Android. iOS, PSP.
http://www.mobygames.com/game/grand-theft-auto-chinatown-wars.

Grand Theft Auto: San Andreas. Windows. Developed by Rockstar North.

Rockstar Games, 2004. Android, Fire OS, iOS, Macintosh, PS2, PS3, PS4, Windows, Windows Apps, Windows Phone, Xbox, Xbox 360. http://www .mobygames.com/game/grand-theft-auto-san-andreas.

Halo (series). The first game was developed by Bungie Studios. Microsoft Corporation, 2001. http://www.mobygames.com/game/halo-combat-evolved.

Halo Online. Windows. Developed by Saber Interactive. Innova Software, 2015. https://www.reddit.com/r/HaloOnline/.

Hearthstone: Heroes of Warcraft. iOS. Developed by Blizzard Entertainment. Blizzard Entertainment, 2014. Android, Macintosh, Windows. http://www .mobygames.com/game/hearthstone-heroes-of-warcraft.

Johann Sebastian Joust. PS3. Developed by Die Gute Fabrik. Die Gute Fabrik, 2014. Linux, PS4, Windows. https://en.wikipedia.org/wiki/Sportsfriends.

Journey. PS4. Developed by thatgamecompany. Sony Computer Entertainment America, 2012. PS3. http://www.mobygames.com/game/journey.

Killer Instinct. Xbox One. Developed by Double Helix Games. Microsoft Studios, 2013. Windows Apps. http://www.mobygames.com/game/killer -instinct_.

Kim Kardashian: Hollywood. iOS. Developed by Blammo Games. Glu Mobile, 2014. Android, Browser, Macintosh. http://www.mobygames.com/game/ kim-kardashian-hollywood.

The Last of Us. PS4. Developed by Naughty Dog. Sony Computer Entertainment America, 2013. PS3. http://www.mobygames.com/game/ps3/last-of-us.

League of Legends. Windows. Developed by Riot Games. Riot Games, 2009. Macintosh. http://www.mobygames.com/game/league-of-legends.

Madden NFL (series). The first game in the series was *John Madden Football*. Developed by Electronic Arts. Electronic Arts, 1988. http://www.moby games.com/game-group/madden-series.

Mafia Wars. Browser. Developed by Zynga Game Network. Zynga Game Network, 2008. http://www.mobygames.com/game/browser/mafia-wars.

Magic: The Gathering. Card game. Designed by Richard Garfield. Wizards of the Coast, 1993. https://boardgamegeek.com/boardgame/463/magic-gathering.

Mario Kart (series). The first game in the series was *Super Mario Kart*. Developed by Nintendo EAD. Nintendo, 1992. http://www.mobygames.com/ game-group/mario-kart-series.

Mario Kart 64. Nintendo 64. Developed by Nintendo EAD. Nintendo, 1996. Wii, Wii U. http://www.mobygames.com/game/mario-kart-64.

Mario Kart Wii. Wii. Developed by Nintendo EAD. Nintendo, 2008. http:// www.mobygames.com/game/mario-kart-wii.

Mario Party (series). The first game was developed by Hudson Soft Company. Nintendo of America, 1999. http://www.mobygames.com/game-group/ mario-party-series.

Mario Party 8. Wii. Developed by Hudson Soft Company. Nintendo of America, 2007. http://www.mobygames.com/game/mario-party-8.

Mario Party 10. Wii U. Developed by Nd Cube. Nintendo of America, 2015. http://www.mobygames.com/game/mario-party-10.

Marvel Mighty Heroes. iOS. Developed by DeNA. DeNA, 2015. Android. http://dena.com/intl/press/2015/03/dena-and-marvel-release-marvel-mighty-heroes-a-real-time-multiplayer-brawler-for-iphone-ipad-ipod-to.html.

Marvel Puzzle Quest. iOS and Windows. Developed by Demiurge Studios. D3 Publisher of America, 2013. Android. http://www.mobygames.com/game/marvel-puzzle-quest.

Mass Effect 3. PS3. Developed by BioWare Corporation. Electronic Arts, 2012. Windows, Xbox 360. http://www.mobygames.com/game/mass-effect-3.

Minecraft. Windows. Developed by Mojang. Mojang, 2010. Browser, Linux, Macintosh. http://www.mobygames.com/game/minecraft.

Monaco: What's Yours Is Mine. Windows. Developed by Pocketwatch Games. Headup Games GmbH & Co., 2013. Macintosh. http://www.mobygames.com/game/monaco-whats-yours-is-mine_.

Mountain. iOS. Designed by David O'Reilly, 2014. Android, Linux, Macintosh. http://www.mobygames.com/game/mountain.

MUD1. Designed by Roy Trubshaw and Richard Bartle, 1978. https://en.wikipedia.org/wiki/MUD1.

NBA 2K (series). The first game was developed by Visual Concepts Entertainment. SEGA of America, 1999. http://www.mobygames.com/search/quick?q=nba2k.

NBA 2K13. PS3. Developed by Visual Concepts. 2K Sports, 2012. Android, iOS, PSP, Wii, Wii U, Windows, Xbox 360. https://en.wikipedia.org/wiki/NBA_2K13.

NBA 2K16. PS4. Developed by Visual Concepts. 2K Sports, 2015. Android, iOS, PS3, Windows, Xbox 360, Xbox One. https://en.wikipedia.org/wiki/NBA_2K16.

Ninja. Folk game. http://ultimateninjacombat.com/.

No Man's Sky. PS4. Developed by Hello Games. Hello Games, 2016. Windows. http://www.mobygames.com/game/no-mans-sky.

Overwatch (Origins Edition). PS4. Developed by Blizzard Entertainment. Blizzard Entertainment, 2016. Windows, Xbox One. http://www.mobygames.com/game/overwatch-origins-edition.

Papers, Please. iOS and Windows. Developed by 3909. 3909, 2013. Linux, Macintosh. http://www.mobygames.com/game/papers-please.

Persona 4 Golden. PS Vita. Developed by Atlus Co. Index Digital Media, 2012. http://www.mobygames.com/game/ps-vita/persona-4-golden.

The Pioneer Trail. Browser. Developed by Zynga East. Zynga, 2010. https://en.wikipedia.org/wiki/The_Pioneer_Trail.

Pokémon Go. iOS. Developed by Niantic, Nintendo, and The Pokémon Company, 2016. Android. http://www.mobygames.com/game/pokmon-go.

Pong. Arcade. Developed by Atari and Atari, Inc., 1972.

Populous. SNES. Developed by Bullfrog Productions. Electronic Arts, 1989. Multiple platforms. http://www.mobygames.com/game/populous.

Red Dead Redemption. Xbox 360. Developed by Rockstar San Diego. Rockstar Games, 2010. PS3. http://www.mobygames.com/game/red-dead-redemption.

Restaurant Story. iOS. Developed by TeamLava. TeamLava, 2010. Android. http://www.mobygames.com/game/restaurant-story.

Risk. Board game. Designed by Albert Lamorisse and Michael I. Levin, 1959. https://boardgamegeek.com/boardgame/181/risk.

Rocket League. PS4. Developed by Psyonix. Psyonix, 2015. Linux, Macintosh, Windows. http://www.mobygames.com/game/rocket-league.

Sally's Spa. iOS. Developed by GamesCafe.com. RealArcade, 2008. Android, BlackBerry, Macintosh, Windows, Windows Phone. http://www.mobygames .com/game/sallys-spa.

Solitaire. Card game. https://en.wikipedia.org/wiki/Patience_(game).

Space Invaders. Arcade. Developed by Taito. Taito, 1978. Multiple platforms. http://www.mobygames.com/game/space-invaders.

Splatoon. Wii U. Developed by Nintendo EAD. Nintendo of America, 2015. http://www.mobygames.com/game/wii-u/splatoon.

Star Wars Galaxies. Windows. Developed by Sony Online Entertainment. Lucas-Arts, 2003. http://www.mobygames.com/game/windows/star-wars-galaxies -an-empire-divided-collectors-edition.

Star Wars: The Old Republic (series). The first game was developed by BioWare. LucasArts, 2003. http://www.mobygames.com/game-group/star-wars-the -old-republic-games.

Starcraft. Windows. Developed by Blizzard Entertainment. Blizzard Entertainment, 1998. Macintosh. http://www.mobygames.com/game/starcraft.

Stardom: The A-List. iOS. Developed by Blammo Games. Glu Mobile, 2011. Android. http://www.mobygames.com/game/stardom-the-a-list.

Stardom: Hollywood. iOS. Developed by Blammo Games. Glu Mobile, 2013. Android. http://www.mobygames.com/game/stardom-hollywood.

StarPower. Live action game. Designed by R. Garry Shirts, 1969. https:// boardgamegeek.com/boardgame/32398/starpower.

Street Fighter. Arcade. Developed by Capcom. Capcom, 1987. Multiple platforms. http://www.mobygames.com/game/street-fighter.

Street Fighter X Tekken. PS3. Developed by Capcom and Dimps. Capcom Entertainment, 2012. PS Vita, Windows, Xbox 360. http://www.mobygames .com/game/street-fighter-x-tekken.

StreetWars. Live action game. Designed by Franz Aliquo and Liao Yutai, 2004. https://en.wikipedia.org/wiki/StreetWars.

Super Mario 64. Nintendo 64. Developed by Nintendo EAD. Nintendo, 1996. Wii, Wii U. http://www.mobygames.com/game/super-mario-64.

Super Mario Bros. NES. Developed by Nintendo and Systems Research & Development. Nintendo, 1985. Arcade, Game Boy Advance, Nintendo 3DS, Wii, Wii U. http://www.mobygames.com/game/super-mario-bros.

Super Smash Bros. Nintendo 64. Developed by HAL Laboratory. Nintendo, 1999. Wii. http://www.mobygames.com/game/super-smash-bros.

Tekken. Arcade. Developed by Namco Limited. Namco Limited, 1994. Android, PlayStation, PS3, PSP, PS Vita. http://www.mobygames.com/game/tekken.

Tom Clancy's The Division. PS4. Developed by Ubisoft Massive. Ubisoft, 2016. Windows, Xbox One. http://www.mobygames.com/game/tom-clancys -the-division.

Tomb Raider. PS3. Developed by Crystal Dynamics. Square Enix, 2013. Linux, Macintosh, Windows, Xbox 360. http://www.mobygames.com/game/tomb -raider__.

Ultima Online. Windows. Developed by ORIGIN Systems. Electronic Arts, 1997. http://www.mobygames.com/game/windows/ultima-online.

Uncharted (series). The first game was developed by Naughty Dog. Sony Computer Entertainment America, 2007. http://www.mobygames.com/game -group/uncharted-series.

Uncharted 3: Drake's Deception. PS3. Developed by Naughty Dog. Sony Computer Entertainment America, 2011. http://www.mobygames.com/game/ ps3/uncharted-3-drakes-deception.

The Walking Dead: The Game. iOS. Developed by Telltale. Telltale, 2012. Android, PS3, Xbox 360. http://www.mobygames.com/game/walking-dead -episode-1-a-new-day.

The Witcher 3: Wild Hunt. PS4. Developed by CD Projekt RED. CD Projekt, 2015. Windows, Xbox One. http://www.mobygames.com/game/witcher-3 -wild-hunt.

World of Warcraft. Windows. Developed by Blizzard Entertainment. Blizzard Entertainment, 2004. http://www.mobygames.com/game/world-of-warcraft.

XCOM: Enemy Unknown. iOS and Xbox 360. Developed by Firaxis Games. 2K Games, 2012. Android, Linux, Macintosh, PS3, Windows. http://www .mobygames.com/game/xcom-enemy-unknown.

XCOM 2. PS4. Developed by Firaxis Games. Feral Interactive, 2016. Linux, Macintosh, Windows, Xbox One. http://www.mobygames.com/game/ xcom-2.

Yahtzee. Dice game. Designed by Edwin S. Lowe. Milton Bradley, 1956. https:// boardgamegeek.com/boardgame/2243/yahtzee.

INDEX

Christopher A. Paul is associate professor of communication at Seattle University. He is author of *Wordplay and the Discourse of Video Games: Analyzing Words, Design, and Play*.